ISBN 978-0-428-95663-9
PIBN 10081489

This book is a reproduction of an important historical work. Forgotten Books uses
state-of-the-art technology to digitally reconstruct the work, preserving the original format
whilst repairing imperfections present in the aged copy. In rare cases, an imperfection in
the original, such as a blemish or missing page, may be replicated in our edition. We do,
however, repair the vast majority of imperfections successfully; any imperfections that
remain are intentionally left to preserve the state of such historical works.

SECOND
IMPRESSION

COLLECTED NOTES

—— ON ——

THE TROPICS

FOR A LIVING

FINANCE
LABOUR
EDUCATION

BY THE

EDITOR OF "TROPICAL LIFE"

[Harold] Hamel Smith] 174901.

25. 10. 22,

LONDON :
JOHN BALE, SONS & DANIELSSON, LTD.,
83-91, GREAT TITCHFIELD STREET, W.I.

—

1922

AUTHOR'S NOTE TO THE SECOND IMPRESSION.

THIS book was originally published under the title that appears as the head line to each left hand page. In those days the question of native labour supplies and how far they would go round, was the dominant factor at all producing centres.

The trouble still exists, although the world is now suffering from a bad attack of under-consumption. When we all settle down and ask for normal supplies of tropical products, the labour question will become acute in the rush to plant up new areas so as to satisfy the demands of those who have gone short for so long. With such a prospect, the future planter and trader in the tropics must be trained accordingly. With an Agricultural College (about to start) in Trinidad, British West Indies, those able to finish their training there, after a sound practical training at home, will be able to learn much concerning the latest time and labour-saving appliances. It will be necessary to do so, as the producers of to-morrow will find labour a luxury that they cannot always afford.

Of late, judging by what one hears, the need of cutting down costs is causing many women to be taken back again into employment after having given up their berths to ex-soldiers. Such women badly need the money and are not "joining up" for fun. As they cannot go abroad as easily as men, especially to tropical centres (although we may yet see a demand grow up for scientifically trained women in connection with laboratory and analytical work or insect and fungoid pest troubles), we must give them every chance to earn their living on this side, and the best, in fact the only way that this can be done, is for the men to look elsewhere for a living and for a chance to help extend the trade and prosperity of the Empire at the same time.

We are told that the United Kingdom has twelve million more mouths to feed than she can properly fill, and that these extra millions should be encouraged and guided to our vast territories overseas. Included in this is a surplus of about two million women, whilst Canada, America, &c., need just that number. We must, therefore, do all we can to start the stream, and to see that it follows the easiest and safest course. I trust that both those who wish to make the journey as well as those who are to act as guides, may find some useful points on how to go ahead in the following pages.

In the section on Finance, I specially commend pages 67 to 70 and 75 to your notice, whilst all that is claimed as to the value of Agricultural Colleges in the tropics should be carefully studied, so that when the cry comes for more colleges, those who have need of their help will realize what a fight we had—from 1906 to 1921—to get the first started.

H. HAMEL SMITH.

5, Great Tower Street,
           London, E.C.3.

July 1, 1922.

DISCUSSING the original issue in 1919, Lord Leverhulme was good enough to say :—

" I congratulate Mr. Hamel Smith on his great and successful labour in his book ' How to Pay for the War.'

" The citizens of the United Kingdom cannot have their attention too strongly directed to the importance and value of the tropical portions of the British Empire. Life in temperate regions is dependent upon the tropics for a very large proportion of its necessaries. Nature has been generous to the tropical portion of the British Empire in giving it a rich fertile soil, capable of production ten-fold to that of the most fertile soil in the United Kingdom. There the rain falls and the sun shines in a temperature which is maintained as in a hot-house, but without the necessity of one single shovel-full of coal or any expenditure upon glass. A few years ago we heard a great deal of what was called ' Intensive Production ' by means of cultivation under glass, and of the enormous increase in yield from land under such a system, but in the tropics we can have our intensive production without the cost of glass roofs or greenhouses or bell glasses, without the cost of hot-water pipes or boilers, and we can have the certainty that any development in the tropical portions of the British Empire will not only give us increased food supplies at home but will help to raise and civilize the natives of those outlying portions of the Empire and, in a few generations, lift them from their present condition, which are in many parts similar to those periods which we call the Stone Age and which it has taken Europe thousands of years to develop herself out of and to reach our stage of civilization.

" The whole human family the world over, of all races and

colour, looks to the United Kingdom and its people for help and guidance in development and progress. It is our duty to respond fully and immediately, without hesitation, to these calls upon us, and we are deeply indebted to Mr. Hamel Smith for his book which indicates so clearly the many directions in which such help and assistance can best be given.

"(Signed) LEVERHULME."

———————————

Referring to Lord Leverhulme's remarks the position as he described it three years ago is, to-day, not only unchanged but accentuated. Feeling this, in the paper I read before the Anglo-Spanish Society on January 17 of this year (1922), when discussing the need of fully utilising both the men and the land at our disposal, I claimed that " It is noticeable that those who cannot make the most of their labour seldom make the most of their land. Too many men live only for the present, when running an estate or opening up fresh land. You must give back to the soil and to the trees the full equivalent of what you take away year by year, otherwise, even in your own time, you will find crops fall off and your own value to the community grow less." . . . improved methods . . . "increase crops considerably whilst reducing costs, for it is cheaper for five men to produce five tons of sugar than ten men to do so. With improved methods all benefit, planter and Government, because the total output of the community producing on the lowest possible basis of costs is sure to increase in quantity and therefore in taxable value."

THE AUTHOR.

CONTENTS.

ILLUSTRATIONS.

SIX CARTOONS BY JACK WALKER.

FOREWORD.

In face of everything that is happening to-day, and may happen to-morrow in connection with Russia, and on account of the immense value of that country to Prussia, if we leave it entirely in her hands to " play with " and to mould to her liking and requirements, I was in hopes that this Foreword might have been written by Sir George Buchanan, G.C.B., our Ambassador at Petrograd until the time that the Bolsheviki made life in that city unbearable.

The need of a complete and well-deserved rest rendered this impossible, for when I approached Sir George Buchanan on the matter, he wrote that " Your letter has been forwarded to me here, where I have been sent for a few weeks' complete rest. Anything that you can do to bring home to the public and to business men generally the necessity of holding out a helping hand to Russia so as to save her from German economic domination in the future will have my fullest sympathy. Russia has still a great future before her and we cannot afford to stand aside and leave Germany a free hand to undertake the work of reconstruction. We must not disinterest ourselves in Russia with her vast future potentialities."

As with Russia so it has been and so it will be with India, Latin America, and Africa. A people that cannot free themselves are not worthy to be free, and if we wish to be free of Germany's domination in times of peace as well as in times of war, we must not allow that country to dominate these markets again as she did before the War. The best governments and the wisest men the world ever knew may do all they can to free the world from the yoke of Prussian militarism and commercialism, but unless the British public rouse themselves and vigorously and willingly support those who show them the way, there will be no casting aside of this abomination; and should it fall around our necks, the misery and torture that Belgium has undergone and is still suffering from will be as child's play to what we shall suffer, and as we shall richly deserve to suffer. It was not the fault of Belgium that caused her people to be reduced to the state in which they find themselves to-day, but were we to go under the heel of Prussia it would be our own fault entirely; it would be on account of our having failed to prove ourselves worthy of being free of such discipline and treatment.

Let us therefore study the case from all points of view. Begin with the valuable reports that have recently been issued on the policy of the Empire to extend our trade and influence after the War, and then do as is suggested in the pages of this book, i.e., develop the latent industries of the Empire itself along the safest, surest, but at the same time the speediest lines possible and keep your eye on India and on Latin America. Above all, hang on to Russia; think of a game of " Soccer " with Russia as the ball. If we allow Germany to get the ball up her end, how can we expect to win the game after the War, no matter how thoroughly we beat the Central Powers in the War itself?

Since passing the final proofs I learn from Mr. Molteno, M.P., that Mr. Bigland " ceased to be Controller of Oils and Fats some months ago.

HAROLD HAMEL SMITH.

INTRODUCTION.

AT the end of January, I think it was on the 29th, Mr. Bonar Law, the Chancellor of the Exchequer, discussed in the House of Commons the constantly recurring demand from a non-wealth-owning class of political economists for a conscription of the nation's wealth. To this I would reply that wealth, like a national army, is always at the disposal of those who enjoy the confidence of its possessors, and who have demonstrated their ability to control and make good use of it if the wealth or the army is placed in their care. Merchant Princes, like the bulk of the officers of the Navy and Army of to-day, have come from every step in the (so-called) social ladder, and even as things are at the present time when considerable improvements could be introduced, such as those outlined on p. 113, there is still an equal chance for all of us to handle, and finally to secure, a portion of this nation's wealth if we are willing to allow our energies and our time to be conscripted to help make use of that wealth for the good of the owners as well as ourselves. Officers of the Navy or Army only enjoy the confidence of their fellow officers and men when by unceasing efforts and constant application to their work they have proved themselves worthy in every way of the trust reposed in them. It is true that an element of chance as well as of great personal risk is introduced into the lottery which brings some men up to the top, leaves others where they are and sends a third section flying down to the bottom; but as it is with the fighting man so it is with the man of commerce and the developer of the Empire's resources. If you wish to reach high positions and to attain great ends you must be capable of enduring much and able to run considerable risks. Faint hearts and slackers have no place in the modern army, military or commercial. It has been their willingness to participate in the great game of Empire-building to the uttermost end of endurance that has enabled our Teutonic enemy to obtain the wealth and the well-organized army with which they have threatened the prosperity and happiness of the civilized world. Will those who, like Mr. Philip Snowden and his colleagues, are so anxious to see the wealth of the Empire utilized for paying the war debt also guarantee that they and the masses in general will be equally generous and thorough in giving the country their brains, their powers of enterprise and endurance, and promise unceasing application to the work set them ? Until such a promise is made and carried out loyally the wealth of this country cannot be increased to the extent necessary to enable the Empire to flourish and so be able to pay for the War within a reasonable time, as it can do and will do if the working classes become as ambitious as the Merchant Princes have been (whose wealth we are now asked to conscript in order that the non-wealthy members of the Empire shall not be made to undergo further deprivation to liquidate our debts) and show themselves equally determined to " make good " both individually and in the aggregate. We all know the cry of the weakling and the slacker from the highest family in the land down to the sloucher in the street whom most people avoid in passing—" If I only had my chance "—" If I was only given a chance "—" If I were Prime Minister I would do this "—" If I were Sir Edward Holden I would do that "—everything, in fact, is promised by these incorrigible talkers and grumblers except continuous effort and persistency of purpose. They are willing to do anything except work unceasingly day in and day out as those who have secured the coveted wealth, or their forebears must have done, in order to attain the position they now hold.

Where the general public make the mistake, I believe, is in only following the career of the rich man after he has already made good, and, like a huge snowball, is able to add to his possessions at such a rate, and with so little apparent effort, as to stagger those who are watching the building up of his fortunes, heedless of the immense effort and unceasing thought as well as toil that he must have put forth at the start to have secured so much wealth. What we all want to remember is that the richest man, like the smallest snowball, had to begin with nothing, and I have always maintained that it is more interesting to watch and much more important to learn from the men who have failed than to covet and grumble at those who have made good. In both cases the seeker after wealth must have been a strenuous, if not always a capable, worker, and it must be agreed that nervousness and lack of application can seldom enter into their daily existence. I am of opinion, therefore, that once we place within the reach of the masses opportunities that we have not enjoyed ourselves for being trained and rendered capable of attracting to their pockets that wealth which we are inclined to covet when it belongs to others, we should find that the national wealth would be more evenly divided throughout the population generally, and would at the same time enormously increase the wealth of the Empire. Once such a training is placed within reach of all, those who continue to complain of others being more wealthy than they are will only have themselves to blame for not having taken advantage of the opportunities offered them to add to the wealth of the Empire as well as to that of their own family and themselves.

I make the foregoing remarks because I see some danger lurking ahead of those who control the finance and wealth-obtaining machinery of the Empire being inclined to place too much reliance on the ability of the few to obtain the wherewithal to liquidate our war debts within a reasonable period, whilst I am of the fixed opinion that this can only be done by the help of the many and by speeding up and increasing the wealth-making capabilities of every member of the Empire, white or coloured, so as to benefit firstly himself and then through himself the Empire at large. Those who claim to be authorities on Labour unrest have been very busy warning us that after the War employment will have to be found for millions of returned soldiers. I am almost surprised that such a statement has to be repeated as often as has been done, and in the threatening manner in which it has been hurled at our heads, when the whole cry of the Empire has been, not for work to be found for its people, but for those who are badly needed to do the Imperial work. That is to say, we need men willing and anxious to go abroad and risk their health and even their lives, as our Empire builders have always had to do, in order to develop the resources of our Empire within its boundaries and to protect and extend our interests and commercial influence in other countries, especially in Russia, Persia, and throughout Latin America, as the Germans have done for many years past. In Brazil alone, one of the richest countries awaiting development, and a centre easily capable of pouring sufficient profits into the Exchequer of any country whose people are bold enough to under-take its development, to pay for the entire cost of this War, there are, or were until recently, 300,000 Germans to possibly under 3,000 Englishmen. Until we have half a million Englishmen in Brazil, the man who stands up in London and says that he needs work should almost be branded as a traitor to his country, for there is, on all sides, far more work to be found if he is willing to undertake it than he is capable of doing, especially later on. Probably such men are neither capable nor willing to undertake the work of developing the resources of this Empire, as they do not want, when it comes to the pinch, to forgo the comforts of living over here and enjoying the fruits of the wealth obtained through the efforts of those who have gone abroad, and as long as we continue to tolerate such a class of beings in our midst we shall never prosper and go ahead as the Central Powers, and especially Prussia, has been doing during the last forty years. If, therefore, the leaders of the Trade Unions continue to complain that this country is not looking after and doing the best for the good of their members, I hope that the Government will tell them that the fault lies as much with the working men as with the workers of all classes in the community, for not coming forward and expressing their willingness to be conscripted in order to develop our national wealth abroad as the men of Germany have proved themselves to be willing to do, and as they have done with such tremendous benefit to Germany and harm to ourselves during the last generation or two.

What, as I have already said, is at present lacking, is the continuity of training organizations to take the children of these men from the very beginning of their educational career and to fit them out both in mind and body to be able " to do their bit " in helping to develop the resources of the Empire abroad, and to put money in the National Exchequer with which to fight the Empire's battles and to defend its people against the brutalities of aggressive enemies, as will have to be done if we mean to hold our

own in the future.[1] I am fully aware that to most people
of all classes the Tropics are an unknown quantity and of
as little interest and as little known to the man in the
street as the North or South Pole. "Lunatics" who
choose to go to any of these places at present awake
neither gratitude nor interest in the minds of those whom
they are benefiting unless it is by coming home and telling
"travellers' tales" of what they have *not* done, and of being
sternly silent of the excellent work they have been putting
in for the benefit of the country to which they belong. To
expect the general public, therefore, to be interested in this
book, and what I have to say, would be almost as silly as
to expect the crowd in a margarine or tea queue to be
interested in a lecturer like Mr. Wilson-Fox who can, and
does, so ably explain to us what the nation needs and how
it can satisfy these wants. It must be owned, therefore,
that probably 80 per cent. of this country, and the Empire
of which it forms part, are unable to realize the important
part that the latent resources of the Empire must be made
to play, and how it is everyone's duty to help them to do
so within the very near future, if we are to pay off our
fair share of the War debt that has been accumulated in
order to save our women and children, as well as our
national industries and prosperity, from the aggressive
brutality and greed of the Huns of Europe. Thus it is
that we are left with only about 20 per cent. of the total
population who are capable of judging how much we owe
to those willing and able to help us develop our resources, or who are in a position to judge how our output
of foodstuffs and other materials can be sufficiently increased, both to feed the public at the lower wages which
are bound to come after the War and still leave a margin

---

[1] See p. 84 regarding the views of Lord Bryce and Professor Hiram
Bingham as to the harm that educated Germans in Latin America have
done and will again do to the interests of this country.

of profit to go into the Exchequer to liquidate our national debt. Everybody knows that if we are to develop the resources of the Empire and add to the existing wealth of its people three things are needed :—

(1) The latent resources to be developed.

(2) The capital to develop them.

(3) The labour, both scientific and untrained, to carry out the schemes proposed.

The first two of this trio we undoubtedly possess, and I think I am right in saying that even when the War comes to an end there will still be sufficient capital left to develop the latent resources of the Empire to a degree that will enable us to pay our share of the national debt, within a reasonable time, huge as it may seem at the moment. The third item alone is lacking, both with regard to the white labour and trained leaders of men on this side as well as to the coloured labour in the Tropics and our overseas dependencies. Until, therefore, we can arrange for these labour supplies to be considerably increased we cannot expect to carry out the tempting, the possible and magnificent schemes that are being dangled before our eyes, without crippling, if not actually squeezing out of existence, the commercial and agricultural enterprises that already exist within the tropical zone. In saying this I am not only referring to enterprises within the British Empire, but would also include those in Latin America, which would never have come into being had not this country invested over £1,000,000,000 to open up and develop the mining and other industries of those magnificent trade centres. Up to the present I would claim that owing to the lack of educated men willing to play their part at Empire construction, whilst this country has found the capital to open up America, south of the United States, Germany has reaped the bulk of the profits accruing from the opening up, with our capital, of the various republics. They have

B

secured these profits because they deserved them through the hundreds of thousands of men that have been willing to sacrifice their home comforts for a time in order to advance permanently the interest of themselves and their families, and at the same time the prosperity of their Fatherland as well. Since this is the state of affairs at the present moment, I hope that every reader of this book will carefully study and give adequate attention to every proposal that is laid before them by men of experience to increase the national wealth, but at the same time I would warn them against being bullied or hustled into accepting such proposals, and voting that they should be adopted, until they know all the ins and outs of the case. Above all, they must ascertain from reliable authorities that the labour as well as the capital and the resources to be developed are in existence without injuring and taking away the wealth of other industries that have already been developed.

I particularly deprecate the attitude of a certain Labour organizer who on more than one occasion asked those present to support the plan laid before them unless they had got a better one to offer. The same attitude has been adopted very foolishly by the followers of Mrs. Besant in India, who are so noisily clamouring for Home Rule for India. I do not pretend to offer any opinion as to which side—the Home Rulers or their opponents—deserve the most encouragement, but I decidedly agree with the *Madras Mail*, when it wrote, a little time back, as follows, against the unreasonable attitude adopted by the Home Rule element towards those who dared to question their right to declare that India as an Empire was in favour of their proposals. Under the heading of

"WHERE IS YOUR CONSTRUCTIVE SCHEME?"
the *Madras Mail* commenced a very interesting leading article by telling its readers that

"A certain class of political critic in this country

appears to think that he can dispose of his European and Indian opponents by asking them where is their elaborate alternative to the Home Rule scheme they condemn. Speaking for Europeans, we frankly reply, nowhere. Not on us is the onus of producing comprehensive and detailed schemes of political reconstruction, for it is not we but the Home Rulers who demand radical changes in the whole existing system. Like our Indian friends, we are well enough aware that there is need of reform at various points in that system, but we flatly deny, as they also do, that the entire system needs to be recast. It is open to the Home Ruler to argue that we are far too complacent over any drawbacks the system may possess, or that it may be obsolete and in need of adjustment. He is entitled to make out such case against it as he can. But he has no right whatever to declare us out of court because we Europeans, believing the system to be in the main sound, and for the rest capable of improvement without general reconstruction, refrain from producing a scheme comparable in ambition and extent to that of the Home Rulers."

I am quite sure that such a policy, whether adopted over here, in India or elsewhere within the Empire, can do no good to those who make use of it, but is likely to cause considerable friction, and will certainly delay the introduction of any system of reform, no matter how badly a change may be needed.

As the public when attending meetings do not go about with a rival plan tucked away in their pockets, this sort of big stick attitude towards the voters of the United Kingdom is not likely to benefit those who have organized the meeting and it certainly is not a course that I would recommend anyone to pursue until they were quite certain that the proposed policy for developing the Empire's resources meets the following requirements :—

(1) Do those who are objecting to pay for the War at the present moment honestly believe that the scheme laid before them is a feasible one?

(2) Are they satisfied that those who are to find the money to finance these undertakings will secure the returns on the capital invested that they are led to believe will accrue and go to help reduce the War debt?

(3) Are the working classes in the United Kingdom the only members of the Empire who have fought and bled and died for the cause of the Allies? Has the United Kingdom been the only centre from which soldiers of all grades and colours have flowed forth to fight the good fight against the military domination of the world?

(4) Have not our Overseas Dominions, our Tropical Colonies and Dependencies also done as well as the working classes in this country, so far as their circumstances would permit, to help win the War?

(5) Since all these various units, the whites, the blacks and the browns, as well as the yellows, have come together and joined in the fight, why should the Labour leaders in this country talk in a menacing manner of the trouble that will accrue when the War is over if the propositions advanced by the E.R.D.C.,[1] including the development of palm products and other industries on the scale outlined by the hon. secretary, are not instantly approved of by the British public, and why should the tax-payers on this side of the water refuse to pay their share of post-war taxation any more than the inhabitants of the British Empire on the other side of the water?

Personally, I am certain that whilst all of us will avoid having to pay heavier taxes than are absolutely necessary it will be found that, once it is realized that the debts must be liquidated, everyone will join in and help to win the

---

[1] i.e., the Empire Resources Development Committee, Hon. Sec., Mr. Wilson-Fox, M.P.

peace as they are now doing to help win the War. But because I object to the tactics that have been called into use to force us to swallow the propositions, none of which have been thoroughly thought out, as they are dished up before us by the E.R.D.C., I have decided to publish the following pages in order to bring to the notice of the British public where and why I disagree with the propositions that I have heard propounded and where I believe they can be improved upon.

I will conclude by repeating here what I have said on p. 39, and which I have copied from my paper, *Tropical Life* : " I admire every square inch of Mr. Wilson-Fox and he has plenty of square inches to admire. I would be only too glad to see the objects he is fighting for become positive facts if their doing so harms no one. It is a pleasure to hear him speak and whether he is out for profit for himself or for the Empire, the more that follow his example the better for the Empire. If you doubt my sincerity when I say this read the article on p. 25 on ' The Outlook for 1918,' and then those who have had the pleasurable tonic of hearing Mr. Wilson-Fox speak will realize what a relief it is to listen to men of his calibre after a dose of those who continue to live only to grumble at the War and its inconveniences and to tell you with woeful countenances that they have had no meat for dinner, no butter or bacon, and, worst of all, that whilst they cannot ride in their motors they have to pay double railway fares when they go away for their holiday jaunts."

As I believe I have stated more than once in the pages that follow this Introduction, the remarks in this book with regard to the raising of crops, &c., refer entirely to areas within the tropical and sub-tropical zones unless stated to the contrary.

I should imagine that all who have read the proposals of Mr. Wilson-Fox will agree that improved and more up-to-date transport systems will have to be introduced throughout many portions of the Empire, and chiefly throughout the United Kingdom, if we are to hold our own and take full advantage of the trade boom that will fall upon us directly the War is over and the trade channels or, let us say, the trade-sluices, are opened and start to flow fiercely and freely again. This country especially, in proportion to the needs of her population, of the volume of trade that should be hers when peace comes, and in face of the chances that she has had in the past to do better, but has only ignored, stands in the greatest need of having her transport systems generally thoroughly re-organized and brought up to date. Unless this is done, and done very soon, we shall not be able to avoid the serious congestion of traffic and the stifling effect this congestion is bound to have on our trade when the War comes to an end and everything and everybody will be, or will want to be, on the move.

Some time ago, in 1904, Mr. E. A. Pratt, a writer who is, or ought to be, well known as an authority on matters dealing with agriculture, home industries, trade unions, and British industries, as well as on the railway systems of this country, told us in his " Organization of Agriculture," that the subject of agricultural (and trade) organization, together with the whole question of the transport of the commodities when produced, has very wide ramifications as between the railways and transport systems and our producers and manufacturers—issues whose ramifications are, in fact, far too wide to be squeezed in between the covers of any popular book. At the same time Mr. Pratt manages to squeeze in much valuable information on the need of the general public helping to bring about the better organization of our transport systems and thus enable them to be more capable of assisting in their turn to develop the agricultural, and the import and export trade of this country.

Then, again, I feel with the E.R.D.C. that consider-able profits should undoubtedly accrue to the State from the successful installation of large irrigation, drainage or land reclamation schemes, as well as from "breaking" new lands, as in Canada, and the establishment of home-steads to be let out on a hire-purchase scheme to settlers on terms that will attract newcomers, and still be able to pay a fair rate of interest as well as contribute a satisfactory sinking fund towards repaying the cost to those who found the capital necessary in the first place to establish these homesteads.

This reminds me that in the Foreword that he con-tributed in 1912 to the first edition of our book "Coconuts, the Consols of the East" (see pp. v to vii of the Foreword, which is also reproduced in the second edition as well), Sir W. H. Lever (now Lord Leverhulme) tells us that: " I see no reason myself why the various Governments affected should not give financial encouragement to the establishment of coconut estates by helping the planter [1] óver the period which elapses before the plantation comes into bearing. If this were done it would open up our tropical possessions [2] in a way that we can scarcely realize. It would increase the ties with the European countries and find good wholesome food for their teeming millions.

---

[1] That is, to finance and otherwise assist the small individual producers and settlers which the returned armies will soon be giving us by the thousand, and who it is to the interest of the Empire to encourage to go abroad in large numbers and plant up and develop the Empire generally, in preference to forcing us to rely on the same quantity of produce from one or two large company-owned properties.—H. H. S.

[2] And so again help to develop the latent resources of the Empire abroad as well as over here by placing on the land in the Tropics numerous communities which would not only send us the vegetable oils, &c., that we are in such need of, but which would, in the aggregate, be more regular and larger buyers of the machinery, estate implements, household supplies, &c., that we have to send them than would be the case if the produce came from only a comparatively few large company-owned estates.—H. H. S.

It would increase the purchasing power of the tropical countries, and would open up profitable opportunities of employment for young men who wish to go there.

" I know of no field of Tropical Agriculture that is so promising at the present moment as coconut planting, and I do not think in the whole world there is a promise of so lucrative an investment of time and money as in this industry. The world is only just awakening[1] to the value of coconut oil in the manufacture of artificial butter of the highest quality and of the by-product, copra-cake, as a food for cattle ; this is of very great value, especially for dairy cows, where food is required that will not give any added flavour to the milk or butter.[2]

" Given reasonable precautions and care, there is very little risk of failure in coconut planting. Experience has greatly increased in the last ten years, with the result that the possibility of failure is reduced to a minimum. A large amount of capital is not required if the planter is willing to grow and cultivate annual crops during the period that his coconut plantation is coming into bearing. The cost of clearing and planting is not of itself heavy ; it is the loss of interest and the long wait and accumulation of expenses during the seven years it takes before a coconut plantation comes into bearing ; but with a planter on his own estate, cultivating other products for

---

[1] This was in May, 1912.

[2] I wonder how many thousands of times this, now historical, paragraph has been "cribbed" by company-promoting schemers and others without acknowledging its source or referring to the context generally, but merely to dangle it before the eyes of the gullible members of the public with funds to invest. It is easy to realize how the name of its author would appeal to such promoters as being likely to "draw" since he has spoken so strongly on the subject. Lord Leverhulme's Foreword to the second and enlarged edition of the book, however, it should be noted, deals very fully with this matter, and with the danger and injustice of putting so valuable a pronouncement to such unfair and even objectionable uses.

the sake of their annual income, the amount of capital required to become the possessor of a rich coconut plantation is not excessive, and should not exceed £10 to £12 per acre, including every expense except the planter's own labour and interest on capital.[1]

" At the present price of coconuts—and there seems no immediate prospect of this price being reduced[2]—the net income to be derived from an acre of fully bearing coconuts would be £10 per annum, so that a comparatively small plantation of a couple of hundred acres would yield a net income of £2,000."

And now we come to what is, to my mind, the most important paragraph of the Foreword so far as the development of the latent resources of the Empire is concerned.

" I may call attention here," Lord Leverhulme went on to say, " to the enormous impetus that has been given to the development of Canada by the very simple help that the railway companies and landowners have given to emigrants in the way of starting them with a homestead into which to move on arrival on the prairies. This simply means that by making it possible for families to move into Canada, that country has become prosperous and successful. The money for these homesteads is paid back by the emigrants, and I believe that no loss has resulted under this system. If planters were similarly encouraged in the Tropics by the help of a little capital and a bungalow, the security being on the plantation, a rate of interest could be

---

[1] This estimate has been challenged as being too low. The challenge, however, has been fully and successfully dealt with in the Foreword to the second edition.

[2] This was of course written nearly five years ago. At present, once controlled prices are removed, I should imagine the value of coconuts would increase. Even to-day, or rather at the end of December, our own West Indian Island of Trinidad—an important coconut-producing centre which enjoys the competitive buying of the New York and United States markets—was quoting £9 per 1,000 for selected nuts, put up in bags of 100, at the producing centre.

arranged sufficient to cover all risks of loss, and to give the Government granting the loan a high return. It is not possible for any private individual to work on these lines, but it is possible for Governments. There are millions of acres of waste land in tropical countries waiting to be developed, and all that is wanted is a little help from the authorities to convert waste tropical possessions into veritable gold mines, producing wealth beyond the dreams of avarice, in occupation as well as in money, and, in addition, providing food for all.

" As a proof of this, let us consider what Government railways have done in developing Nigeria. Surely with this striking object lesson in front of them, Governments could assist in some other way[1] to further develop coconut planting and allied tropical industries, so as to insure that we make the most of this enormous field for human activity."

Going back to the E.R.D.C. and their proposals, I certainly consider that those who financed the cost of building and making a success of the Assouan Dam have not derived, in direct payments, such monetary benefits as they might have done and no doubt would have done, without hurting anybody, had such a scheme been carried out according to the present ideas of the E.R.D.C. On the other hand, can it not be claimed that the Egyptian Government has received its full share of profit (as well as of richly-deserved praise) many times over, indirectly if not directly, in the increased taxation, in the larger import and export duties, as well as in the fresh businesses that have been established through the building of the dam which has brought vast additional wealth to the land of the Pharaohs, additional wealth which is estimated by Wilson-Fox at £100,000,000 at least.

---

[1] But only by keeping close control over those carrying out the schemes, not by leaving the Development Board a " free leg " to act as it—i.e., the Board —thinks best.

What the E.R.D.C. has to tell us, through its honorary secretary, concerning the possibility of increasing all sections of the electrical industries, and of developing a more general, more efficient as well as a cheaper power supply, both on this side as well as in other portions of the Empire, is undoubtedly correct and should receive the closest attention on the part of the public. We must, however, see to it that those who undertake such schemes are made responsible to the country through the House of Commons for the success or failure of the work under-taken by them.

A far better system also is needed, both when obtaining, as well as in the distribution of our fish supplies, not only in this country but elsewhere as well. On p. 40 it will be seen that I called attention to this want some years ago, especially in connection with the fishing industries of our West Indian Possessions, as well as with those along the coast of Brazil.

One day, perhaps, we shall have, not the Minister of Production and Wheat Supplies, mentioned on p. 39, but rather a Minister of Imperial Development (and I am willing to admit that Mr. Wilson-Fox could fill such a post with advantage and credit so long as he was held in check by, and made responsible to, the House of Commons), whose department will cover all these schemes, and others still to come.[1] Such a minister should enjoy Cabinet rank and even be a member of the War Council, since he would be responsible for the production of food-stuffs, &c., needed to feed the troops, whilst at all times he

---

[1] For instance, the cleaning and polishing of our rice crops, and also the cutting and polishing of our diamonds within the Empire and not in Holland and elsewhere outside. In Chapter XXI, p. 130, I also discussed the cutting and grinding of lenses and optical goods generally within our midst instead of going to Germans to do the work, either in Europe or in America, which, to a German, is one and the same thing, especially for the optical trade.

would have to see to it that we were not only adequately fed, but also enabled (and, if necessary, forced or, to use a more gentle phrase, shall we say, educated up to the need of realizing that everyone of us will have) to carry on our various trades, industries, and professions, at the quickest rate possible, at the lowest cost compatible with quality and finish, and with the least amount of fatigue and consequent wear and tear to our minds and bodies that human ingenuity and care can enable us to enjoy.

The trouble with a book of this description is not what to put in it, but what you can leave out, as leave out I have had to do with the public's purse-strings growing tighter and tighter, and so requiring cheaper and not more costly books, as the present price of paper, printing, &c., urges one to issue. As, however, it is the public who have to be pleased and not my own inclinations, I have had to exclude all details—the most interesting portion of my scheme of How to Pay for the War—and only discuss in this volume the broad outlines mentioned in the index, viz., Finance, Education, Raw Labour, Imperial Expansion, Dry-zone Farming, and an Anglo-Slav *v.* a Teutonic trade domination of the Russian markets.

If, however, the public show sufficient interest in this book to warrant my issuing a supplementary volume, I will then discuss such subjects as the following, each and all of which I was foolish enough to imagine could be included in this volume without causing a rise in the price to be paid. Having been taught otherwise, the undermentioned items have had to be cut out :—

(1) Facilitating the settlement of ex-soldiers, officers and men, in agricultural and commercial centres abroad to carry on and extend the trade, influence and wealth-earning powers of the Empire.

(2) The possibility of building up a china clay and china manufacturing industry in British Malaya, as was

discussed by Mr. William Jones, Assistant Geologist to the F.M.S., and other authorities, as far back as May, 1915, and probably before that.

(3) The establishment of egret, pheasant, and other plumage-bird farms in order to use their plumage for bird millinery, thereby increasing the numbers of these birds (whilst improving their plumes), and not reducing them as some claim is being done.

(4) To establish chinchilla, silver fox, and other valuable fur-animal farms, in order to prevent these animals from becoming too scarce, and also to improve the quality of their fur for trade purposes.

(5) To encourage the breeding of cattle on coconut and other vegetable-oil-yielding estates, so that margarine can be manufactured locally (by such firms as Messrs. Lever's, the Maypole Company, Ltd., the Wholesale Co-operative Society, and other typically British firms, as Messrs. Tata are reported to be doing out in British Cochin), since both the oil and the milk are there, and the poonac, or seed-cake, on which to help feed the animals, can be had for the asking.

(6) In the same way to rear pigs and poultry in huge quantities, to the advantage of the crops, and also of this country and other centres to which the meat if shipped in cold storage would be very welcome. Properly encouraged the raising of pigs in the Tropics would become as remunerative as the rearing of cattle in Argentina, Paraguay, &c. India shows that the animals take kindly to the climate, and once care is taken to keep them from running *too* lean, the profits obtained are incredible. Their bristles alone are extremely valuable, the longest and best having recently been sold at over 50s. per lb. (£2 10s. for 16 oz., or more than 3s. per oz.).

(7) Whilst waiting for the area under sugar-cane to be planted we could not only expand the palm-sugar industry

within the Empire, but also collaborate with America in drawing supplies from the nipa, coconut, and other palms in the Philippines and elsewhere.

(8) We can, as I urge in this book, enormously increase our wealth from Latin America, by going into the handling of the trade products there and sending them to our own countrymen as well as to the ports and consuming centres of our Allies. Since I wrote (with Mr. J. F. Woodroffe) " The Rubber Industry of the Amazon," my knowledge of what we could do in that remarkable country and throughout Latin America has been greatly increased.

(9) The raising of remounts and the breeding of mules on coconut estates and elsewhere in the Tropics and throughout the Empire. This industry needs support not so much for the revenue and profits it would yield as for the chance it would offer to the Empire of having remount depots (like coaling stations) dotted about the world, so that no matter where we needed the animals, a supply would be available at a reasonable distance. With regard to the need of increasing our own supplies of mules, I cannot understand how and why this important industry has been so absolutely neglected, especially in comparison to our requirements throughout the Empire. One firm alone in the United States, it was reported in May or June, 1916, sold 120,000 mules to the British purchasing agents. If this is correct, I wonder how many animals— mules, horses, &c., in all—have been purchased during this War, and where our supplies will come from in future if some such plan as the one suggested in this paragraph is not adopted ?

All this and much more we could do, for I am sure we have the money. The only links missing in this chain of Imperial development that we want to see passed round the world are willing helpers, properly trained for the work, and surely these will be forthcoming as soon as the War is over and the men come back to civil life. It is in order to attract and train such men as soon as possible that I have devoted so much space in the following pages to the need for training colleges, and have spoken so emphatically on the desirability of catching hold of every one who seems in need of " a job " and insisting that he does " his bit " to help win the peace as he has done to help win the War. To enable him to do this we must start at once and arrange for an Imperial development system of education capable of coping with the demand for such courses, and, whilst this is being done, elect a Minister of Imperial Development and Food Supplies, with Cabinet rank, who will see that the necessary financial and other assistance is not lacking, once the men (and women) can be turned out fully trained and ready for action.

In conclusion I would like to say this. Before we can start to pay for the War on the basis that I am about to suggest, we have to win the War in a way that will ensure a permanent peace, and that means that a " clean knock-out " defeat must be inflicted on the Prussian militarism and all the bestiality and brutality that that militarism stands for. The belief that war pays has been consistently taught to the people of Germany since the days of Frederick the Great. They have been forced to accept this doctrine with a far greater faith and belief than the belief they profess to have in a God and a Bible as we understand the Deity and that book. All this will have to be changed once and for ever, unless we want to pay not only for the cost of our own share of the War, but Germany's share as well.

As Lord Denbigh told us, as members of the London Chamber of Commerce, when speaking of our enemy's war aims, Germany has grown to be what she is by war and war alone, and especially by the three short successful and lucrative wars of 1864, 1866 and 1870. Germans have been taught to regard war as a paying business, and the military party still wants the public of our chief enemy to continue in that belief.[1]

Germany has for long been intensely jealous of England, the Earl went on to say in his decisive, racy manner, bringing out his points and driving them home—"burning them in," to use his own phrase, one by one with a vigour that astonished but pleased the huge audience that faced him immensely—and has for many years been working with infinite cunning for the undoing of the British Empire and British Trade, and thereby securing the military domination of the world.

Germany hoped to attain her ends by "peaceful penetration." She deliberately prepared and brought on this war when peaceful penetration was not going fast enough. This is why I am so keen on displacing the educated German, one-third merchant and two-thirds spy and military strategist, throughout Latin America.

Germany aimed at getting what she wanted by seizing Belgium and the coast of Flanders, invading and defeating France and Russia, and by establishing the great scheme known as "Central Europe" or "Mittel Europa." This immense belt of territory, stretching from the North Sea to the Persian Gulf and served throughout by the Bagdad Railway, would then be entirely under the control of Berlin, and Germany would thus dominate and divide Europe. Germany could then destroy Britain's position in Egypt and the East, seize her trade route to India and eventually wrest India itself from Britain.

---

[1] As if to make me emphasize this portion of the book (which I did not mean to introduce, but having heard Lord Denbigh speak I feel loth to leave it out) a lively cannonading is going on over my head whilst writing, between the German airmen and our own "somewhere in England," on the evening of the day after the Chamber of Commerce had been told about the war aims of Germany, especially those of Prussia.

One of our greatest dangers, yet one that is little known in England, is the projected ship canal, already begun, to connect the North Sea rivers with the Danube, and thereby facilitating the free transfer of light cruisers, destroyers and submarines across Europe to the Black Sea and Dardanelles. Issuing from behind the protection of the Dardanelles they could dominate absolutely the whole Eastern Mediterranean. These waters would thereby be rendered most dangerous to British ships, so that, with Turkey, Bulgaria and Rumania remaining in the power of Germany, our position in the Eastern Mediterranean would be in constant peril.

Germany is fighting for the domination of the world and supremacy on sea and land. She says to us: "You are no longer any use as fighters. You are a decadent race. We see you are afraid of Germany from your constant appeal to us to reduce armaments. You are a mere nation of shopkeepers. Get out and get Under." That is her watchword. "Get out of your Empire and get under Us."

Our reply is: "You are a race of arrogant and brutal bullies; we have in this war proved to you that we are the better fighters. We are not going to get out of our Empire at your bidding. We are going to stick it, and we are now engaged in showing our people what will happen if they don't stick it, until America comes in with all her force."

German " Agents " are now busily engaged all over the world designing to bring about a peace by negotiation. Such a peace under present circumstances *would be a German victory*. If peace were made leaving Germany in possession or control of the territory she now occupies either in the West or in the Near East, she would have won the war and obtained a position from which she could most certainly break up our Empire in the near future.

One side or the other must win. A drawn war is a German victory. Dr. Paul Lensch, Socialist member of the Reichstag, said recently : " Germany will have won the war if she does not lose it ; but England will have lost the war if she does not win it."

We hope, after this war, to see an improved standard of living and better social conditions. We hope that as all classes have fought and died together in this war, so all classes may join in creating a happier and more contented England.

How is this possible if Germany threatens us at vital points, forcing us to maintain a large and expensive army at home and corresponding garrisons abroad ?

Our one chance of a lasting peace is to beat Germany in the field—proving to the German people that with all the world against her on account of her faithlessness and brutalities—Militarism *does not pay*.

The above are the War Aims of Germany in a nutshell, as outlined by Lord Denbigh. My readers therefore can fully realize how necessary it is to make " a clean sweep " of the " gang " now terrorizing those under their heel, and if we do not want to suffer even worse horrors than those meted out to Belgium and France, we must not listen to any pacifist arguments, and above all we must cease from tolerating (and with some among us of almost encouraging) those parasites of free democracy, the conscientious objector and non-protector of our women and children, as well as of the Empire as a whole. Their absence in the midst of Germany is a great disadvantage to us, but then, as every one knows, such people cannot batten and fatten on those who are ruled by autocrats as they can and do batten on a democratic social system such as prevails over here.

Many thanks are due to the publishers of *Tropical Life* for allowing me to reproduce several articles which I had written for and published in that monthly on such questions as the need of tropical agricultural colleges, the need of increasing the labour supplies of the Tropics, and also of financing and encouraging those who are striving so earnestly to extend our trade from this side and to develop the resources of the Empire and of the countries of her Allies abroad. I have reprinted these articles sometimes in the first, sometimes in the third person as they were in the original. This is as it should be, for the development and increased prosperity of the Empire is not a one-man job, " we " alone can do it by joining together and working in unison. So long as everything goes well what does it matter who gets the credit, if the Empire and Mother England get the prosperity. If, however, faults have been committed, or injustices done, unintentionally, to anyone, then, and only then, will " I " take the place of the editorial " we," and be quite ready to receive a " wigging " (if I deserve it), and told how to avoid doing so another time.

Apologies are due to the publishers of the *Mysore Economic Journal*, of Bangalore, for the article I contributed to their columns and have (practically) reproduced in this book, without waiting for the Editor's permission to do so. I have also to thank my friends in America for my paper *ex* the report of the Eleventh Annual International Dry-farming Congress. The *Daily Graphic*, of London, kindly allowed me to include the cartoon on p. 112.

In conclusion, may I call attention to the Appeal on the back cover of the book, and urge everyone, where engaged in developing the latent resources of the Empire, to remit at regular intervals a percentage of the salary and profits they receive. We must all remember that if these blinded men were not at St. Dunstan's many of us might be reduced to their state—worst of all, we might, like Belgium, be in the grip of Prussia.

BIBLIOGRAPHY.

———

As will be seen when reading the coming pages, I have made use of articles contained in the following publications, all of which I hope my readers will study in the original.

The Contemporary Review, October, 1917.

The Nineteenth Century and After, October, 1917.

The West India Committee Circular, January 10, 1918, and other issues.

The Journal of the Royal Society of Arts, December 15, 1918.

United Empire. Organ of the Royal Colonial Institute. Several issues.

West Africa : 28, Fleet Street, E.C. 4. Several issues.

The Mysore Economic Journal, Bangalore, Mysore. The January, 1918, and other issues.

The Agricultural Journal of India, issued by the Agricultural Research Institute, Pusa, India. Several issues.

The British Citizen and Empire Worker, London.

The Labour Leader, Manchester.

The New Europe : 10, Orange Street, Leicester Square, W.

The Round Table : 175, Piccadilly, W. Several issues.

Current Opinion, New York : 65, West 36th Street. March, 1918, and other issues.

The Madras Mail, Madras, Southern India.

The Pan-American Magazine, 70, Fifth Avenue, New York, U.S.A.

"Paying Britain's War Debts by Easy Methods": a brochure by Mr. John H. Harris, Denison House, Victoria, S.W. 1.

The Proposed Imperial Bank of Industry : a plan drawn up by the Committee of the British Empire Producers' Organisation. Evelyn House, Oxford Street, W. 1.

"Metals as a Base of Imperial Strength": a paper read by Mr. Octavius Beale before the London School of Economics on February 9, 1917.

How to Pay for the War.

SECTION I.

IMPERIAL EXPANSION.

CHAPTER I.

The Native Factor in the Economic Development of the Empire.

" The Wealth of the Country depends less on its natural resources than on the vigour, the energy, and the training of its people."—The Prime Minister (Mr. Lloyd George) at the Royal Albert Hall, October 22, 1917.

IF the reader will turn to the note at the foot of page 783 in the October issue of the *Nineteenth Century and After*, he will there see a statement by the present American Ambassador to the effect that " The Rule of Conduct which serves as the fundamental basis of democracy in the United States of America is that every human being should have an opportunity for its utmost development." A wiser saying has never been uttered and this statement of Mr. Hines Page, followed so soon after by that of our present Prime Minister which stands at the head of this page, should sink into the mind and brain of every Britisher, worthy of the name, for on it depends the success of the future as regards the fortunes of the British Empire when we one and all, man, woman and child, will be or ought to be working to the uttermost of our powers to help develop the resources of the Empire in every way possible and thus win the Peace as we mean to win the War. Unless each and all of us are given the opportunity to develop our own latent resources and capabilities to the uttermost, and until we are all willing to seize such opportunities and to make the most of them, it will be impossible to develop to the full the latent resources of our Empire.

As this is the work that lies ahead of us I for one cannot be too grateful both to the American Ambassador and to our own Prime Minister for having uttered such words at so opportune a moment, for, by urging that every man and woman, above all, that each boy and girl, should be given every opportunity possible to develop their powers of thought and action, the development of the Empire can alone be properly and adequately carried out.   What we all need is to be trained to think things out for ourselves, for this constitutes the only sure means of turning our thoughts and abilities to use and of being able to develop them for the benefit of the immediate district in which we live as well as of the Empire at large.   Every statement, therefore, as well as every institution brought into being that helps us to think and, having started our thoughts in the right groove, that helps us to develop them for the common good, is rendering an inestimable service and providing the surest means of helping us to build up the future prosperity of our State.   Those who think otherwise and want us to believe that the State should develop itself rather than allow individuals to do it for her, run a bad chance, so it seems to me, of stifling the ambitions and the initiative of the more pushing of the population and of not making use of the vigour and energy of us all to help the common cause, or of giving us the opportunity of developing ourselves to the uttermost for the good of the State.   State development by the State must tend, on the other hand, to use its people on the whole like so many labourers, each to do his or her allotted task which has been set for them by others whom chance or perhaps favouritism has placed above their fellow creatures and against whom there is always liable to be a grudge, probably quite undeserved, on the part of the workers who imagine that they have not been given an equal chance with those who are above them. If I am correct in this, then State development must, in the long run, prove less successful both for the country and for its people than would be the case if we were all trained to develop first ourselves and then the particular business with which we are to become connected and through that the prosperity of the State by our individual action and enterprise.

This is why I believe that individual self-development brought about of course by State or philanthropic-aided colleges or similar institutions must prove far better and safer in the long run than if the State were allowed to be developed by a privileged few, jealous of their position and anxious to maintain it, perhaps unwittingly, at the expense of the general population. If this view is correct we could look for nothing but trouble and disappointment later on if the views expressed by Mr. Wilson-Fox in the paper that he read before the Royal Society of Arts on December 13, 1916, when Lord Selborne was in the chair, and, more recently, in his article on " The Development of the Empire's Resources " in the October Number of the *Nineteenth Century Review*, were agreed to by the Government and the public because, as stated by one speaker who claimed to be a Labour representative, Mr. Fox had outlined an attractive and easy method of paying for the War.[1]

Mr. Fox is quite right when he claims that the resources of the Empire could be and should be developed to a very

---

[1] See also the paper read by Mr. Wilson-Fox before the Royal Colonial Institute on January 9 as well as the address delivered by Mr. Alfred Bigland, M.P., before the Members of the London Chamber of Commerce on January 30, of which a full report has been published, I was glad to see, in *West Africa* (London), of February 9 (1918).

much greater extent and at more rapid rate than has hitherto been the case. In the same way the trade of this country and the production of manufactured goods within the United Kingdom not only can be increased very considerably, but will have to be increased both per man employed and per horse power of the machinery called into use to help the human factor, for, if we do not turn out our goods at a quicker rate and at a comparatively lower cost at post-war rates than we were doing up to the time hostilities broke out, we shall not be able to hold our own against our competitors, whether they be our American cousins or our German enemies. The dormant resources of the British Empire at home so far as her manufacturing industries are concerned will have to be developed in every way possible, as will the dormant resources that we are fortunate enough to possess in the Tropics. For this reason I wish everyone who sets himself up to remedy the defects that are hindering this development all success in their crusade, so long as they do good to the present generation and do not lay the seed of future trouble for those generations who have yet to come. So far as the Tropics are concerned I cannot help sounding a note of warning lest our well-meaning friends in their anxiety to help the present generation and to relieve the enormous taxation with which we are faced in order to pay for the cost of the War, should cause a permanent injury to befall future generations out of all proportion to the benefits that they will confer upon us to-day. So far as I can make out from the propositions laid before us, either the suggestions thrown out cannot be materialized in the near future and so will not be available to help reduce the war debt as we want to see it reduced, or else, if we are to obtain £50,000,000 per annum from palm products in Africa and the South Seas, or 2,000,000 tons of sugar from British Guiana, we must speed up and exploit the natives who are to produce these enormous amounts (in spite of the anger of Mr. Wilson-Fox against those who use the word "exploit" in reference to his suggestions), or else such propositions must be ruled out of court altogether as being impossible to attain within reasonable time to meet our debts. If these are the only results that we can look for, what is the good of asking us to adopt such a policy when on the very face of it the proposition is impossible on account of the lack of labour and the many years, if ever, that it will take to achieve. Having read or listened to four statements given forth I believe with the approval of the entire Committee interested in drawing up schemes for developing the resources of the Empire, I gather from what we have been told that neither Mr. Wilson-Fox nor Mr. Bigland have been speaking for themselves, but on behalf of the Committee which we are told is composed of leading men with world-wide experience in economics. If this is so, why have we been told on more than one occasion that the members of the Committee are not experts, and until we get a satisfactory answer to this query, I think the British Public would be wise to ascertain whether every member of the Committee is or is not an acknowledged expert as regards the affairs of the Empire, and therefore should be and must be either ignored or else held responsible for the results that will arise for good or for evil from every word that they utter, and the proposals that they lay before the British Public for their acceptance.

At the present stage of the controversy I feel sure that we should have much more confidence in the Committee if it were to issue a joint manifesto and let us know the names of all those who are interested in the scheme so far as the Tropics are concerned, and whether both at the present time and in the future they intend to carry on the work individually or collectively merely out of love for their country or whether they will expect to be paid for their services. Before the public can be asked to approve of the scheme we must know the whole of it and be told what industries are to be dealt with, and how it is proposed that those already connected with established industries will be treated should the State decide to take them over and develop them.

Up to the present everything is extremely ambiguous : so far as I can gather the Committee is only considering large-scale proposals and therefore no one can say where their influence will extend to or where it will cease, and this is bound to cause great unrest and anxiety among those who have already done so much to develop the resources of the Empire. Every man in the Tropics is fully aware of the fact that any further development of an industry, or an increased output from the soil, must mean an increased number of labourers engaged in that particular work, and so they are wondering where all these labourers are to come from. Let the Committee enlighten them on this matter before they continue to receive propositions and to dangle tempting methods before the eyes of the ignorant British Public (ignorant so far as tropical development is concerned) of how to help pay for the War out of our tropical possessions by obtaining such sums as £50,000,000 a year out of palm products or 2,000,000 tons of sugar from British Guiana.

Of course, having settled the Labour difficulty, if ever it be possible to do so, we then come to the question of Capital, for it must be remembered that an income (that is a net profit) of £50,000,000 a year on palm products alone from two centres that do not include India or Ceylon, will need an enormous amount of capital to develop, and so will Mr. Bigland's 2,000,000 tons of sugar which he insists can be obtained from British Guiana. Such capital, of course, could be obtained by the State from out of the pockets of the public, supplemented possibly with private capital, as was done in the case of the British Cotton Growing Association which, in its time, has eaten up quite a substantial amount of money, though what benefit the Empire has derived from it in comparison with the substantial capital that the Directors have had at their disposal, is very difficul tto estimate. If the British Public gives the members of the Board to be nominated in the hereafter according to the views of the members of the Empire Resources Development Committee, the capital that they will need it is to be hoped we shall get a much larger return per £100 invested than has been received by those who subscribed to the funds of the British Cotton Growing Association. If we do not do so the whole aim and object of the E.R.D.C., viz., to help pay for the War, will come to naught, and the public will have to stand the racket and pay for the cost of the War as well.

This is an important item, especially as it comes on the top of the lack of labour, taking the Tropics as a whole, that already exists, and which will be further diminished if the men needed to carry out the schemes of the Committee on the scale proposed by its honorary secretary are to be forthcoming. In face of this I do not think I am asking too much when I want to know if the members of the Committee, who are mentioned by name in the October issue of the *Nineteenth Century Review* (p. 836), are really working to benefit the Empire, or whether, if they are not careful, they will not rather be putting money in the pockets of a privileged set whose names will, so I take it, have to be made known to the public later on.

In any case they should come forward as a group in the same way as Mr. Wilson-Fox has come forward personally, as well as Mr. Bigland, in a lesser degree,[1] and state

---

[1] It is only fair to state that Sir Starr Jameson was to have addressed the London Chamber of Commerce, but owing to his death, so greatl

definitely—and it must be definitely—not on the ambiguous terms hitherto used—what other tropical interests besides vegetable oils, sugar and fibres, the Committee or the Board yet to be nominated, mean to develop, and to let us know at the same time exactly how they are to secure the labour, &c., necessary to obtain the produce with which they mean to deal.

As I have already stated elsewhere (*Tropical Life*, May, 1917, p. 73), " I understand that it is proposed that a beginning should be made by establishing monopolies of vegetable oil products such as oil palms, coconut palms, and other oil-bearing trees, and presumably later on, to include cacao beans. Do such concerns, I would ask, grow on gooseberry bushes, or can they be produced in the Tropics without much risk ? Can the right, therefore, to exploit or, if the Committee finds that term too harsh, to develop these industries be granted by the State to any board or committee without confiscation or, in plainer English, without committing an action which morally, if not legally, amounts to pure robbery."

If industries already established are not to be taken over, I do not understand where these enormous quantities of trade products are to come from, for surely we are not expected to wait until the trees have been planted and the crops come to maturity, before starting forth to help pay for the War. I may be wrong to think so, but taking

---

deplored by every Imperialist, Mr. Bigland had to take his place. It could well be claimed, therefore, that the Committee had arranged for three prominent members to lay their views before the public. Meanwhile it is to be hoped that Lord Selborne will be induced before long to let us know his views ; it should not be difficult for him to do so, since it could well be claimed that Mr. Bonar Law gave him the lead when he spoke in the House of Commons on January 29, of increasing the revenue of the country by developing the immense latent resources of the Empire. See the report of his speech in the House of Commons in the *Times* of January 30, pp. 7 and 8, showing that he made his remarks the day before Mr. Bigland addressed the London Chamber of Commerce.

the scheme as a whole as laid before us up to January 31, and making every allowance for the modified statements uttered by Mr. Bigland at the Chamber of Commerce regarding the elimination of profit-grasping middle-men, either it has been proposed that the tropical industries already started by individual effort are to be absorbed by the State, and worked with the help of the planters as well as of the merchants, through the monopoly or board, or else the State is to start planting and producing the crops on their own account. If neither of these schemes be the ones sought for, the whole proposition as regards the Tropics is unfeasible, and is in fact an attractive fairy tale which may please the mind of the public over here as it seemed to please the labour organizer who spoke in defence of it. Even if the entire proposition is only a fairy tale, no one can deny the fact that the resources of this Empire of ours sadly need developing, and that if the rising generation were properly trained from the start, that is, whilst they are still at school, but more especially when they have left to attend the secondary schools and colleges, they could help us enormously. Again, many of the younger ex-soldiers, provided that the Tropics did not affect their health, should be induced to take an interest in such work as with their assistance our Overseas Possessions can and will give in many cases, so far as Dame Nature goes, five and ten times the present output and thus increase our National and Imperial wealth to a degree that will prove very useful when the time comes to liquidate the War debt. So far, however, I have found nothing in the schemes put forward to show how any increases can be secured in the near future, say within the eight or ten years that Mr. Bigland mentioned in the Chamber of Commerce, and until we have been satisfied to the contrary we must take it for granted that the vastly increased output that we are asked to look for can be obtained only by speeding up the present producers. To do so would cause trouble with the natives, and if we start that then, far from increasing our production, we shall obtain smaller outputs and encourage serious race trouble as well. This is a little point that the Labour organizer already referred to would be wise to digest, for on the two occasions that I have heard him speak in support of the Committee's scheme he has asked us to adopt the propositions put forward, because if we do not do so there will be trouble with the "lads" when they come back from the War, since they do not mean to pay for the War as well as to fight in it. Perhaps a speaker at the London Chamber of Commerce was not far out when he said that there probably will be trouble when the men come back from the War, but that it will be between the men and their trade organizers and strike leaders before anyone else. In any case, the people of this country, if they trouble to read the foreign papers, know perfectly well that revolt and riot are not the exclusive property of the white race, and if from want of tact and judgment they cause the coloured people to revolt as Germany did, the cost of doing so is increased twofold to us, because we first have to quell the trouble and then have to go without the help of those who have been helping us to collect the tropical produce that we cannot do without, through their having been killed or driven away during the riots. If the British workman is a valuable asset to the Empire, those who imagine that the natives abroad are not equally useful are making the mistake of their lives. For this reason, if the whole scheme so far as the Tropics are concerned is to be based on the proportion of an income of £50,000,000 per annum from palm products from Africa and the Pacific alone, then I would claim that the whole idea, if it is to be of any use in helping to pay for the War within the time of the present generation, far from being a fairy tale, will become a horrible nightmare; nay, more, it will develop into a tragedy as serious as any tale of the Spanish Conquistadores, and the Indians of South America, or of the German and other races with the negroes cf Equatorial Africa.

With the present population that exists in the Tropics it is foolish to expect to develop our resources over there to anything like the proportions suggested and those who· try to do so must either fail in their object or else they will kill out the natives at an alarming rate (to say nothing of ruining present development work on which these natives or the bulk of them are already employed), because the discipline and pressure under which the men would have to work would reduce them to such a degree of temperamental and physical misery that they not only would, but they will rather die than go on with it. This means, therefore, that those who are to come after us will have to starve or else reduce the rate at which our population is increasing because, as we stand to-day, the white race cannot progress without the raw materials and the foodstuffs that we are drawing from the Tropics, and which we shall need in ever-increasing quantity as fresh generations come and go and the population of this country, of America or elsewhere grows larger and larger. Already farseeing practical men are realizing at last that if the natives in the Tropics continue to be killed off even to the same extent during the next ten or twenty years that they have been in the last score of years, it will be found that the people with the white skins will also become considerably reduced as regards their numbers, wealth and power. This is not surprising, as without larger supplies of native labour than we already possess we shall lack the food, the raw materials and the trade called into being by these coloured races who alone can cultivate the soil and handle the crops in the full Tropics.

Commenting generally on one or two points in the

article by Mr. Wilson-Fox in the *Nineteenth Century Review*
I cannot help noticing that on page 837 he points out
that "it must, however, be emphasized that the Committee
does not command the services of an expert staff and is,
therefore, unable, even if so desired, to express an authori-
tative opinion upon any proposal submitted to it." With
all goodwill towards Mr. Fox and his ambitions, I must
say that I do not like this short paragraph, for it gives you
the idea that the Committee is ready to make proposals
and then seeks to shirk any responsibility concerning the
results. I have a sufficiently high enough opinion of
Mr. Wilson-Fox's knowledge and experience to suggest
that he is an expert staff in himself, and in any case I do not
see why such a statement should have been included. If
the Committee has not sufficient confidence in their
opinions to be willing to stand by them whatever happens,
why do they come before the public and ask them to accept
what they themselves are not sure of?

Again, on the same page, he goes on to tell us that "it
can hardly be questioned that the realization of the
Committee's aims would be highly desirable." To this
we will all agree, but I again disagree when he adds the
words with only a comma in between, "always provided
that such realization were not accompanied by evils which
it failed to take into account." "It" signifies of course
the Committee, which seems to me in face of this statement, and of the one quoted above, to be trying to face both
ways, so that whatever happens, whether success or failure
comes out of their proposals, they will be in a position to
turn round and say, "I told you so." If this is not making
proposals and then shirking responsibility over the results,
I should be curious to know what constitutes doing so.

Taking the whole of the Committee's proposals, as laid
before us so far by the hon. secretary and Mr. Bigland, I
take it for granted that the scheme or schemes put forward

are with the one idea of greatly increasing the output of tropical outputs within the Empire, and of speeding up the rate of production throughout our tropical possessions, in order to help pay for the War as soon as possible. I am quite willing to agree with the Committee that we have by no means done as well in the past as we should have, but in our hurry to make amends in the future we must be sure that the change is for the better and not for the worse.

Such schemes as the ones proposed to be carried out on the huge scale suggested in connection with palm products and sugar gives one the idea that the Committee wants to start at once, or, at any rate, as soon as possible. To carry out such an undertaking, whether now or in one or two years' time will, besides the capital needed, require whole armies of natives (and here I am using the term armies in quite the modern sense of the word, amounting to hundreds of thousands at a time) if we are to produce the crops and to transport the products from the fields and the forests down to the shipping ports. Where, I am again obliged to ask, are these armies of natives to come from, and also, even if the labour supplies are forthcoming, who is to enjoy the profits if the scheme proves successful, and who is to stand the losses if the venture proves a failure? Already we want larger labour supplies to do the work that we have in hand than are obtainable at the time of writing, and without such increased supplies we shall not be able to develop the resources of the Empire on the lines already mapped out.[1] This means that one hundred Committees like the E.R.D.C. cannot increase or further develop our Imperial resources unless

---

[1] See p. 37 in "The High Price of Sugar," where I urge that "If India restricts labour supplies for the West Indies and elsewhere she must increase her outputs." See also in this book, p. 134.

they first secure substantial numbers of natives from some place that they alone must know of if they expect their proposals ever to materialize. So far as I know the world and its labour supplies I cannot understand how this Committee or anyone else can expect to further increase to any appreciable extent within the next ten years or more the output of the Empire's products on the scale suggested, without causing serious inconvenience to, and probably permanently crippling, established and flourishing concerns already in existence. When you come to an end of your supplies of labour, so far as numbers are concerned, and you still want to increase your output, there is only one thing left to be done and that is to increase the proportion of work per labourer per day. In other words, if we are to obtain fifty or even twenty-five per cent. of these enormous outputs from the British Tropics we shall have to force the pace and to drive the native to work at such a rate that even if the present generation is satisfied with the results nothing but harm will befall those who have yet to come. Possibly this is what Mr. Wilson-Fox is thinking of when he tells us that the realization of his ideas might be accompanied by evils which his Committee has failed to take into account. If this pamphlet comes before their notice, as I have no doubt it will do, neither Mr. Wilson-Fox nor any member of his Committee will be able to say that they have not been warned to take this possible and highly probable evil into account.

On the other hand, as I show more fully in various articles reproduced from *Tropical Life* in the latter part of this book, much can be done by judiciously supporting, financially and otherwise, enterprising men with energy and push who prefer to " make good " in the Tropics than to rust at home ; and also, by scientifically training planters and agricultural experts we can insure not only that our present crops are not reduced on account of pests and other troubles, but that the present outputs will be increased by extending the areas planted and increasing the crops generally by means of scientific and up-to-date methods, as well as by improved machinery and other appliances. This scheme for developing the resources of our Empire has already been discussed by me in " The High Price of Sugar " when commenting on the danger of overworking the natives on tropical estates. After showing how scientific training could increase the output of sugar per man and per acre without over-burdening the labourers, I conclude by stating on p. 12 " what an immense saving of labour, which could then be devoted to other industries, these increased yields would mean compared with our requirements under existing conditions. The fact that in the near future every worker will be, if he does his duty, worth two ordinary ones before the War should alone cause the authorities to see that those who have the land and employ the labour to cultivate it, know how to appreciate and how to use both the land and the labourer to best advantage, and that too without the labourers being overworked to a degree that can render them useless to their family or to themselves and a burden to the community at large." In the book that I wrote with Mr. J. F. Woodroffe on " The Rubber Industry of the Amazon " I also devoted much space to a discussion of the South American Indians and *Caboclos* and the amelioration of their lot whereby, whilst their level of comfort would be considerably raised, their output of produce could be increased far beyond the extra cost involved in the better housing and feeding of these workers.

To speed up the development of the resources of the Empire on the lines and at the rate suggested by the E.R.D.C. would create in any case a demand for native labour far in excess of the supply. Before I conclude, therefore, by giving my views as to how the resources of our Empire can be safely developed for all time and for the benefit of everybody, both of this as well as of future generations, I would like to say a few words on the danger of "forcing the pace" of the coloured races in the Tropics, and I am doing so, not from any humane reason, but out of pure selfishness, because I do not want my children or my grandchildren to run short of the necessities of life in the time to come. I am doing so because, on paper, I do not profess to care one jot or tittle what happens to the blacks, the browns and yellows of this world, but merely because I believe in the idea that it is wise to grab from the Tropics year by year, both now and in times to come, every ton of material that can be secured and to take all steps possible to increase that output in every way. To do this, however, we must set to work cautiously and in such a way that we shall secure much larger native populations everywhere, and not the continually smaller ones that seem to be the rule at present even under the most favourable circumstances. Judging from all we have heard recently, the natives whenever subjected to over-pressure have been killed off, or discouraged, or otherwise prevented from breeding or of rearing their children when they do come along, the result being in every case where such circumstances exist that the population has gone steadily back. With this view in my mind when I read the English translation of a book written by Adoph Cureau, published about two years ago and entitled "Savage Man in Central Africa," I could not help wondering how many of the British public realized what a stern necessity the Tropics of to-day are to the reputedly civilized nations of the temperate zone; furthermore, that an abundant and ever-increasing native population, a far larger one than exists at present, will be an even greater necessity in the

-days to come if the so-called civilized nations are to
continue to increase by being able to satisfy their ever-
increasing demand upon the foodstuffs and raw materials
that the Tropics can alone produce for us and which
Europe, America, Australia must all have, as the Central
Powers, and especially Prussia, have learned to their cost.
Meanwhile, I would claim that those who have had to do
with natives and especially those who have watched the
white and coloured men when handling the labour gangs,
kindly or otherwise (and through not understanding the
men, through impatience, fatigue or other causes, it has
too often been a case of otherwise), will agree with
Monsieur Cureau when he tells us, on p. 37 of his book,
that we must remember that every man has in front of
his judgment something which is like a bit of coloured
glass and which represents an aggregate of inherited or
acquired ideas, prejudices, interests, desires and sensations
that are derived from tradition, physiological or pathological peculiarities and surrounding influences. Thus it
is that men should be made to study anthropology and be
trained before being placed in charge of native labour,
because otherwise when the untrained white man tries to
understand and fix the ideas behind the black man's mind
in his own, he is inclined to fail, since, as with a kaleidoscope, every time he looks into it the ideas take on new
shapes and colours and the unexpected is ever happening.
Thus it comes about that the untrained man being unprepared for the emergencies that arise is inclined to lose
his patience and friction, loss of time, reduced output and
other troubles frequently result. For several years past
I have been trying to realize that, since we are already
feeling the shortage of coloured labour (and we shall feel
it with a vengeance when the War is over and all the
nations fly to the Tropics to feed themselves to repletion
and to lay up a stock, in order that they shall not go

2

without in the near future, after so many years of fasting),
what will happen in fifty or a hundred years' time when the
white peoples in spite of this horrible War will have
become much more numerous than they are to-day, and
the coloured races run a very good chance of becoming
much fewer in number.   Since it has been proved that the
native races alone can raise the crops and collect the
materials in the Tropics that are needed by the white
consuming centres, and as we know that the native
populations, as things are at present, are growing less, it
can only happen if this reduction in numbers is not checked
and increased populations made the rule, that the white
races *must* also grow less, and considerably less, as there
will be a lack in the wherewithal to supply their needs
and to generate the volume of overseas trade necessary to
give them an income.

I think that a far safer means of developing the
resources of our tropical dependencies as they should be
and could be developed lies in the establishment of agricultural colleges and institutes of research in the Tropics,
so that we could train the boys fresh from the secondary
schools or colleges over here, or the young men as they
come home from the Front, and make them capable of
carrying out this valuable work of tropical development on
all sides.   Such work must be done not only in our own
dependencies, but throughout Latin America also, as
there Germany has been coining money in the past that
would have come to us had we had as many young Englishmen throughout that Continent as there have been Germans
at the command of our chief enemy.   These scientifically
trained men would encourage individual producers to
further efforts by making them thoroughly *au fait* of the
work that would be required of them ; and also by enabling
them to establish estates themselves or to manage those
belonging to other people, the trained men would help to

increase both the individual wealth of the owner of the estate as well as of the Empire at large ; incidentally these trainers of men would command large salaries to their own benefit. Whilst this is going on, these newcomers would set an example to the local and native owners of how estates can be managed to best advantage and pests, diseases, &c., kept at a distance, and so prevented from · reducing the outputs which are so badly needed at the consuming centres. Such an action and example is bound to improve the general output of tropical produce, as the natives quickly follow the example of those whom they see obtaining better results than themselves. One successfully managed farm or estate run on up-to-date lines is far more valuable to the Empire at large as an object lesson to encourage other more backward planters to change their methods than several years of theoretical training.

It is by such means as these that we can best achieve our object of increasing the resources of the Empire to the uttermost capacity of the workers available, both white and coloured, and, by pursuing such a policy, the profits that will accrue from these industries instead of finding their way into the pockets of Germany, or of a privileged few in this country, which is not beneficial to the general welfare and trade of any nation, will be spread among a large number of people of all colours and creeds living in many lands who will thereby be rendered more useful to the manufacturing industries of this country as suppliers of raw materials, &c., as well as regular overseas buyers of the goods we turn out.

In conclusion, whilst urging upon every one to carefully study every word that Mr. Wilson-Fox, Mr. Bigland, or other members of their Committee have to tell us regarding the serious need that exists of developing the resources of the Empire in order to help pay for the War, and to note the propositions with which they agree and on which they can collaborate with the Committee in developing, I would like them to consider whether it would not be wise to have the following queries asked and answered in the House of Commons before sanctioning or even of seriously con- sidering any scheme of development being carried out in which the State is directly interested and which it is to be asked to finance :—

(1) Will the Committee, or those who will ultimately carry out the scheme proposed, state definitely before laying their proposals before the public for acceptance, which crops and industries they propose to start upon, and also to give a complete list of the various undertakings which they believe they can develop to the advantage of the Empire?   In making this request it must be remem- bered that I am only referring to industries in the tropical and sub-tropical zone.

(2) When is it proposed to start the scheme in connec- tion with each of the various industries, and how, and in how many years, do those in charge of the work propose to secure the much larger supplies of produce that we are told can be obtained ?

(3) What output per annum can be looked for from each of the industries to be named ?   How many labourers will be necessary to secure these results ?   How will these labourers in each of the centres to be named by the Committee be secured without affecting existing industries, native or otherwise ?

(4) Who is to find the money for these various under- takings ?   If it is to be the Government, that is the British taxpayer, on what security is it to be advanced ?

(5) It is suggested that a share of the profits should go into the National Exchequer to help liquidate the cost of the War, what will be the proportion of this share ?   Will it be at the rate of the present War profit tax, viz , 80 per

cent., or what return can be looked for on the capital expended? Are those who put this scheme into execution to be indemnified against any financial loss if the scheme turns out to be unsuccessful?

(6) Will a complete list be published of the names of everyone who has taken or is likely to take an active part in developing the scheme and especially those who are to be placed in charge of it, if sanctioned by Parliament? Such lists to be divided under two headings: (*a*) those who have done the work purely out of love for their country and look for no monetary reward whatever, and (*b*) those who are working for payment or in the expectation of receiving a profit later on.

When satisfactory answers are forthcoming to all of these queries then I hope and believe that the general public, as well as those already established in the Tropics, will support Mr. Wilson-Fox and the Empire Resources Development Committee in every way possible, but until these queries have been satisfactorily answered I do not believe that anyone in the House of Commons, or anyone who has expert knowledge of the Tropics and their industries, will support the Committee in the way that we have been asked to do.

The following articles have been reproduced from *Tropical Life* and other journals showing how we can *Help Pay for the War* by extending and developing the Agriculture, trade and commerce of the Empire, by means of the following: (1) Financing and encouraging all classes and grades of workers; (2) educating and training the "brains" and "pushers" in our midst to guide and lead others to do their "bit" as well; (3) conserving and increasing the present raw labour supplies throughout the Empire, and training them to increase production with less strain on themselves; (4) encouraging expansion, not only within the Empire, including India, but also in Latin America and elsewhere ; (5) raising food crops, &c., in semi-arid zones by extending the principle of " dry-farming "; (6) maintaining our faith in Russia as a nation and cultivating her markets in spite of the present state of affairs.

CHAPTER II.

Are the Working Classes in England being urged to Exploit the Tropics ?

Tropical Life, December, 1917.

PLANTERS, merchants, and even the officials attached to the various agricultural departments in our tropical and Crown-Colonial possessions and protectorates should take note of the British Workers' League, which is being boomed by the *British Citizen and Empire Worker*, of which Mr. Victor Fisher is editor. At the same time he is the hon. treasurer and secretary and backbone-in-chief of the British Workers' League, and is also a pillar of strength in supporting Mr. Wilson-Fox's scheme. This is shown by the remarks incorporated by the hon. secretary of the E.R.D.C., in the paper he read before the Society of Arts last December, when he told those present that a well-known German writer has recently laid it down that " the general principle is, the more an industry lends itself to the formation of syndicates, the more suitable it is for State participation. . . . He (Professor Naumann) realizes, and he is quite right, that no one likes taxation, and he therefore very properly casts about for some alter-native plan," and Mr. Wilson-Fox unfolds his plan, which has been described according to the spectacles through which the critic views them as being purely philanthropic, or a carefully-drawn-up plan for State participation, hardening up to such terms as pure monopolistic exploita-tion on German methods.

Previous to this (p. 79 of the *Society of Arts Journal*, December 15, 1917), he told his audience : " This statement of the proper limits of State action is not my own. . . .

I rejoice to tell you that it is taken from an article recently contributed by Mr. Victor Fisher, one of the ablest members of the Labour Party," and it could have well been added, " editor of the *British Citizen and Empire Worker*, and hon. secretary and treasurer to the British Workers' League " ; but these facts were not mentioned. We include them now, however, so that our readers can realize what a leading position Mr. Fisher appears to occupy in the imperial politics of the Labour Party, especially now that he has, according to the *British Citizen*, been chosen by Stourbridge as their prospective parliamentary candidate. We entirely disagree with what we gather to be Mr. Fisher's views on the economic development of the Tropics, but apart from that, we should imagine that his presence at Westminster would be a distinct acquisition to the House of Commons. Judged by the articles he contributes to his paper, we should imagine, for instance, that Mr. Fisher fully agrees with the views expressed in the following articles. Meanwhile, with so strong a support behind him, Mr. Fisher's position in connection with the British Workers' League makes the objects of that body of paramount interest to our readers, especially the first two, bracketed together, which run as under : —

To promote, demand, or support legislation to ensure :—

(1) The application of the lessons of the War :—

(*a*) That unrestricted commercial competition in,' and the private ownership of, vital and key industries lead to waste, inefficiency, fraud, and national disunion ; and

(*b*) That the full utilization and development of National and Imperial resources, in Peace or War, mainly depend on the PUBLIC OPINION and control of vital and key industries.[2]

We shall be interested to know what those who have risked so much to develop our colonies and protectorates, and to bring them up to the level at which they stand, will think of a league whose primary objects are as stated, and also what they imagine such a misleading and potentially mischievous agitation can lead to. We should imagine that if the League succeeded in working up its members to the desired degree of enthusiasm, such objects would do more to dismember the Empire than the Kaiser, the

---

[1] And so we are to have State monopolies as a remedy.

[2] The capitals are not our own idea, but as printed in the advertisements of the League.

Crown Prince, and the whole of the German War Party put together. The *British Citizen* is an excellent publication, we read it very carefully, and find it full of views with which we are entirely in agreement, whilst its policy is virile and go-ahead, but we cannot agree with anything it has to say as to the best way to develop the economic resources of the Empire, and sincerely trust that its views will never be accepted by the country at large until softened down and considerably modified.

In answer to the above criticisms, Mr. Victor Fisher, the founder, as well as the honorary secretary of the League, addressed the following letter to us :—

THE BRITISH WORKERS' LEAGUE.

To the Editor of TROPICAL LIFE.

SIR,—In your issue of December last you published a critical article in regard to myself and the British Workers' League touching the question of Empire Development.

The point in the League's programme which has apparently roused your opposition is the statement : " That the unrestricted commercial competition in, and the private ownership of, vital and key industries lead to waste, inefficiency, fraud, and national disunion."

The question here raised is the question between a system based on unrestricted individualism and a system based on national co-operation, and it would take up far too much of your space to discuss so great a problem. I must, therefore, limit myself here to pointing out that the economic system characterized by unrestricted competition between individuals has, as a matter of fact, already practically ceased to exist in the commercial and industrial worlds. It is no longer a question of *laisser faire* individualism *versus* co-operation based on nationalities, but rather as between the latter system and joint-stock undertakings, tending to develop into trusts or cartels. The British Workers' League is of opinion—speaking in general terms—that the modern State cannot much longer afford to allow rings of private stockholders undiluted control of *vital* industries. This does not in the least mean, what is suggested by your footnote, that we are in favour of State monopolies. We do believe, however, that in a steadily increasing degree, both in the interests of the consumer and in regard to public revenue, public authorities will have to control in varying degrees the commercial undertakings affecting commodities vital to national security. Such control, as applied, would have to be tentative, and would obviously have to be maintained by a service very differently equipped and organized from that of a State bureaucracy.

It cannot be supposed, however, that the last word has been uttered on commercial and industrial organization. That organization, as it exists to-day, differs immeasurably from the commercial, industrial and financial organization of a hundred or even fifty years ago. Can it be supposed, that these vital matters are in a static condition? Is it not rather wiser to assume that these, as everything else in life, are in a state of constant development and decay, and that as individual ownership in many industries merged imperceptibly into joint-stock ownership, and joint-stock ownership into trusts; so, with the flux of time, that also will reach its climax, and some other system will take its place? Do not all the tendencies of the age go to show that it will be modified in its turn by increasing public control?

I enclose the full text of our proposals in regard to National and Industrial Reconstruction, which have been worked out after many months of study, and I venture to ask for these proposals your sympathetic consideration.

Faithfully yours,

VICTOR FISHER,

London, January 4, 1918. *Hon. Secretary.*

CHAPTER III.

The Outlook for 1918—and After.

How Long are we to Continue trying to make Bricks without Straw, or to Develop the Resources of the Empire without Trained (White) Workers?

Tropical Life, December, 1917.

THE wealth of a country, Mr. Lloyd George, our Prime Minister, told us the other day, depends less on its national resources than on the vigour, the energy, and the training of its people. In short, the country that lacks discipline, organization, and technical knowledge cannot compete with others whose people possess these qualities.

This statement is true when applied to any country, but

it is doubly correct when applied to ourselves. To prosper
and be happy in this world one must work[1]—really work,
a fact that many, even in old England, seem quite oblivious
of. By this we mean that many of those who are above
the poverty line do not know what *real* work is. To get
up, to go by train or tram, to do routine work in an office
or factory so as not to be dismissed, to strike for more pay
yourself whilst others are getting less, this is not real work,
especially in these days, and the country that is farther
removed from living such a life is bound to come out top—
in the end. Those who do not think so will be well
advised to sit up and watch this War out and the five
years that follow the declaration of peace. At the end of
that period we are quite sure that it will be seen that our
view is the correct one. It is not enough to exist, to move
automatically and be indifferent of the world outside. For
an empire to prosper its people must think and struggle
to be always doing better, if not for themselves then for
their country. Routine workers, or lotus eaters, whichever
you like to call them, should be tied by cords to heavy
chairs, and left in a room with food about which they can
only get at if they manage to extricate themselves from
their bonds. Muscles, mind, and method would all be
developed to an astonishing degree after a course of this
treatment was ordered for those who imagine that life is
easy in spite of the War, and that the country goes on
because the average man or woman exists and does the
minimum of work for the maximum of pay that he or she
can bully out of the world. But this is a mistake.

If this country means to prosper and keep ahead, her
people must give up being lotus eaters ; everyone must be
trained to give up keeping their eyes just in front of their
nose or with an expression in them as if bored to death,
as some still do who have escaped joining up. Every man,
and even every woman, should be trained to specialize in
and become more or less expert in some country abroad,
so that the nation as a whole would be correctly and fully
informed of what is going on in all parts of the world. To

---

[1] Tolstoy is very emphatic on this, as when he makes Levin, in
"Anna Karenina," say, "I must have some physical exercise or my
character will spoil. . . . To sleep you must work and, to be happy,
you must also work."

"I will not be kept alive to do nothing," said the late Sir Charles
Dilke.

have a vote one should have to pass two examinations : one to prove efficiency in the work from which he (or she) is earning his (or her) living, and the other on a subsidiary study of some country or industry abroad in order to prove that, since the bulk of the wealth and power of this country comes from abroad, the citizen has proved himself to be as well versed in and appreciative of that which is building up the wealth of the Empire generally, as he is of the routine work which gives him (or her) the daily, weekly, or monthly wage on which they live.

Until something is done we shall always be behind as a developing power, and through that defect we shall always be handicapped when out to secure a place on the highest summit of World-Success. Is it an exaggeration to say that if, before the War, the work of a few thousands, perhaps even of one or two hundred only, of our leading men who had specialized in foreign and overseas develop-ment trade, had been checked and their business connec-tions shut down, our trade and the main sources of our wealth would have also been checked, and would even have, very soon, like a sluggish stream in the Tropics, dried up under the tropical sun of foreign competition ? In those days, who among the 90 per cent. of those whose happiness and food cannot be assured without the help of the remaining 10 per cent. would have cared if these producers of the Empire's wealth had died out and so caused the wealth that they created to have been cut off ? We believe that, until this 90 per cent. whose welfare depended on the trade developed by and dependent on the others, began to feel the pinch, they would have continued to be indifferent to what was happening around them, and would have awakened to realize the irreparable value of these few leaders, gone beyond recall, only when it was too late to replace them. As we said long ago, if only the Tropics could be placed out of all reach of non-tropical countries for six months, how much more we should appreciate them when we got them back.

Can an Empire like ours continue to prosper in these competitive times if our views of the case, as just men-tioned, are correct, and no steps are taken to remedy the ignorance and indifference of the masses as to whom they owe their welfare, and whence the bulk of our wealth comes from in the first place ? Ask yourselves whether, even to-day, with the daily papers full of news from every country and centre under the sun, has the

case really been improved? Does the public to-day, the
stay-at-home, suburban public, the dwellers in the large
cities, and larger and smaller towns which depend on outside trade (whether the inhabitants know it or not), do all
these know and realize this? Are they aware that,
because they only make goods or build houses or sell wares,
they are not nearly so important to the stability of the
wealth of the Empire as those who are engaged in wealth-
producing industries as mining, fishing, or agriculture,
both here and abroad; industries which alone really
increase the wealth of the world?

We are obliged to mention these details, which are no
details in our minds, though they bore others to death even
to glance at them. We do so, however, because we know
perfectly well that 90 per cent. of the townsmen of this
country take no useful and sustained interest in the outside,
and especially in the overseas world, and therefore will be
of but scant value to the Empire when in the near future
she wants to develop her trade abroad. As our educational
system is arranged, the majority of our people *never will* be
of any use when it comes to a question of developing the
resources of the Empire, but rather will they prove a
hindrance, as the new ideas are beyond their understanding, and they object to the extra work involved in trying
to master the details sufficiently, if only to decry it (no
matter how excellent the plan may be) in the train, tram,
public-house, or elsewhere when they come together.
This is why it would be as well for the future of the
Empire if an examination was made compulsory for all
adults, in order to prove that they were efficient in whatever work they did to earn their bread and cheese, and
also that they were worth troubling about on the part of the
strenuous ones who produce the bulk of the trade, food,
and wealth generally from abroad. Without their help
the lotus eaters would soon cease to exist or else would
drift into the workhouse until those abominations are
abolished and tramp-prisons or labour-farms established
for the able-bodied slacker, and real home-like institutions
for the unfit and for the old folks.

Somewhere in some part of the world the natives are
extraordinarily expert in knocking down birds, monkeys,
&c., by means of slings when they need a meal. This
skill, we believe, is obtained by their having been taught
to sling stones from childhood in a simple and practical
manner. A prepared meal is placed on the top of a post,

the height of which varies according to the age of the
child, and the child and the meals, to say nothing of the
birds in the air, vultures or otherwise, are left alone for
the best one to win. If the child knocks down the food
with a stone from his sling he has a meal; it he does
not he goes hungry; no wonder, therefore, that the child
soon becomes expert at stone-slinging. All we ask for
is that every citizen of the Empire should be equally
trained until he can help to a useful degree to obtain his
meals, the meals for himself and his dependents by helping
to increase the production and trade of the Empire to a
far greater degree than most of us are doing at present.
Until they can do so, such people should be restricted as to
the size and variety of the meals or other comforts and
advantages which they have been enjoying, since they
never would have come their way if it were not for the
labours and forethought of others, who have secured the
energy and training mentioned by the Prime Minister, to
get the better of the vultures and so become expert food-
producers for themselves and the lotus eaters as well.

The time has arrived, however, when these lotus eaters,
as well as the inefficients, shirkers, half-timers, or advocates for reduced outputs must no longer be tolerated.
They are as dangerous to the welfare of this country as
the undermining and peaceful penetration tactics of the
Germans. From now onwards everyone must be trained
to add his full quota of utility to the good of his own
country—of the Empire at large, or else be treated, no
matter what his or her station in life or share of wealth
may be, as all tramps and won't-works should be, viz.,
sent to a labour-home and fed on dry bread and water
plus meat and semi-luxuries according to the amount
of food-stuffs they raise or of other useful work they
do. This refers equally to the public everywhere within
the Empire as well as to landed proprietors in England,
princes in India, or black chiefs in Africa. If they do
not justify their ownership and control of the land that
is theirs by law, then by the same law must we take it
from them in trust and develop it for the good of the
community until another member of the family owning
the property comes along and proves himself able and
willing to do what his kinsman failed in doing. And as
it is with the wealthy landowners, so it must be with
the workmen throughout the Empire—artisans, engineers,
or transport men here, and peasant proprietors and field
workers in the Tropics. They must be trained to put, as

a body, more mind and muscle into their work, and so produce larger returns per man and per acre. If they do not do so, then this country, with its comparatively small white population, will go down before the pushful, enterprising country with a much larger, more willing, and better-trained army of workers that has long been doing so. If this is what the English and British people wish to occur, why, we feel bound to ask, are they sacrificing their best men and so much money to win this War?

The greatest obstacle (judging from what I have seen going on around me during the half century that I have dwelt in the suburbs of London) to a satisfactory and speedy expansion in the development of our Empire is our present and past educational system; a system which has always and is still narrowing and not expanding the visions and aims of the young and old alike. Those who have "thought Imperially" have done so in spite of the strait jacket that the Government has placed us in under the impression that they were teaching us to do our duty to our King, our Empire and ourselves. Never has a more serious mistake been made; worse still, it is to-day as rampant and mischievous as ever. Until the entire system is swept away and a truly Imperial thought-compelling system built up in its place, the people of the United Kingdom, and especially those residing in and around our large cities and centres of industries, will never realize the importance and wealth of this Empire and all that it means to those within it and to the world at large : that is, if the world is to remain, on the whole, Anglo-Saxonized and not go under the heel of Prussia.

Sir Harry Johnston touched on this same serious defect in the able address that he delivered to the African Society when he said, ". . unless the authorities can become infused (and ' enthused ') with the New Learning, can take the educationists by the neck and force them to drop their out-of-date nonsense, whereby an inapplicable and useless education is being invariably imparted to the young of all classes, to the future soldiers, sailors, merchants, mechanics, ministers of religion, editors and journalists, &c.—unless, in short, we see to it that the New Education deals very considerably with African subjects we shall not only fail to appreciate the importance of Africa, but shall be unable to shape a right African policy and to turn our hold over Africa to the legitimate profit of our Home State and to the rest of the Empire."

"LEST WE FORGET!"

"THE Rule of Conduct which serves as the fundamental basis of democracy in the United States of America is that every human being should have his opportunity for his utmost development."—Dr. Hines Page, the American Ambassador, in the *Nineteenth Century Review*, October, 1917, p. 783.

"The Wealth of the Country depends less on its natural resources than on the vigour, the energy and the training of its people."—The Prime Minister (Mr. Lloyd-George) at the Royal Albert Hall, on October 22, 1917.

"It is not only additional men that are wanted [to help the Government], but it is the getting of men of an exceptional type both in ability and experience."—The Chancellor of the Exchequer when discussing the appointment of additional members to the Treasury. House of Commons, January 29, 1918.

"When I was at the Colonial Office I was struck by the evidence of immense natural resources in many of our Colonies. I thought it was possible that the time might come when we could pay off part of our national debt by rapidly developing, through the State, these resources. . . . I need not point out to the House how many objections would be raised to that kind of proposal if one were seriously to put it forward. . . . You would find people saying that to try to develop the resources of our Colonies for the benefit of this country in that way would be exploiting them."—The Chancellor of the Exchequer on Paying for the War. House of Commons, January 29, 1918.

"Under the scheme we want to see established, of granting agricultural scholarships from the lower schools in the United Kingdom to the secondary ones, and then up to the agricultural colleges at home or in the Tropics, everyone will have an equal chance with his fellows. The Empire needs such help, and we must therefore see that all those under training live healthy lives whilst being taught. Steady work, strong limbs, sound health, tenacity of purpose, keenness to seize every opportunity to push yourself and your country ahead, these are the monopoly of no single class, or, if they are, such qualities are perhaps more frequently found in those who have never had all that money could buy. . . In our Imperial development scheme, every man who means to get on shall get on."—*Tropical Life*, August, 1917, p. 124.

SECTION II.

HOW TO EXPAND.

CHAPTER IV.

By not Discouraging the Expansion of Agricultural and other Industries throughout the Empire.

PATRIOTS AND PARASITES.

Tropical Life, September, 1915.

IN our issue of October, 1909, we called attention to the report issued by the Departmental Committee appointed to inquire into and report upon the subject of agricultural education in England and Wales, before which our Editor gave evidence, and urged that scholarships (or their equivalent) should be established to enable the holder to travel abroad to study the agricultural methods of other people and lands and compare them with their own. This point was accepted by the Committee, which "strongly urged the Board of Agriculture to provide—as is done in other countries—scholarships enabling the holder to undertake post-graduate research, and also travelling fellowships to enable teachers and other suitable persons to study agriculture abroad" (see Report, p. 29, paragraph 103). In the right-hand column against this recommendation are placed the names of the three witnesses, Mr. William McCracken (formerly Professor of Agriculture at the Royal Agricultural College, Cirencester, and at that time, in 1909, agent for Lord Crewe's estates in Cheshire), Professor Winter, M.A., Professor of Agriculture at University College, Bangor, and the Editor of *Tropical Life*, who urged the establishment of such scholarships.

We were reminded of this by the receipt of the late Professor King's wonderful work on the agricultural methods that have been slowly evolved out of forty centuries of experience by the farmers of China, Korea,

and Japan.   On pp. 4 and 5 of this book the author writes:
"It could not be other than a matter of the highest
industrial, educational, and social importance to all nations
if there might be brought to them a full and accurate
account of all those conditions which have made it possible
for such dense populations to be maintained so largely
upon the products of Chinese, Korean, and Japanese soil.
Many of the steps, phases, and practices through which
this evolution has passed are irrevocably buried in the past,'
but the maintenance of such remarkable efficiency attained
centuries ago and projected into the present with little
apparent decadence, merits the most profound study, and
the time is fully ripe when it should be made.   Living as
we are in the morning of a century of transition from
isolated to cosmopolitan national life, when profound
readjustments, industrial, educational and social, must
result, such an investigation cannot be made too soon.
It is high time for each nation to study the others, and by
mutual agreement and co-operative effort the results of
such studies should become available to all concerned,
studies, too, that have been made in the spirit that each
should become co-ordinate and mutually helpful component
factors in the world's progress.

" One very appropriate and immensely helpful means for
attacking this problem, and which should prove mutually
helpful to citizen and State, would be for the higher educational institutions of all nations, instead of exchanging
courtesies through their baseball teams, to send select
bodies of their best students under competent leadership
and by international agreement, both East and West,
organizing therefrom investigating bodies, each containing
components of the eastern and western civilizations, and
whose purpose it should be to study specially set problems.
Such a movement, well conceived and directed, manned
by the most capable young men, should create an international acquaintance and spread broadcast a body of
important knowledge which would develop as the young
men mature and contribute immensely towards world-
peace and world-progress.   If some broad plan of international effort, such as is here suggested, were organized,
the expense of maintenance might well be met by diverting
so much as is needful from the large sums set aside for the
expansion of navies.   Such steps as these, taken in the
interests of the world-uplift and world-peace, could not fail
to be more efficacious and less expensive than an increase
in fighting equipment.   It would cultivate the spirit of

3

pulling together, and of a square deal, rather than one of holding aloof and of striving to gain unneighbourly advantage."

Such ideas appeal to us strongly, and we cannot help adding that there should be no need to issue such an appeal in the first place, nor, having been issued, of such a prophet crying in the wilderness to apparently deaf ears, as he has to do, since no one seems willing to listen to his excellent advice. As we stand to-day, both in England and America, the lower-class politicians (socially speaking), who have crept into the " most-high places," where they are doing excellent work on every point but this one, seem unable (either they or their subordinates who look to them for light and guidance), owing to their previous training and general environments having narrowed their outlook on life, to appreciate what they owe to the Tropics, and how this country would miss the supplies of necessities and semi-luxuries that they send us if they were cut off. Their inability to realize this has always had the tendency to cause the Tropics, the industries that exist there, and above all the men who have made those industries, to be looked upon as so many milch cows, which only exist to be milked as dry as possible for the good of the exchequer at home, and the public have yet to learn how much more milk can be obtained and how the quality can be improved by careful training and selection and by supplying the animals from the start with all they need. Meanwhile the ordinary man-in-the-street on this side, the borough councillor and town employee, &c. (none of whom are engaged in wealth or food-producing industries and whose labour and pay tend to become more or less parasitic on the wealth-producers), since they are selfish (or wise) enough to stop at home in safety and comfort instead of risking their health, lives, and money in pushing the trade and influence of the Empire abroad, are thus able, being resident on this side, to secure enough votes to enable them, in the aggregate, to do the wire-pulling necessary to secure an almost unfairly large share of the benefits of the settled life and administration over here, whilst they are tending, at the same time, to shift their share of taxes on to those who least deserve to be burdened with them because their labour on the whole is of far greater use to the Empire. On no one does this burden fall so heavily in these times of war as on the smaller individual, tropical pioneer, exporter, trader and agriculturist residing on this side, or who is running an office here, while he is doing the heavy mental and physical spade-work abroad. The borough employees and the working men have had their wages raised since the War started and still complain, whilst the tropical worker is receiving 25, 50, or even 75 per cent. less income, and still goes on his way uncomplaining, his only anxiety being to last out or, if secure, to obtain the shipping necessary to carry on his share of the nation's trade and so keep the exports going and thus help pay for the War. Surely it is ' the old tale of the two mule teams during a sugar campaign in the Tropics, when all is bustle and hum to bring in the canes to be ground. The load, to save time and trouble, is taken from the cart of the jibbing team and piled up on to that of the willing animals, who thereby, *because they are willing*, have to draw the double load, whilst it is quite likely that the useless jibbers, pushed aside as a nuisance, even get into the stables first and have the pick of the feed because the others are foolish enough to be willing, and so are worked overtime to make up for the absence of the jibbing team.

The leading papers support us in these views, which are put forth in no party spirit and are even more noticeable in some points in America than here. The London *Westminster Gazette*, most democratic of dailies, perhaps, hit the nail hardest on the head when it told us (on the front page of its issue of August 18) that: " We must so mobilize our military and naval forces as not to demobilize our industries beyond the point necessary for our credit " . . . to do this " We are obliged to divide our man-power between three equally important services—with the Army, with the Navy, and service in the industries *which must be kept going if the War is to be financed*" (italics ours). Napoleon was unable to understand " that he was being beaten by our imperturbable habit of going about our business while he was draining the life-blood of his people . . . In the long war of endurance on which we are now embarked, the industrial *rôle* of Great Britain is as important now as it was a hundred years ago, and we should do far more harm than good to the Allied cause if we destroyed it or gravely compromised it by withdrawing too many men from industry in order to put them into the fighting force."

All this is very good—on paper—but what has our Government done, or what is it doing, to put it into practice? If we are to go ahead we must be just as well as generous to *all* the taxpayers at home and abroad, and be both just and generous towards those who are willing to sacrifice the comfort of home and risk the dangers to health abroad for the benefit of the Empire. As already stated time and again, we must train the tropical and agricultural industrial army to enable them to extend the wealth of the Empire in the same way as we are training, and always have trained, the Navy and Army to defend it. Up to the present this country, as a whole, has not only *not* done so, but refused to take any interest as a nation in such acts on the part of some of its well-wishers who have tried to take the first steps towards seeing that our industrial army is properly and adequately trained. With the reorganization of the nation's resources that is now being carried out, we trust that an adjustment will be made in favour of the Tropics.

CHAPTER V.

By Ascertaining the Best Way to Develop the Resources of the Empire.

Tropical Life, January, 1918.

ELSEWHERE in this article, as well as in others which I have written, I have criticized the views, as I gather them to be, outlined by Mr. Wilson-Fox and his colleagues for developing the latent resources of our Empire in order to secure the much larger profits which they can undoubtedly yield to help pay for the cost of this War. "The post-war revenue which the Government will have to raise by one means or another," pointed out Mr. Wilson-Fox on January 9 to the Fellows of the Royal Colonial Institute, "in order to discharge its ever-growing obligations cannot now be expected to be less than £600,000,000 per annum, and may even exceed £700,000,000." The amount is stupendous, and it is high time to consider how we can best meet such a course. On this we are agreed, *we* being Mr. Wilson-Fox and his colleagues, Mr. Victor Fisher (see his letter on p. 36 *re* our criticisms in the December issue, p. 182), and his British Workers' League, and *Tropical*

Life. The main points[1] on which we are inclined to differ substantially include (but are not necessarily exhausted by) the following. If these can be modified, therefore, it would help forward the progress that we all want to see made:—

(1) As Mr. Wilson-Fox leaves no doubt that he strongly objects to being told that his scheme, so far as can be judged by what he has written or told us, will cause the natives to be "exploited," either he must modify his estimates very considerably, or else tell us how many years' it will take for the Government and the Development Board to secure an *annual* income, as estimated before the Society of Arts, of £50,000,000 (see their journal of January 6, 1917, also the paper before the Royal Colonial Institute, p. 5 of rough proof given out to the Press). How can any organization on this earth expect to obtain such an income *per annum* from the two centres mentioned, Africa and the Pacific, or even in the entire world, in the lifetime of Mr. Wilson-Fox, Mr. Bigland, or Mr. Victor Fisher?

If there is no hurry, and if this huge income is not to be forthcoming in our lifetime, then the scheme (which a Labour Unionist at the R.C.I. meeting said should be tried because it is so attractive and bright) will not appeal to the working classes, as it does at present, because they, the same as ourselves, apparently think or thought these £50,000,000 a year alone from palm products in Africa and the Pacific would be ready when the £600,000,000 to £700,000,000 a year already mentioned falls due, i.e., on the declaration of peace.

(2) If the E.R.D.C. wishes to gain the confidence of the tropical public, they must not hide themselves behind the excuse of not being experts when talking to those who have been entirely wrapped up in tropical development for years and generations back. Above all, they must not allow Mr. Bigland, M.P., and Controller of Oils, &c., to tell us, time after time, his funny story of being able to produce 2,000,000 tons of sugar from British Guiana "if I am ordered to do so." To those who know British Guiana and its labour conditions, this statement is such

---

[1] As outlined by Mr. Wilson-Fox in the paper he read before the Royal Society of Arts in December, 1916, and reproduced in their Journal of December 15, 1916, in his article in the October issue of the *Nineteenth Century Review*, and now in his paper before the Royal Colonial Institute (see *United Empire* for April, 1918). Mr. Fisher's views can be "guessed at" by a study of his paper, the *British Citizen and Empire Worker.*

absolute nonsense, that to trot it out after so important a
paper as that Mr. Wilson-Fox read before the Royal
Colonial Institute this month or Captain Jebb (see *Tropical
Life*, June, 1917, p. 89) a little time back, is as undignified
for a man holding so important a position as Mr. Bigland
does, as it is annoying to his audience.[1]   Also, it removes
all confidence in the entire scheme of these alleged non-
experts when their "corner-man" indulges in such jokes.

(3) It is a great pity also if the E.R.D.C. is to gain and
to hold the confidence of the public that it should be so
much of a one-man-show as it has been so far.   Let us
hear what other members, especially Lord Selborne, has to
say.   Earl Grey, now, alas! no more, would have filled the
biggest hall in London had he been advertised to speak on
the subject when the Committee was first formed.   What
a pity he did not do so, even by proxy, just to let us all
know to what degree he was in a line with Mr. Wilson-Fox.

(4) Why should the Committee expect those who know
the Tropics intimately, and not as the Trade Union officials
or even Mr. Victor Fisher know them, to tolerate the most
magnificent scheme in the world, when they know that its
foundations do not even rest on sand, but only on water, to
be washed up and hoisted on anybody who will accept it?
It is *absolutely* impossible for Mr. Wilson-Fox to do what
he has outlined, or leads one to believe he will achieve, *in
the near future* unless he uses Germany's methods on the
native.   He assures us that he never hinted at doing so, and
I am quite sure he did not.   In face of this, however, he
will fail to carry his working-class followers, and I do not
envy him the consequences.   When Tommy comes back
from the War, and each goes back to his trade, determined
not to pay the increased taxation *as well as* to fight our
battles, the more dazzled he is at the prospects held out to
him by the E.R.D.C., the fiercer will be his hatred, and
greater his punishment, on the heads of those who misled
him.   Unless the E.R.D.C. base their estimates to fit in
with the depleted labour forces that still remain in
equatorial Africa and the South Sea Islands, the wrath

---

[1] When addressing the London Chamber of Commerce on January 30,
Mr. Bigland commented on this statement, and then went on to read
paragraphs from elsewhere, showing that there was sufficient *land* in
British Guiana to produce 2,000,000 tons of sugar.   This appealed to me
as being very "poor cricket."   No one denies that the land is there and
waiting.   It is the labour that is totally missing, as we say in this paragraph, and as Mr. Bigland must know, since he poses as such an expert
on sugar production in British Guiana.—H. H. S.

of the disappointed ones will be on their heads, and much as one would regret to see the drubbing they would get, they will have no one to thank for it but themselves, unless it is optimistic Mr. Bigland and his two million tons of sugar from British Guiana.

All the same, I admire every square inch of Mr. Wilson-Fox, and he has plenty of square inches to admire. I would be only too glad to see the objects he is fighting for become positive facts, if their doing so harms no one. It is a pleasure to hear him speak, and whether he is out for profit to himself or for the Empire, the more that follow his example, the better for the Empire. If you doubt my sincerity, read the article on " The Outlook for 1918 " (reproduced here as Chapter III), and then those who have had the pleasurable tonic of hearing Mr. Wilson-Fox speak will realize what a relief it is after a dose of those who still grumble at the personal inconveniences of the War, i.e., no meat, no dinner, worst of all, no motor rides, and double railway fares to pay for their holiday jaunts.

Allowing that the scheme of the E.R.D. Committee is capable of achievement, and that it will relieve the working men and women, fighters and workers, from the extreme pressure of a £600,000,000 budget, no one can deny that immense numbers of native labourers will be needed to carry it out, and that these men must have white superiors to guide them. Let the scheme, therefore, start on this side *at once* by means of the following :—

(1) Insist that men shall be trained for the work at colleges on this side and in the Tropics to guide and supervise the coloured labourers, as outlined on p. 124 in our August issue (right-hand column). (See Chapter XVII, p. 105 with the cartoon *ex* the September, 1917, issue of *Tropical Life.*)

(2) Arrange for banking facilities to be made available for them, i.e., the British working men and small manufacturers over here to be able to do " their bit " by helping to turn out British-made goods at rockbottom (and not factors') prices against German competition, as outlined in our article as far back as September, 1914, when the War started, under the heading of " The Trade War with Germany. If I were the Chancellor of the Exchequer," and later in December, 1916, and January, 1917, on " Financing 1917—and After. The Need of Supporting our Pioneers of Industry Overseas."

(3) Give us a Minister of Wheat Supplies (and, if you like, of rice, beans, and cereal food-crops) who would rank

equal with the President of the Board of Trade, as asked for in our issue of June, 1917, p. 93. Such a Minister to be responsible for keeping satisfied the Empire's requirements of such food by arranging for the utilization, drainage, and opening up of such lands as are known to be suitable. for the crops named, but which lands cannot be " broken," drained, and " licked into shape " by small private owners. To-day we must encourage the small owner and discourage the large men. This is done by setting up central collecting stations and financing, threshing, storing, and selling the wheat on a co-operative basis.

Mr. Wilson-Fox, Mr. Fisher and others will, I believe, agree that we are one on these points. If so, all the better, and let us get ahead on them, as well as on organizing the fisheries off our coasts and those of our Allies, not forgetting the West Indies and off Brazil, to which I drew the attention of Sir George Doughty and others years ago, and they did not even answer my letters. But do not talk of £50,000,000 a year or even half that amount as an annual income from palm products, and, above all, please suppress the little joke of two million tons of sugar from British Guiana, unless you do not mean to start paying for the War until long after this generation has gone to join those who have fallen for the Empire in their last long sleep.

*　✹　*　*

Our best thanks are due to Mr. Wilson-Fox for what he is doing, and it is a pity that many others who are so busy " gassing about " all that they would, and could do, do not come forward and give us the benefit of their views as Mr. Wilson-Fox has done. Absence of competition and lack of criticism are the worse enemies that progress has to contend with, and the absence of rival schemes to those put forward on the occasions mentioned is greatly to be regretted at this somewhat critical stage in the prosperity and the development of the latent resources of the Empire. I say that the absence of rival schemes is to be regretted because, although we want hustlers like the member for Tamworth, I do not favour some of the definite propositions he has made, and I like still less (or dread still more) the rumours in the air, that tend to increase in number, of eliminating as far as possible (an ambiguous, and hence an unsatisfying and somewhat dangerous term) the middlemen between producers and consumers. This idea was somewhat modified by Mr. Bigland when addressing the merchant members of the London Chamber of Commerce on January 30 (1918). I believe that everyone who carefully reads Mr. Wilson-Fox's statements will conclude, as I have done, that he is in favour of such a proposal. If he is not, then I have entirely misunderstood him, and not only myself, but many others who have had lifelong experience of the Tropics and tropical labour as well.[1]

I mention this now because the entire matter, both the definite statements made by Mr. Wilson-Fox, as well as the rumours floating through the atmosphere seem to me to be only waiting to take shape as soon as the approval of the public here, who have votes in the House of Commons, show any inclination to accept them and to dictate terms to the pioneers and builders-up of the Empire on the outer edge of our possessions who are safely out of the way and cannot bother this Government with their adverse remarks and votes.

Mr. Fox addressed a meeting of the Royal Colonial Institute on the very day that the first portion of these notes was sent in to press (see p. 37), so I could not, at the time, wait to include any comment on what he and his friends then said.• I would, however, call the attention of cacao planters and exporters to the following " quotes " from what was said in the article contributed by Mr. Fox to the *Nineteenth Century Review* for October (pp. 835-858 =: 24 pages):—

(1) " Their " (i.e., the Empire Resources Development Committee, a self-appointed committee on which, so far as can be ascertained, no practical planter or trader whose interests are at stake has been included. Hence they are being judged in their absence and without a hearing) " common belief is . . . . that a system under which practically all production is left to the uncorrelated and uncontrolled activities of *private individuals has had its day*."

---

[1] With regard to the possible effect that speeding-up the output of the Tropics would have on the labour forces, see the following, among other articles, in :—

"After the War—The West Indies for ex-Warriors." *T.L.*, January, 1916, p. 11.

"Savage Man in Central Africa." *T.L.*, February, 1916. p. 27, or in this book, p. 16 *et seq.*

"After the War and the Domination of Latin-America." February, 1916, p. 31.

"State Exploitation of the Tropics" (being *T.L.'s.* views on the paper read by Mr. Wilson-Fox before the Royal Society of Arts on December 15, 1916).   May, 1917, p. 73.

"The Proposed Imperial Development Board" (based on Captain Jebb's proposals laid before the Royal Colonial Institute). June, 1917, p. 89, or this book, p. 50.

(2) The distinguished statesman who presided (name not given for some reason) on October 31, 1916, expressed the view that probably the only remedy for the situation was to be found in development by the State for the State of the natural resources of the Empire.

(3) (p. 837) "in some instances it might be advantageous for the State to take direct and single-handed action on its own account."[1]

(4) (p. 837) "It must be emphasized that the committee does not command the services of an expert staff." If this is so, why should this committee (which is standing up against century-old experts who have made the British cacao and other industries abroad what they are) be listened to and tolerated as dictators of how the latent resources of the Empire can be best developed to the advantage of us all? We say this because of what Mr. Fox himself pointed out at the Society of Arts. In face of this, if we are not asked to lean on a reed that has already been broken, and is therefore unequal to the strain, we are at least invited to trust our ˙fortunes and the prosperity of the Empire to one that has a bad "kink" in it, and is not as strong as one would wish. " I have heard it said" (see the report of Mr. Fox's remarks in the *Journal of the Society of Arts*, December 15, p. 79), "how is it, if State development is practicable, that the British South Africa Company cannot show better results after all these years?" Evidently Mr. Wilson-Fox has a conscience, and on that occasion it was pricking him, and thus caused him to make this statement, headed by the words, "Physician heal thyself." Evidently there have been internal as well as

---

[1] This sentence taken as a whole said, " and that while, in some instances it might be advantageous for the State to take direct and single-handed action on its own account, in the majority of cases co-operation with persons already engaged in, and having special experience of particular branches of production, industry and trade, might be expected to give the best results." This seems to me to flavour of one set of middlemen, who have acted for years as pioneers of our Imperial enterprise, and have "made good" at the risk of health and wealth, earning and drawing their pay " by results" obtained by their ability and enterprise, being pushed aside in favour of a body of Government paid officials, similar I suppose to those engaged by a body like the British Cotton Growing Association, whose work is well known to all equatorial Africans. If this is the idea, and the public can study the statements in the original if they doubt my views, then I would claim that the State Development of the Tropics, its vegetable oil, cacao and other industries, will be as successful and well thought of by others as the undertakings known as the British Cotton Growing Association and the British South African Company are to-day.

external critics of the British South Africa Company, its policy, and successes or failures.

Now we come down to the statements directed immediately upon the Tropics (p. 438). " The second report related to a suggestion that the State might similarly participate with general advantage in the distribution and sale, and possibly *also in the production*[1] of vegetable oils and fats, for the production of which the tropical territories of the Empire occupy a specially favoured position. After reviewing the circumstances of the trade, the sub-committee[2] expressed the opinion that a beginning should be made in connection with the trade in palm products of the tropical possessions of the Crown in Africa." I am a little doubtful myself as to what portions of tropical Africa can be counted upon as a tropical possession of the Crown, since Sir Hugh Clifford, as pointed out further on, tells us that, " The Gold Coast Colony of to-day, rightly viewed, is not a territory which Great Britain has conquered, but a federation of small independent States."

That is all the room that I can spare for this cloud that is threatening the well-being of our tropical industries, except to ask my readers whether the following question, put to the E.R.D.C., has ever been answered : " Does your programme include European financial ' control ' in any respect whatever of the successful cacao-producing enterprise of Britain's dependencies? " Until an emphatic answer in the negative is received, the cacao producers within the Empire will be wise to act upon the idea that they are no more likely to escape than are the fishery, vegetable oil, fibres, and other industries mentioned by name by Mr. Wilson-Fox, who, it must be remembered, stated last July that his committee had under consideration proposals whereby not only the traders and middlemen were to be eliminated, but, as far as possible, the control of the Civil Service as well. This means that the Tropics are to be given up to the mercy of the State monopolists without even the nominal " Protector " that we have given to indentured coolies. The E.R.D.C. evidently have no

---

[1] I put these four words in italics because one of my most prominent critics wished to contend that Mr. Wilson-Fox had made no mention of cutting out producers as well as the middlemen, but only of buying the crops collected or produced by others. Anyone reading this sentence can judge for himself which of us two, my critic or myself, has put the most correct interpretation on Mr. Wilson-Fox's views.

[2] Names not given, nor reasons why the members' opinions should be worthy of attention.

opinion of the value and ability of the Civil Service, since they have discussed their removal as well, so that "effective business management would be assured, together with protection from political interference." Old Leopold in the Congo was free from political interference I believe ?

       *   *   *   *

I have said enough, I trust, to warn our readers and the British Tropics generally of what is in the air, so we will now get on to pleasanter but not less important matters, and discuss the cacao market whilst there is still enough freedom left to enable us to have something to talk about. Rumours concerning the limitation of the price of raw cacao thicken in the air, but so far they are confined to British growths because, on paper, foreign kinds are not imported. There is, however, such a thing as Prize Cacao, and when one looks through the weekly returns, taking London alone, and you think about the fat piles of foreign cacao that have been offered from time to time, you cannot help wondering whether Cameroons are to remain at the astonishing price they realized the last time they were sold, or whether Arribas will stop at 112s. and Bahias at 98s., whilst fine Ceylon are put below 85s., West African under 55s., and Trinidad, Grenada, &c., proportionately low. I mention these figures because they are in the ether of the air, and even if they are not registered, when the message comes to be put down on paper there are those who would like to see them agreed to. When one thinks of the height to which raw cotton has reached without being checked (because the bulk comes from America), and when one watches the widening out of the proposal of Mr. Wilson-Fox and his friends, care must be taken lest the proposal to make the British Tropics pay for the War may not fail in its object owing to British capital and enterprise going to anywhere and everywhere *outside* the Empire in order to carry on their new plantations away from such trade stiflers, and so leave those who cut down prices and grab old-time industries "for the good of the State," as Germany has always done, in possession of the deserted fields. Of course, those who cannot move will have to stay, but the rush to plant and to help feed the Empire after the War can be, and will be, diverted to places outside the Empire to an astonishing degree if those who have the ear of the Government, as well as the Ministers themselves, are not careful. Cacao planters and others, in West Africa and elsewhere, have done well for the Empire in every way ; it remains to be seen how these (at present) irresponsible committees and profiteering manufacturers will treat these planters and merchants in return. The public are not likely to benefit, since the profits " are to be divided with the Government," and as " divided " means that the profits go to more than one party, one wonders who is to share the spoils. So far this has not been made clear, but I wager that neither the producer nor consumer will benefit, as no one has, as yet, even hinted at cutting down the profits of the manu-facturers, whose goods go up, up, up, whilst we are told that the price of raw cacao must come down, and those of copra, &c., have been drastically limited. It is our duty to support our Government, and we shall all do so, of course, but only so long as self-constituted committees are not allowed to influence and govern the Government, as some views spoken and written show a tendency to be the case, relying on the next elections to carry the votes of the working classes against the interests of the Tropics.

CHAPTER VI.

By not allowing the ex-German Colonies to go back to that Country.

Tropical Life, April, 1917.

EVERY Englishman and pro-Ally must have listened with unalloyed pleasure and satisfaction to the concluding remarks made some little time back by Mr. Walter Long (our Secretary of State for the Colonies) at the West-minster City Hall when, referring to the future fate of the ex-German colonies, he told us that " We have acquired possession of different German colonies in various parts of the world. Now, I speak with knowledge and with responsi-bility, and I speak as the representative for the moment of those Overseas Dominions which are the pride and glory of our Empire to-day, when I say—Let no man think that these struggles will have been fought in vain. *Let no man think that these territories will ever return to German rule.*"

This weighty statement had, of course, been duly considered and approved of by Mr. Long's fellow Ministers before being uttered at such a well-advertised and crowded meeting as the one mentioned, which had been held in support of the War Loan. It can, therefore, be looked upon as official, and as showing what the views of our own Government and those of our Allies are with reference to the fate of the ex-German colonies after the War.

If there is anyone outside Central Europe who does not agree with Mr. Long's pronouncement that their colonies must never be returned to Germany, and we can hardly believe that there can be, we would strongly recommend him or her to study the following books that have recently made their bow to the public :—

(1) "The German Peril and How to Crush Prussian Militarism" (published by The Russia Society, price 1s.), by Gabriel de Wesselitsky, London correspondent of the Russian paper *Novoye Vremye*. The book reproduced the paper read by its author before a meeting of the Russia Society, which crowded to overflowing the Great Central Hall at Westminster, to hear what this eminent authority had to tell them concerning the chief enemy of our country and of every one else.

(2) The *Round Table* for March, No. 26 (2s. 6d.), especially the series of articles on "The New German Empire" (pp. 253-284), which discusses "The Spirit of German Policy, Germany's War Aims, The Eastern Plan, The New German Empire.

(3) "Germany's Lost Colonial Empire and the Essentials of Reconstruction," pp. 87, price 1s. net. (Simpkin, Marshall and Co., Ltd.), by John H. Harris, author of "Dawn in Darkest Africa," of which book the late Lord Cromer wrote in the Preface that he contributed to it: "Mr. Harris has acquired a firm grasp of the main principles which should guide Europeans who are called upon to rule over a backward and primitive society, and of the fact that prolonged neglect of these principles must sooner or later lead to failure or even disaster. He writes as a fair-minded and thoroughly well-informed observer."

Lord Cromer was right. Germany never has been able, apparently, to acquire a firm grasp of any sort of principles, whether they concerned the white or black race, and most assuredly has failure overtaken all her efforts, built up as she has been on concrete a hundred feet down, and surrounded by men a thousand deep with drawn bayonets always bristling for war. The very weight of the base has caused it to sink in the mud of Germany's iniquity and blindness to everything that makes life durable for the average man. The very terror of her armed Huns and pirates has instilled energy and distrust, if not down-right hatred, even into the hearts of the phlegmatic Chinese and the ease-loving Latin American. One and all are against Germany and her ways ; one and all agree that such a people must never again be entrusted with the lives of the terribly reduced population that Germany left in her colonies, nor must she be allowed again to own territories outside of Europe to exploit and drain of its riches in order to decimate the civilized nations, as she annually decimated the black tribes that had the misfortune to find themselves under Prussia's iron heel.

"What sort of peace does Germany still hope to secure?" are the opening words to the first of the articles embodied in "The New German Empire" series in the *Round Table.* "The question," the author goes on to explain, "can be answered in a sentence : A peace which will enable her to fulfil, in the next war, the aims she has failed to fulfil in this." Under the Kaiser Germany developed into a hungry Power. The object of the Em-peror—and therefore of Germany—was to make her a "world-power," dominant throughout the globe as others had already made her in Central Europe. Already pre-dominant in Europe as the first military Power, Germany was to become an extra-European or a "World-Power."[1] Even the Socialists are reported to have joined in the cry, for we are told, that in an article dated as recently as January 17 last, one of the leading Socialists demanded for Germany "an extensive Colonial territory which will enable her to import from within her own sphere of government the tropical products which cannot be grown on her own soil."[2]

If it were not for the misery that the German occupation of tropical centres has always entailed upon the subject races under their control, whether coloured people abroad or Serbs and Belgians at home, it would be interesting to watch for how long she would continue to import the tropical products she requires from her own territories. It

---

[1] See the *Round Table*, p. 259, where the question is fully and carefully discussed as to "What sort of a Colonial Empire did Germany hope to attain?" Hope to attain, we would add, in the Latin American continent, as well as in Africa and elsewhere.

[2] Robert Schmidt, in the leading Socialist monthly, *Sozialistische Monatshefte*, for January 17, 1917.

would not be for many years, for the simple reason that in a generation or two there would not be a native left to cultivate the soil and prepare the crops for their taskmasters. Germany, judging from what she has done in the past, would have soon exterminated the coloured labour had the colonies remained with her, and since no Germans want to go there (as they prefer our own colonies, with their just, humane laws, which enable them to fatten on and to fleece us as merchants, instead of tilling their own soil as settlers), the end of their colonies as important producing centres would not have long delayed, even without the War.

" Thirty years after the birth of Germany's great dream of colonial expansion," writes Mr. Harris on p. 16 of his important book, which has appeared in the very " nick of time," " the creators find that their work in its main objective has been utterly futile, because her sons and daughters, having discovered that the areas prepared for them are uncolonizable, bend their footsteps elsewhere, mainly to the territories under the flags of Great Britain and the Americas. The colonies of their own country had no attraction for them. . . . From 1880 to 1910 the population of Germany had increased from 45,000,000 to 65,000,000, and during this period there were over 2,000,000 emigrants from Germany. Whither ? To those colonies upon which German statecraft, the Colonial Societies, and every allied agency of government had lavished such care in preparing them as homes for these emigrants ? *Nothing of the kind* . . . less than 1,000 male emigrants settled in Germany's Colonial Empire each year.

For political reasons, therefore—that is, to prevent Germany from having bases throughout the world, and the means to suck in money with which to equip her armies to fight her civilized neighbours, as well as for humanitarian reasons—our chief enemy must be deprived of all her extra-European possessions. This is especially important during times like the present, when civilized nations are striving so vigorously to increase the coloured labour supplies throughout the Tropics, and not exterminate them year by year as the Germans have been doing so systematically, as shown by Mr. Harris's book on p. 27, where he reports : " . . . allegations had frequently been made of atrocities inflicted upon the natives, including the barbarous treatment accorded to natives, of women and children captured during the Herero War, thousands of whom, it was said, were either murdered, driven into the waterless desert, or interned on barren rocks on the sea coast, there to die of hunger and thirst, until it had been estimated that the Herero tribe had been reduced by between 30,000 and 40,000." "In view of the figures published," sums up Mr. Harris, "a population of 'at least something over two persons to the square mile—against ten in Angola and eight, even to-day, in the Belgian Congo—gives as the original numbers, from 750,000 to 1,000,000,' and to-day the remnant cannot total more than 200,000. In Togoland in 1894 official figures put the population at 2,500,000 natives and the Europeans at 56, aud yet twenty years later—in 1913—the native population was given as being only 1,500,000. Truly can Germany, especially the Prussian element in it, pride themselves on their thoroughness in depleting the Tropics of its coloured labour supplies, which to-day are an absolute necessity if the soil is to be cultivated and the crops prepared and sent over as foodstuffs and raw materials, for without these no white country can exist for long, and Germany least of all, as she will always be the last nation on earth to successfully run colonies of her own. She can only fasten and fatten herself, barnacle-like, on the colonies of other nations so long as the other nations are foolish enough to allow her to do so.

With such facts before us, it was pleasant to hear Mr. Long say that her Colonies will never be returned to Germany, especially as the question has not, so far apparently, attracted much attention among the non-German Americans. While President Wilson is reported by the *Round Table* for March, 1918, p. 248, to be in favour of an absolutely impartial adjustment of all colonial claims in which the interests of the populations concerned " must have equal weight with the equitable claims of the Government whose title is to be determined." . . . . . On the whole, American opinion is more alert as to the African tropical colonies, but it is still quite fluid. Very little is known as to the essentials of that problem. Few of the facts about German maltreatment of the Aborigines have reached American ears, and there is no wide appreciation of the gravity of General Smut's warning " as to Germany's military aims throughout the interior as well as along the coast-lines of *Mittel-Afrika*. American public opinion is as yet not at all interested in the fate of Germany's South Sea Islands."

CHAPTER VII.

By Studying the Suggestions of the Proposed Imperial Development Board.

Tropical Life, June, 1917.

WE think it but right that we should in a book of this description call attention to the carefully-thought-out paper read by Captain Richard Jebb on June 5 (1917) to an influential audience of the Royal Colonial Institute, when the vigour, sincerity and determination shown by the leading men who took part in the debate to bring things to a head, so as to be able to start off without delay to make things " hum " once and for all time, was very noticeable.

Differ as the speakers may have done between themselves or with the opinion of the audience before them, there was no getting away from the fact that *all* were agreed that those vast resources within the Empire, which have hitherto remained dormant and idle (and hence, like all idlers, had often been allowed to get into mischief and benefit our enemies instead of ourselves), must now be developed to the utmost without delay. "If it is decreed that the Empire needs 2,000,000 tons of sugar, then we must have them," vigorously insisted Mr. Bigland, M.P. (one of Mr. Wilson-Fox's lieutenants), and those present, including ourselves replied " Hear, hear," as on this point we found ourselves in accord with the member for Birkenhead. Other leading spirits who are urging us all to develop the Empire also spoke with the same vigour and sincerity, including Lord Desborough (in the chair), Mr. Sandbach Parker, Hon. Gideon Murray, Governor of the Leeward Islands (who made an excellent speech), whilst the heavy guns, which scored hits every time, were manned by Hon. J. G. Jenkins, late Agent-General for South Australia, and Mr. F. M. B. Fisher, of New Zealand, the latter gentleman speaking in the most convincing manner that we have yet heard. " Those who support the Unseen Hand, and the idea of trading with the Germans," he exclaimed, " should go and live in Germany. This Empire is no place for them, and they should have no place in this Empire."

From our point of view, as the general mass of our

people stand at the cross roads to-day (*laisser faire*, retro-gradation, development, progress), waiting for the mandate of our Empire-builders as to the conduct and movements in the future, it is absolutely necessary that no time should be lost in telling us to go "full-speed ahead" for many reasons, but especially for two: (1) To feed our people, and keep our factories well supplied with raw material so as to extend our trade. (2) As with a military war, to help us oust the competition of the enemy from all points of vantage, and to secure both the import and export trade of the chief centres of the world for ourselves and our Allies. For this reason, whilst the cry must always be the British Empire for the British, we must never again allow South America to be dominated by Germany. There we must nail to the masthead a flag with these words: " Latin America for the Latin Americans and the Allied countries in North America and Europe." In no part of the world will civilization and genuine culture and progress have to fight the mediæval Hun and his modern evil ways as in Latin America. Therefore, the question of the development of the resources of the Empire must always include the Latin-American markets as well. Above all, the begetting of wealth must always go hand-in-hand with the begetting of welfare. In a word, wealth + welfare = lasting power; wealth − welfare = Prussianism.

Captain Jebb, we believe, favours the views we expressed last month in our leading article. Like ourselves, he claims that the resources of the Tropics should be developed whenever possible by the indigenous races and *by methods appropriate to the development of an indigenous civilization*, and not by the exotic methods of our own industrial system which, in our own case, has already illustrated the old adage that wealth is not always equivalent to welfare. "We must hope," Captain Jebb will tell you, "to liquidate the War debt, or at least to meet the interest bill, by developing the resources of the Empire, just as our forefathers contrived to meet the bill for the Napoleonic wars by the industrial revolution that took place after the military campaign[1], but to be successful we

---

[1] This is the reason, with a virile and progressive nation determined as a people (and not as a ruling class, dominating only serfs and "gun-meat") to go ahead, why great wars so often bring great progress in their train. Those who remain are then forced to bury their prejudices and forgo their privileges, thereby allowing the land, &c., to be opened up, and all classes and creeds to come in and help make their country and themselves wealthier than before.—ED. *T.L.*

must start with a firm grip of the idea that in the Tropics, as elsewhere, the foundation of wealth must be welfare. *If* we cannot have tropical produce cheap, let us have it dear, and arrange our costs on that basis." Those who know what the near future holds in the palm of its hand for us will agree that Captain Jebb is right, and be glad that the Royal Colonial Institute gave him the chance of expressing his views at so propitious a moment as now. We certainly are, and so will others be, when they have read the paper and subsequent debate.

CHAPTER VIII.

By encouraging Ceylon or elsewhere within the Empire to Produce Camphor.

Tropical Life, January, 1918.

THE American papers have, from time to time, been mentioning the words "Camphor Production in the United States," especially the *Oil, Paint and Drug Reporter*, of New York, in its issue of February 17 last, which dealt with the matter at some length, and more particularly with the experimental work carried out by the Satsuma concern, which, we are told, had at that date (February 17) about a thousand acres under cultivation, with another thousand being planted up. These two thousand acres it is reckoned will contain about 1,000,000 trees. This means 500 to the acre, and so might seem at first to be rather closely planted, but Macmillan[1] tells us that about a thousand acres were estimated to be under camphor in Ceylon in 1908, when about 15 cwt. of the commercial product was exported, against about 5,200 tons as the world's total supply, almost entirely raised, of course, in Formosa. The area in Ceylon was coppiced or cut back to a height of about 4 to 5 ft., in order to obtain successive clippings. If planted 6 ft. by

----

[1] See p. 507 of "A Handbook of Tropical Gardening and Planting." By H. F. Macmillan.   Price 15s. post free of *Tropical Life.*

6 ft. that would give 1,210 trees to the acre. In Ceylon it was estimated that about 14 lb. of clippings could be looked for from each tree, which should give 170 lb. of commercial camphor per acre, say 1 to 1½ per cent. of pure camphor, besides the oil obtained as well. In Formosa a yield of 120 lb. per acre is spoken of, whilst in America a yield of up to 200 lb. is claimed at times.

In Florida, it seems that the plantations of the Satsuma Company, which is closely affiliated with the Celluloid Company, forms a portion of an earnest attempt which is being made to render the United States less dependent on the Formosa output which has to feed so many markets. Another camphor-producing concern is controlled, if not actually owned (in the United States), by the Du Pont interests, and is, or was, known as the Arlington Co. If America finds it worth while to plant camphor, and we quite agree that it is so, it must surely also be to the advantage of this country to extend the number of centres carrying on camphor-growing experiments, as well as to increase the areas where the drug or gum has already been planted on a commercial basis. It must no longer be urged by the people of this Empire in future as it has been in the past : Why should we bother ? We can get all the camphor we want from Formosa. We can buy all the sugar we need from Cuba, Java, &c. ; the latter centre will also send us bark or quinine at a ridiculously low cost, and so on. All this must be altered once and for all time, because the most incorrigible dreamer, pacifist or slacker must have been able to realize by now, whether he is willing to acknowledge the fact or not, that whatever supplies this country and the Empire at large may be able to obtain in normal times are of no account, and need not be considered when it comes to times of war, and the man who really believes that there will be no more war, and hence no need to prepare for it, had better go and live in Berlin until he has learnt otherwise. Those less doubtful should read William Archer's " Gems (?) of German Thought," where their pastors show by their views how righteous it is for Germany to fight all nations now at war with them. " To attack London," says Karl König, in his " Six War Sermons," "is to attack a den of murderers." This is quite equal to Bernhardi, when he urged that " the efforts directed towards the abolition of war must not only be termed foolish, but absolutely immoral and unworthy of the human race."

In face of such statements, with what a true ring to the

ear comes back to one's mind the Old Roman saying, *Homo solus est aut deus aut demon*, i.e., Man alone is either a god or a devil. The German Emperor, from all accounts, honestly believes that he is the equivalent of a god; we are still more certain that he is nothing of the kind.

It must be agreed, therefore, that we shall have to prepare for yet another war, the postponement of which can be achieved only by the ability of the anti-Prussian nations to be self-supporting, to stand alone, and to be able to exist, not only without the help of Germany in any way, but to exist and to prosper in spite of the rapidly increasing German population still being on the earth's surface.

Since this is the real state of affairs as we stand to-day, we must not think of providing for ourselves as if we are to have peace, but in the firm conviction that there will be another war, for if it does not come in our time, it will only be on account of our economic preparedness, which will prevent the wolves from starting to attack. This is the compelling force that is already driving us forward " to do or to be done," and which is insisting that we shall start at once, as Germany is doing so far as she is able, to make this Empire of ours self-supporting in every way, so that we shall no longer be obliged to go to Germany for perhaps fifty per cent. of our imports, and to other countries for twenty-five per cent. more. Brutal, blustering, boastful, bull-headed, egoistical and insanely unmoral as the Prussians may be, according to the papers from which we have collected these adjectives, the people of the Allied nations will also, if they are wise, remember that they are equally patient, dogged and determined to win at all costs, and that if they have made many mulls this time, that only means less mulls in the war to come.

And so, we claim, it is high time for the British public to acknowledge the fact, and when they have done so this country will be well advised to do the same as Germany, and put her Imperial house in order and prepare for the next war. People, in the past, have been far too busy looking at big guns, watching reviews, and reading speeches that are published deliberately either to stir them up and make them panicky, or else to make them stupidly indifferent to what is going on around them. We prefer to ignore such " kites," as it is better to keep our eyes on the economic development *within* the Empire, which properly carried out will do more to postpone the next war than all the manœuvres, big guns, and political " gas " yet invented.

Among these economic products must be included sugar, coco-nut products, vegetable oils, cotton, cereals, and camphor. There are others, but these will lead, no matter what else may follow, and camphor, cotton, and vegetable oils must always be in the forefront.

Returning for the moment to the work being done in America in connection with camphor production and extraction, that country is wise enough to realize what a lot depends, if the industry is to prove a permanent commercial success, on the satisfactory and, therefore, remunerative recovery of the gum from the leaves and twigs, for it is claimed over there that the industry can be run to pay without the destruction of the tree itself, in order to secure the wood chips to distil from. To what extent such a view is correct remains to be seen. In reference to this, one regrets that fuller particulars have not been published concerning either the original or the newer machine used in Florida for clipping the leaves and twigs from the trees, especially as, according to the reports, " The success or failure to grow camphor trees on a scale large enough for commercial purposes stands or falls on the successful operation of this machine."

CHAPTER IX.

By making Trinidad or another West Indian Island the " Hong Kong of the West."

Tropical Life, April, 1915.

SOME twenty years ago Mr. R. H. McCarthy, C.M.G., who is now in charge of the Colombian Railways in London, occupied the post of Collector of Customs at Port of Spain, the capital of the Island of Trinidad, which celebrated its hundred years of British Rule in 1897, when our Editor was in the Island, and had the pleasure of serving on the Committee that arranged the public festivities, which included a ball, dinners to the poor, fireworks, and illuminations on a most lavish scale.

Shortly after this Mr. McCarthy, addressing a closely

packed audience, which included the then Governor (the late Sir Hubert Jerningham), described the future possibilities of trade between the United Kingdom with Latin-America and our West Indian possessions, which would make Trinidad the Hong Kong of the West, to receive and pass on this trade of the real El Dorado, which so many had dreamed of and risked their lives for, and where wealth untold still lies unknown and unappreciated, awaiting its day of discovery. Trinidad, owing to its proximity to the Orinoco, and the important trade centres along its course, will always be very popular and much sought after as a transhipping depot, especially now it has such convenient harbour accommodation and a dry dock, to say nothing of possessing the best hospital, we believe, for a vast area around, both island and mainland. Barbados, already connected by steamers with Manaos, will, with tact and wideawake management, secure her share, and having the bigger river and the most important traffic to draw upon, she may yet secure as valuable a connection as Trinidad, although further away from her quarry. With the Canal open and trade rapidly increasing between Latin America, Australia, Japan, and the East, no one can yet estimate what can be done with the other islands if capable heads and willing hands go thence, East and West, to say nothing of the island entrepôts in between, to develop, encourage, and guide the trade-to-be, and see that it goes to their own folks. Such work will benefit both themselves and the Empire as a whole. To do this, however, the Empire must help them a little at the start, and up to now no one can pretend that the Old Country has done much in that way, nor does it show many signs of even recognizing that it should. So fierce has been the game of grab at home (we are talking, of course, before the War, or outside war politics) that no party seems able to find time to attend to the Tropics which none of them can do without for a month, or if they could spare the time and money, they want so much for their own fads and fancies that there is, apparently, nothing left (even with a £200,000,000 Budget in peace times) to help trade-builders overseas, or who want to go there, although they are often better men and more deserving of help than those who get the money at home. Let us hope that when the War is over a grateful nation will realize that this Empire of ours will have a little annual bill, running around some thousands of millions, to pay for interest and principal as the cost of this War. Knowing how necessary it will be to provide for or, better still, to try and entirely replace this amount the people at home must learn a little of what the Tropics has meant to them and done for them, in men, money, and foodstuffs, and so be induced to give West and East each an Agricultural College, and an Institute of Scientific and Commercial Research. We have already suggested that the West Indies should follow the example of the Federated Malay States, Canada, South Africa, and the Australian States, and have a museum of specimens and samples attached to a bureau of information and publicity in a wide-windowed shop facing the popular side of a leading thoroughfare. By some such means alone can we advertise the unique advantages offered by these possessions as centres for planting and trading, and so draw to them those men, with capital of their own or at their command, who will be available and anxious to settle down, but not within the four walls of a city clerk's office or storekeeper's establishment and the everlasting streets of a big city or town.

SECTION III.

FINANCE.

CHAPTER X.

The Budget and the Tropics before the War.

A £195,000,000 PRE-WAR BUDGET, BUT NOT A CENT FOR TROPICAL MEDICINE AND EDUCATION.

Tropical Life, May, 1913.

" A PROPOSAL deserving to be heartily supported is that of Professor Dunstan for the establishment of a tropical school of agriculture. The time is very proper for this step to be taken. Until within very recent years the Tropics exacted a heavy sacrifice from the able and promising young men who went out to them. Either they died at their posts or they came back broken in health and constitution. The schools of tropical medicine have gone far to achieve a complete victory over the adverse climatic conditions, so that operations can now be carried on where formerly they were impossible. Thus energetic and ambitious youths have a wider field open to them. At the same time there has been a great development in the growing of rubber plantations, which, with tea-planting, has become a very important form of tropical agriculture. These industries are both carried on in Ceylon, and in that island there is already a nucleus of what might become an Imperial college of tropical agriculture. Professor Dunstan suggests that Ceylon is, ' on the whole, the country best suited for the establishment of this college.' The idea would be for the student to undergo a course of training at one of the English agricultural colleges, and then follow it by one in tropical agriculture."[1]

---

[1] Sir Henry McCallum, ex-Governor of Ceylon, also strongly supported the claims of that Island in an able letter to the *Times* of May 12. We feel, therefore, now that East and West have both had their cause fully and carefully laid before the Government and the public, it is for them to see which centre should have the first college, until, we hope, in the near future, each will have its College of Agriculture.

Thus spoke *Country Life* of May 10, and we fully endorse all they have said. At the same time we cannot help feeling how very little the Government of this country has done to improve matters, as described above, and to show its appreciation of the energy and enterprise, as well as of the set-backs and suffering which have been the lot of those pioneers who have dived into the hinterland and un-known areas of the Tropics, in order to send us unstinted supplies of raw material and foodstuffs, to keep our factories busy, and to feed the great British public. And are the British public, or the Government elected by them, grateful ? We fear not—neither grateful nor appreciative. In their ignorance or indifference as to where the supplies come from they take no precautions to safeguard the con-tinuance of them ; they do not even set aside a small fraction of what this country spends to carry on the work of the Schools of Tropical Medicine or to establish Colleges of Agriculture in the Tropics. What has been done to further the first of these two worthy and indispensable " Insurance " schemes has hitherto been done entirely by private effort and exertion. Mr. Lewis (now Viscount) Harcourt says nice things about the idea of establishing tropical agricultural colleges, and Mr. Austen Chamberlain is doing magnificent work, as a private individual, by dragging in tens of thousands of pounds for the London School of Tropical Medicine, and we are sincerely grateful for the same. What we maintain, however, is that a leading man like Mr. Chamberlain should never have been compelled to give up his time to go begging for that money which a really appreciative country should be only too ready to expend on those who sacrifice so much to feed the public and keep them in employment. If the Exchequer is driving us crazy or into prison to make us spend millions on national health insurance and national education ; schemes which tap the lowest strata of this country, those who are a hindrance and no help ; surely a fraction of the amount thus spent would be wisely expended on a tropical health insurance and a tropical educational insurance on similar lines for the benefit of planters, if only to safeguard and improve the workers overseas, as we are doing to the public here, so as to enable them to be of greater use to this country than they can ever be without this help. Although, undoubtedly, this ought to be done we do nothing ; we do even worse than nothing—we put exceedingly heavy taxes on the produce shipped to us by our children overseas, to help educate, and insure, and downright pamper the working men and the lowest classes here, whilst the Government so far has done nothing for the tropical planter abroad —has done nothing, and does not seem ashamed of the omission.[1]

Tempora mutantur, nos et mutamur in illis (Times change, and we with the times). In the old days the prodigal son went abroad and rioted, and then came home and ate the fatted calf that had been carefully tended by the steadier folks at home. To-day it is the prodigal who stays at home, and wastes *ours*, not *his* substance, and it is the tropical planter who goes abroad to help make the fatted calf (now a golden one) for the prodigal at home to gloat over and glutton at, and to give nothing in return. " This year will be, I anticipate, the most glowing year that British trade has ever known," Mr. Lloyd George, Chancellor of the Exchequer, and therefore Prodigal-in-Chief (*pro tem.*), told the House of Commons on Budget night (April 22), and on the strength of that statement presents a bill of £195,000,000[2] for this country to pay,[3] in which not one farthing is to be voted to establish agricultural colleges in the Tropics or to further consolidate and assure the work of the London and Liverpool Schools of Tropical Medicine. What money these necessary institutions will get must come in the form of charity, *i.e.*, out of the pockets of everyone but the general public, who to-day cannot possibly exist without the Tropics, for as Europe and America develop their industrial enterprises agricultural pursuits must be, and will be, driven more and more elsewhere, *i.e.*, to the Tropics and sub-Tropics. Had the Chancellor of the Exchequer voted (as he would do if

---

[1] See Indian Tea Association Notes, p. 86, column 2.

[2] Long ago we warned our readers of the certainty of *£200,000.000* Budgets, even in times of peace ; see, for instance, p. 55 in our March (1910) issue, when we said : "This country must have more money for revenue purposes. This means that more of us must go abroad to extend the trade of the Empire. To-day we grumble at *£150,000,000*, in a few years we shall want *£200,000,000*. Let us therefore change our educational methods. Let us teach the children we can get control of to become agriculturists and colonizers."

[3] If the Tropics fell out of existence, how much of this amount could be raised? Of course, it must be remembered that the experienced and educated man who has invested his all in the Tropics has no vote. The working man, be he industrious or a waster, helpful or a hindrance, has a vote, hence, we suppose, he takes all for himself, and gives none to those who equally need and deserve it, if only because they send food and work for the voter who stays at home.

he could realize what the Tropics means to this country) but £250,000 a year (that is about *one-eighth* of 1 per cent. only on the total amount demanded) for two or three years, then the foundations and assured success of the agricultural colleges and the work of the Schools of Tropical Medicine would be well and truly laid, and the future prosperity, happiness, and general welfare of the public "insured" far more certainly than the National Health Insurance, costing millions a year, with its panel doctors and sanatoriums, will ever bring about. We are too late, we fear, for this year, but we do hope, most sincerely, that our future prodigals will see to it (if only for selfish reasons, *i.e.*, if they want to continue to feast on fatted calves and to demand that they become bigger year by year) that the tropical planter is at least given the same medical and educational facilities that are offered and forced on the lower classes on this side, especially as the cost for the first will be but a fraction of that for the latter, and the benefits that will accrue from the latter cannot be compared in any way with the benefits offered by the Tropics.

CHAPTER XI.

Financing our Imperial Pioneers.

IF I WERE CHANCELLOR OF THE EXCHEQUER.

Tropical Life, September, 1914.

IN the first article in the August issue on " Why and How the War will Benefit the Trade of the Empire " we urged our readers to remember that the question of finance must not be overlooked. This, of course, is what we have contended and striven to drive home to those in authority over us in every way we can, viz., that in future the leadership of the world lies with the nation who owns the heaviest purse,[1] and so it behoves us to develop our possessions and spheres of influence in every way possible. We have had over twenty-five years' experience in merchants' and

---

[1] As those seeking to float war loans, either at home or abroad, very soon discover.

traders' offices, both here and in the Tropics, and know exactly the shiploads of enamelware, china, earthenware, glass, lamps, and thousands of other household and estate supplies, as well as machinery of all kinds that went out regularly from the Continent, all of which could just as well and far better have gone from here. The cost may be a little higher, but the quality is far superior, and since the freight, charges and insurance, and all the expenses of transport up country on the other side are the same on the cheap rubbish (which often arrived leaking and broken) as on the fair-priced and strong, useful articles that were made to last, even in the Tropics, a benefit out of all this evil may still accrue to British makers if this War eliminates the trade in cheap rubbish, and substitutes well-made articles that will last a fair time and still cost reasonable prices. The only thing needed to extend such a trade are the banking facilities asked for further on when a " banking machine " similar to those splendidly managed concerns which have helped to make Germany what she is, is described and we ask that similar facilities be extended to the small manufacturers and traders under the Union Jack.

We appeal, therefore, to engineers, manufacturers, and traders generally not to pull back on account of the War, but to press forward more vigorously than ever and make hay whilst the sun shines in the Tropics if not over here, and take this heaven-sent chance to place out British goods of British quality on the African Continent, Latin America, South Seas, Asia, Malaya, &c., where we fear hitherto they have not been as prominent a feature in the shops and stores overseas as we should have liked them to be. In doing so they will help the Empire, keep their work-people and staff going, and also help themselves at the same time.

This is " Great Britain's opportunity," the London *Evening News* told us a few days after we had circularized English manufacturers on the matter, because :—

" Germany has supplied Argentina with 23 per cent. of her imports in spare parts of machinery, 40 per cent. of her imported electric wire cables, 51 per cent. of her galvanized wire, 41 per cent. of her jewellery, 74 per cent. of her dynamos and electric motors, 27 per cent. of her spare parts of carriages and automobiles, 34 per cent. of her tramway material, 61 per cent. of her household utensils, 49 per cent. of her glassware, and 26 per cent. of her copper manufactures."

If this is so with a single Republic, and the one, too, in which this country has the largest stake, what must the total German trade be throughout Latin America generally ? It is contended, and we believe rightly, that the German houses have handled business on terms that neither English nor American firms can entertain, and that they have done it with bills drawn on London houses and discounted in Paris, and so gambled with our money and pushed us out of markets, because by financing them we enabled them to do so. Hence the forty millions of German bills one hears so much about. We do not profess to know anything about finance, but if there is any truth in the above statements, then it is for this country and France to apply the remedy in future; and we cannot believe they will not do so. The South American trade, we know from personal experience, has been done (on the surface) at half price for years back, and we have many friends who have had to leave it alone as English wages, &c., make our costs exceed those of the Continental houses. We have heard the trade described as kite-flying, and those who flew the kites have now cut the string, and we have lost our property. Maybe we shall regain it; when we do so, it is to be hoped that the kite-flying will be done by our own countrymen, and not aliens. If we are going to risk our money, and lose some of it, let us lose it to our own people, not to unfriendly competitors.

The first portion of these notes was issued by our Editor as a leaflet to the leading firms, Chambers of Commerce, and the Press of this country. It brought back a fair number of answers agreeing with the statements, and stating, as a rule, that the writers were already taking steps to push out in those centres where the absence of German competition leaves a void. " But whilst we do not believe in growing rich at other peoples' cost through quoting impossibly low prices," they add, " we hope other firms, when the boom does come, will not, on the other hand, lose their heads and ask prices that are too high."

Having dealt with Argentina, let us discuss the German grip on Brazil, as outlined in an excellent work, " Brazil—To-day and To-morrow," by a well-known authority, Miss L. E. Elliott, Literary Editor, *Pan-American Magazine.*[1]

---

[1] New York. 338 pp., including Index. 24 Illustrations. 3 Maps. Price $2·25, or 10s. net, in London. Weight, 38 oz. The Macmillan Company, New York, London, Toronto, Bombay, &c., or *The Pan-American Magazine*, 70 Fifth Auenue, New York.

This book came to us at the right moment. It shows how Brazil, the greatest of all American countries, is, practically speaking, the least developed, and it also shows in Chapter II what steps have been taken by Germany to try and colonize Brazil. When one hears how these men have been behaving over there, Brazil can well be thankful that the European War came when it did, to show her patriots what an enemy she had in her midst, and how harmful they meant to be, and can still become (with a few noteworthy exceptions), if steps are not taken to expel the dangerous and undesirable element as speedily as possible, and keep the others in order.

The first official, deliberate importation of colonists to Brazil, we are told (p. 56), began in 1817 with some Swiss settlers. A second batch brought no less than 342 Germans. Germany at this period had not begun her industrial expansion which later kept all her people at home, and so, for about twenty-five years, she became the largest shipper of settlers to Brazil.

The second official colony, that in Rio Grande do Sul, was started in 1825, and consisted entirely of Germans. That Colony is now reported to have developed into one of the chief towns of the State, with 40,000 inhabitants. Its establishment was followed rapidly by that of Tres Forquilhas and S. Pedro de Alcantara, in Rio Grande, both German settlements. Then came, in 1826, S. Pedro in Sta. Catharina, and, in 1828, Rio Negro in Parana, formed by disbanded German soldiers. Petropolis, the model city in the hills above Rio, was founded by Germans and Swiss. German colonizers created the Sta. Isabel Colony, down South, in 1845, and started five new centres in Rio Grande between 1849 and 1850. In 1850 Blumenau, in Sta. Catharina, was founded by Herr Blumenau of Brunswick, as German a centre as Hamburg itself from all accounts. To-day Blumenau is a hustling city, with 50,000 inhabitants and a big trade. Then came the " Colonizing Union " of Hamburg, which established a fine town at Joinville, with a population to-day of 25,000, and, later, Mucury in Minas; so there must be at least half a million people in Brazil who are pro-German in birth, breeding and sympathy, and believe that the cause of the Fatherland should come before all.[1]   The author

---

[1] The authoress says 250,000, but as she owns that 128,830 Germans are known to have entered Brazil, and as we believe in the saying, " Once a German, always a German," we are sure that our estimate is nearer the

deals very fairly with our chief enemy, and gives them all the credit they deserve for having shown the determination they always have done to hang on to Brazil in spite of the most serious drawbacks. The climate, the Indians, and the total lack of communication at first, still left them undaunted, and, as we have always claimed, it is a great shame to think how the people of this country, spoilt and pampered at home, have not swarmed out to South America, which has been so liberally financed with our capital, to develop the continent along lines that would prove of mutual advantage both to the visitor and visited— to Brazil as well as to our own Empire.

After the War it is sincerely to be hoped that this mistake will be rectified. The girls and women can stop in the offices, and the men can go and push British interests over there, and assure Brazil's future by means that will not leave her with an unpatriotic growth in her midst that can injure her future, as Germany seems anxious to do at the moment, if given a chance. Brazil, by cutting off negotiations, will no doubt be able to put her house in order. We wish her all success, and she ought to be very grateful to Miss Elliott for having published so important

---

truth from a political point of view. It might also be as well to remind readers what President Wilson told the American Federation of Labour at Buffalo when he addressed them on November 12, 1917 : viz., " There is no important industry in Germany upon which the Government has not laid its hands to direct it, and, when necessity arose, control it. You have only to ask any man whom you meet who is familiar with the conditions that prevailed before the War in the matter of international competition to find out the methods of competition which the German manufacturers and exporters used under the patronage and support of the Government of Germany. You will find that they were the same sorts of competition that we have tried to prevent by law within our own borders. If they could not sell their goods cheaper than we could sell ours, at a profit to themselves, they could get a subsidy from the Government which made it possible to sell them cheaper anyhow ; and the conditions of competition were thus controlled in large measure by the German Government itself. But that did not satisfy the German Government. All the while there was lying behind its thought, in its dream of the future, a political control which would enable it in the long run to dominate the labour and the industry of the world. They were not content with success by superior achievement ; they wanted success by authority. I suppose very few of you have thought much about the Berlin to Bagdad railway. The Berlin to Bagdad railway was constructed in order to run the threat of force down the flank of the industrial undertakings of half a dozen other countries, so that when German competition came in it would not be resisted too far, because there was always the possibility of getting German armies into the heart of that country quicker than any other armies could be got there.'

a chapter in her book just when the information was so badly needed.

We are glad to see that the present Chancellor of the Exchequer shares our opinions, for, according to the London *Daily Telegraph*, in replying to a deputation, he referred to the important part which finance would play in the War in these words :—

" In my judgment the last few hundred millions may win this War. The first hundred millions our enemies can stand just as well as we can ; but the last they cannot, thank God, and therefore I think cash is going to count much more than we can possibly imagine at the present moment. We are only at the beginning now. Of course, if we have great victories and smashing victories that is all right, but then they may not come yet. We may have fluctuations, and things may last long.

" We are fighting a very tough enemy, who is very well prepared for the fight, and he will probably fight to the very end before he will accept the only conditions upon which we can possibly make peace, if we are wise.

" We financed Europe in the greatest war we ever fought, and that is what won. Of course, British tenacity and British courage always come in, and they always will; but let us remember that British cash told, too. When the others were absolutely exhausted we were getting our second breath, and our third and our fourth, and we shall have to spend our last before we are beaten."

In order, however, to obtain these millions to spend in the art of war, some one, and many a one, has to make them in the arts of peace, and that takes us back to the question of the trade war, to carry on which the manufacturers and merchants of the Empire are being trained and mobilized. This War also needs financing, although, thank goodness, only in pence or even farthings compared to the millions that will go into the melting-pot before peace is proclaimed.

For this reason, if I were the Chancellor of the Exchequer, I would arrange through the Board of Trade and the leading mercantile houses to consolidate the Empire's commercial interests in some such way as the following, so as to enable the rank and file of young Englishmen who have hitherto been discouraged from carrying on a trade war overseas, to do so now with as great a vigour and with the same chances of success as is likely to be ours in connection with the other war on the Continent.

In the same way as Lord Kitchener asked for 100,000 and then 500,000 men to fight our enemies with sword and bayonet, the Board of Trade should appeal for suitable men to go and push our trade and interests in all parts of the world overseas, both near the coast and up-country. The question of language need deter no one; it can be picked up by anyone who means to get on whilst he is learning the general business routine. I say this as no war can be carried on without soldiers of all ranks, and our trade soldiers are at present lacking for want of leaders and absence of prospects, for at present those who make the start must, more or less, compete against existing British interests, and these, instead of collaborating with the newcomers, will fight them, not join forces with them to fight the common enemy. We want to change all that. The Board of Trade should appoint a general and the staff necessary to finance and guide this new army, and render them independent of the old guard and their old-fashioned ideas, and then we should soon see the rank and file flow in to help. The fall in the price of rubber in the Tropics has cut many men adrift, experienced ones as well as just " creepers "; these should at once be eligible. Again, when the War is over thousands of young men will be only too glad to enter any channel of trade, and many of these would also be very suitable for training as traders overseas.

The first thing to do, however, is to finance these soldiers. Nothing can be done without money, cash or credit, and, unlike our competitors, this has been lacking to the English trade-adventurer, and until it is forthcoming nothing can be done, for the making of machinery and other goods is easy enough; it is the selling of them at a profit and to get in the money that is so difficult, and yet those who do the first get financial assistance far more easily than even the big trader. There are, however, many thousands of the smaller manufacturers in London and elsewhere who could increase England's trade to an unprecedented extent if a little help along the lines indicated was forthcoming. The big, old-established houses may object to this competition, but it would be a mistake to do so ; properly managed, if they helped form the banks it would increase their revenues and diminish their risks. Besides, for the good of the country and of those who have turned out to fight, the interests of the few whose trade is being protected without their having to go out to fight must not be considered when the advantage of the many is at stake, and it is undoubtedly better for a country to have a large number of smaller merchants and traders than a few very large ones.

Having discussed the fighters, we then come to the sinews of war, cash and credit, especially the latter, for very little cash is needed ; it is mainly a matter of banking facilities. We want at least two big banks to which present banks, financiers, merchants, and the Government would subscribe, or otherwise arrange to run on a co-operative basis. Then we want a big discount bank to handle the bills, managed by men capable of advising and guiding merchants, manufacturers, and traders when all goes well, or to liquidate failures, thereby preventing unnecessary losses when mishaps occur. All these banks must be quite independent of each other in every way, so that if one gets into difficulties the credit of the others need not necessarily be affected. On the other hand, they must work in perfect unison, and, for the sake of brevity, I will call them "the machine." Besides these we shall need smaller banks, *not* branches but independent concerns, in the large towns and manufacturing centres, and at the chief trade centres abroad, independent of, but financed and guided from headquarters. If we already have banks there, they can be incorporated or arrangements made to finance traders through them.

Having thus secured financial facilities we come to the trading. A merchant in England sends out six young fellows to push on his trade (and our trade) abroad, or those on the other side want to make a start. At first every-thing is tentative until the new soldier having had some training, gains nerve, becomes acquainted with local habits, tastes and patter, and generally "feels his feet " ; then he spreads out, and sells, barters, and trades on his own responsibility, but financed by those behind him until, of course, he is quite independent. Meanwhile, the orders, and produce or cash, begin to come in and are sent home. Each unit throughout, except actual branches of a firm, must be absolutely independent of each other so far as book-keeping goes, so that in case of a failure through inexperience, illness, or *force majeure* the others would not be compromised beyond the unit's debt. Should a failure occur, then the local merchant, or the big firm at home, or even, in the case of a serious " smash," the machine itself steps in and works to minimize the loss. One unit is simply replaced by another, or if the ·business is to be transferred this is effected, book debts, goodwill, stock, &c.,

without having to accept a ruinously nominal price as must be done at present. Some losses are certain to occur, but the profits on the many mount up whilst the losses are minimized, and since each unit is entirely " on his own," to sink or swim according to his ability and fate's decree, and is *not* a paid servant, each one naturally strives his best to keep going, and so the whole machine is run by picked men, without favour, and goes strong. Brains and energy help capital and experience ; sometimes . you tell the man or men to go ahead, and indemnify them against loss when you wish to secure a new centre ; elsewhere, those at home or at the shipping port may warn the up-country man to " pull-in " for reasons that are not apparent where he is. To the steady and gifted man promotion is sure and often rapid. No posts must be given by favour, and so the way is open for those at the extreme outposts to be drawn homewards and, with their long practical experience, to gain control of affairs, provided, that is, they have saved their money and gained the confidence of the majority. One point more regarding the manufacturers, and especially the smaller men, to whom progress is denied at present owing to the absence of financial assistance. Here the banking machine could assist to consolidate and facilitate the co-operation of mutual interests as follows : Modern factories to-day, as a rule, are strong believers in division of labour, and instead of making everything themselves they buy the parts from various firms, and put them together with such additions as their own workshops turn out. With the banking machine behind him, even a small manufacturer could execute an order which at the present time he has to pass by, and so we are told there are thousands of pushing firms in London alone who could make great use of the financial assistance which others ought to be equally anxious to offer them. With " the machine " a manufacturer called A. obtains an order, say, for a mill that costs £500 or £1,000, of which he actually makes only 25 per cent. He should be able to go to his bank and, once they approve of the firm giving the order, they assist the man to complete the work—that is, they send him to other customers to secure the parts, and they are paid through the bank by having their accounts credited with the amounts due. Except for wages no money is needed, and when the machine has been delivered and paid for, probably A.'s account will be credited in the same way, and by then he is busily engaged in doing work for orders obtained by B.,

C. and D. on the same terms. This is as it should be; we must learn how best to organize and utilize the energy and enterprise of the, at present, unattached unit, or, in other words, the nation's commercial interests must be consolidated so as to enable all, millionaire and hundred-pounder alike, to do their share in pushing the trade of the Empire abroad, and increasing the demand for labour at home.

But at present " the machine "—that is, the organization and co-operation of the various units—is altogether missing. I hope the present crisis will call attention to this important omission and bring about its establishment, not only for the good of the individual, but also to enable the Empire as a whole to obtain those " last few hundred millions " which this Journal, and now our Chancellor of the Exchequer, recognizes as being the one thing necessary to always place us ahead of our competitors and to keep us there.

CHAPTER XII.

British *v.* German Methods of Expansion in Latin America.

Tropical Life, November, 1916.

WE are glad to see that the Trade and Industry Committee of the Royal Colonial Institute has received the following statement as to the possible extension of British trade in Latin America, which entirely bears out all that we have claimed in connexion with this country's indifference to our neglect of the magnificent trade openings out there, openings as numerous, as vigorous, and as endless as the waterways of that continent; it also supports our contention that British interests are not, by four-fifths, adequately represented throughout Latin America; that is to say, there should be at least five Englishmen out there after the War to each one that we could boast of before August, 1914.

What this country and its Overseas Dominions particularly want to establish in Latin America are several strong commercial and trading banks on the lines suggested in our February issue to place within the grasp of enterprising British subjects the financial assistance that is so willingly given to their German competitors. The United States outside German circles over there are, we believe, waking up to the need of establishing such banks, so it is to be hoped that John Bull will do the same and also encourage the excellent Anglo-Latin-American banks already established to spread out and include new districts in their lists of branches and agencies. Our old friend the Colonial Bank, for one, should get out to Manaos and Belem (Pará), and also down to Santos and Rio, and have, a branch in Petrograd, and agencies at the chief trading centres in Russia, and so be able to participate in the large profits in the Russo-tropical trade that will spring into being when peace gives trade a chance to come into its own again.

Referring to the United States penetration of Latin America, the *West Coast Leader* of Lima, Peru, tells us that another factor in the situation is that the approaching opening of the new American bank in Lima (Banco Mercantil Americano) is bound to cut heavily into the remnants of American and other business which the German bank still retains.

Returning to the Royal Colonial Institute statement, this claims that British trade has lost ground in Latin America, or to put it in another way, British people do not possess and have not had as much trade as they ought to have done for one main reason, viz., *there are too few purely British importing houses in Latin American countries.* In Central America, in Mexico, and in the South American countries, the stores are largely in the hands of Germans. These firms, pursuing the national idea, such an idea being practically unknown to British people, always prefer to import from Germany, and they have a definite policy in promoting German trade. This is a laudable object on their part, and British people should take the lesson to heart, have a definite policy also, and always try to "go one better" than their enemies have done.

Most of the German firms are of mushroom growth. Young men have come out for a small salary of about 200 marks, or even less, per month. They were serious, hard-working young fellows, of great adaptability, content with very few pleasures, but by dint of close attention to business able to make themselves valuable to their employers. They are a reliable class, and all credit is due to them from their own country's point of view. In due course, with a little luck coupled with much patience and attention to business, these juniors are often able to become partners, even one of the heads of the firm that they went out for, or of a firm that they have started for themselves. Such men, later on, can go home, open a house in Hamburg, and settling down there, only make an occasional trip abroad. Thus the process of development goes on with the patriotic and pushful Germans. Have we not a sufficient number of patriotic and pushful British-born subjects to do likewise, and on the same scale for our Empire?

The same thing applies to the agricultural part of Latin America, where large numbers of coffee and sugar estates are owned by the Germans. To increase British trade you need initiative of this character. It will do little good to send out travellers, catalogues, samples, appoint agents, and spend large sums on propaganda in countries where such a condition of affairs as I have indicated prevails. What we need are men to manage banks—our banks, to start business houses—our business houses, and to form cacao, coffee, and other estates on all sides, owned and financed by British individuals and banking concerns.

It would be worth while for some of our Manchester, Birmingham, and London exporting firms, or of those trade-associations that we hope to see formed, to open up branches in the principal towns of Latin America. We would suggest that the Board of Trade, Chambers of Commerce, and public-spirited men should take the matter up, so that by propaganda the young fellows at home shall become interested in the work and grow more reconciled to the idea of going abroad, especially when by doing so they realize what a lot of good they can do both for themselves as the young Germans have done, and also for their country as well.

As we said in February (1916) strenuous times are ahead of us, and the nation who goes even a shade slacker than the pacemaker will get ridden down. In September, 1914 (*see* p. 61), our Editor, discussing "The Trade War with Germany," urged that, in order to obtain the millions to spend on the art of war, someone, and many a one, has to make them in the arts of peace, and that takes us back to the question of the trade war that will follow when the clash of arms is silent in Europe. The trade war will also need its soldiers, eager, ambitious men, determined to win, and the first thing to be done is to arrange to finance these trade warriors later on.

Negroes, like children, or rather because they are nothing else but big children, often bring the truth home to you at very unexpected times and in very forcible ways. We remember an old shabby negro at our elbow admiring, the same as ourselves, the very beautiful and decidedly costly interior of a church. "Seems to me," he audibly soliloquized, apparently to the air, certainly to no one in particular, "it takes a 'mazing lot of money to get to glory," and so it will do when the glory referred to is that of winning the Trade War after the Peace of Europe has been declared. Preparations for this commercial campaign after the military war is over are already apparent on the part of our adversaries in a widespread and dangerous degree for this country unless we can start "right now" to beat our enemy at his own game. As Lord Sumner told us at the Æolian Hall at the beginning of last November, the maxim that everyone must follow from now onwards must be—"produce all you can, consume as little as possible, waste nothing, work hard." This is what the Germans are doing and will do long after the War is at an end. If we do not do as well and better, even if we win the War we may lose the peace, as we shall not be in a position to recover our economic balance (get our second wind in foot-racing parlance) as quickly as the Central Powers.

Having carefully studied and digested the foregoing ideas on the urgent need of this country in general (which means, of course, London in particular, since she is the hub of the Empire and of the financial world as a whole) bringing about a radical and drastic change in its attitude towards its sons who have brains and ideas, determination and push, but no money to turn these talents to the advantage of the Mother Country, we hope our readers who have the interest of the Empire at heart will see that a start is made to give such men their chance. At present we claim that such men are not encouraged by the general community, and are directly discouraged by the big merchants and banking establishments (whose Boards are largely controlled by these same autocrats), who are conservative in their habits, and therefore slow to change and encourage enterprise on the part of others. Such men look askance at these irrepressible fanatics (in their opinion) for pushing on the trade and commerce of the Empire, lest (if financed) they fail and cause these millionaires to lose a few pounds, or what is far worse, lest they should succeed, and by mounting up the ladder of financial success become strong enough to push down these old-fashioned, out-of-date houses, who have hitherto had the game all to themselves. Enterprise in all and every shape abroad is not, and has not been, encouraged in this country for many a year, if ever, certainly not since the merchant adventurers and the Lombard goldsmiths settled down and formed the foundation of the wealth of London and the Empire within a few yards of where these lines are being written.

But times change, and go on changing—outside London. Unlike the Latin proverb, however, *Tempora mutantur, nos et mutamur in illis*, London no longer seems to change with the altered times, and certainly not in the way that she should do, if the best interests of the Empire and its future are to be considered.

Since such are our opinions, and always have been, as anyone who glances through the files of *Tropical Life* must own is the case, we were exceedingly glad to receive the December number of the *Round Table* No. 25 (Macmillan and Co., Ltd., price 2s. 6d.), and to notice among the other sections that the one on " Industry and Finance " (pp. 31-66) deals vigorously with the matter of our neglect of our prodigal sons abroad, whose efforts deserve support in the same way as our Teuton rivals not only support theirs, but also train others at home and egg them on also to go abroad and fight for the trade of the Fatherland in a way that we cannot but admire, and regret that our leaders have not followed, or, better still, excelled in.

Such are our views on the methods of Germany as compared with our own, but we cannot say whether the Court of the *Round Table* would agree that such views are what they mean us to gather from their articles.

We will, however, quote certain sentences from the four articles that go to form this section, and then leave our readers to secure a copy of the magazine and form their own opinions as to whether our contemporary goes far enough or whether we go too far.

The four articles are headed :—

(1) The Higher Direction of British Industry.
(2) The German Banking System.
(3) English and German Banking Compared.
(4) The Financing of Industry after the War.

To any man who knows one-fiftieth part of the possibilities of development that lies wrapped up in the future of the Tropics, what vistas of delightful but fierce, strenuous trade-fighting these four headings unroll before the mind's

eye. We all know, who know anything of what Germany
has done to develop her trade (and to fill her coffers at
other countries' expense to carry on this War, or, shall we
say, this dream of a World-Empire, that we only wish the
people of this country had had the " go " in them to dream,
much more to carry out), how very different the banking
system in Germany is to our own. In Germany banks
exist to finance enterprise, here they exist to gather in the
savings of the millions and to lend it to the few big houses
whose influence enables them to secure loans on advantageous rates. It is true that the doors of the banks are
equally open to all, but we should like to see the face of
the manager or of the Board of Directors at the men with
ideas but no cash, the pioneers and prodigal (pushing)
sons from the fringe of the Empire (prodigal only of their
strength and love of their country and its welfare), who
dared to walk in and ask for assistance. We unhesitatingly
maintain that such men in many cases deserve such assistance if the good of the Empire at large is considered, far
more than the merchant who faces them as a director of
the bank, or who rubs shoulders with them (and in either
case scowls at them as a rival) as they go in, each to lay
their case before the manager. What is the result ? The
man with ideas hangs on, and finally gets into the clutches
of the company promoter, from whom he gets very little,
and the public still less, except by a fluke. Listen to
what the *Round Table* has to say on the matter : " Even
before the War, notwithstanding the reputation for in-
tegrity, which British industry and finance enjoyed, and
which still inclines foreign countries in our favour, the
tendency has been of late years for Russian, Chinese, and
South American enterprises to go to Germany or the
United States." The United States, into which our
enormous war orders are pouring fabulous sums, until
their industries will be vastly more wealthy and powerful
than our own ; until, in future, we shall have two enterprising and powerful rivals, the U.S.A. and Germany, to
compete against. " A contributory cause to this," our
contemporary goes on to say (p. 64), "is undoubtedly the
roundabout, slow and costly methods of negotiating financial
business through company promoters, trust companies and
so forth, in London, compared with the immediate and
thorough consideration given to them elsewhere by powerful and combined financial and industrial interests." Now
turn to page 61, where you read : " In other very well-
informed quarters there is considered to be a serious and

immediate need for a financial institution, not necessarily with any banking functions, but with very large resources, so that it should be in a position immediately after the War to provide large sums to enable British industry to compete with the powerful combinations of German and American trusts and cartels. . . ." (Page 63) : " If the world's trade is to be fought for by great foreign combinations and cartels, we, too, must build our industry, on a large scale,[1] and large industries require large methods of financing. . . ." (Page 61) : " It would be prudent that any such scheme should start on a modest scale, and that its operations should at first be limited and cautious, . . . there are few institutions, either of a financial or industrial kind, which have not been built up from small beginnings." Probably at first it would be wise (for the institution to be established) to act mainly as " Sociétés d'Etudes " ; but soon, very soon, we hope, a strong, wide-spreading fighting machine would be evolved and set to work ; such a machine as has been discussed in previous articles.

Let us now comment on and quote those sentences which express our views on the drawbacks of our present financial system compared with Germany's, when it comes to a matter of pushing the influence and trade of this Empire abroad in competition with those of our rivals. The future domination of the world, the ability to come out and to remain " top dog " in the international struggle for supremacy lies, we have always claimed, with the country owning the biggest purse. For this reason, the time has come when banking institutions should be pressed into the service of the State and framed to help those who have shown themselves able to help themselves. To pick and choose such men will be quite easy ; in any case, it will be as easy as it now is to choose which out of the sea of men that look up to the Throne, are to be picked out and honoured with a knighthood, baronetcy, peerage, &c. Instead of that honour, impartial judges will choose among the pushful, and probably penniless, pioneers of the Empire, those whose brain and grit, whose perseverance and knowledge, possibly through long years of a lonely uphill fight in a foreign country, have increased

---

[1] But to do this we must have the pioneers or trade scouts out all over the world to scent out the new openings and pave the way for the regular trade soldiers to follow.—ED., *Tropical Life.*

our knowledge of trade-openings abroad, and to such men shall be given the far more genuine honour of being deemed worthy of financial assistance, cautious at first, but generous when the chances are satisfactory, to go and make good for themselves and the Empire against our competitors overseas.

Firstly, we want all our readers interested in such an idea to secure a copy of this December issue of the *Round Table*, to study carefully the information it con-, tains and which we cannot reproduce here. To encourage them to do so, however, we will dangle before their eyes the following notes, regretting, as we do so, that the article was not written twenty years ago and more, when we were trying to make good, and to make bricks without straw, in the Tropics. Had we known as much then as we do now, in all probability *Tropical Life* would never have been started, but knowing, even at the time, how and why we failed, we have been trying ever since to help others to avoid the breakers that we got upset over. After this we will begin quoting :—

" There has been developed," the *Round Table* tells us, p. 44, " a far closer connection between banking and industry in Germany than in this country, and many functions are performed by German banks which would be considered in this country to be outside the sphere of legitimate banking. These functions include the tasks of acting as close financial advisers and even controllers of many industrial concerns, of carrying through reorganization and promotions of industrial companies, of issuing industrial securities, of encouraging new ventures, and of syndicate business of every description," in a word, to save the trade pioneer from the clutches of the company-promoter. Since this country has no institution to do this, then the sooner one, and more than one, are formed, the more likely shall we be to win the coming trade war against our enemy competitors.

Such institutions bring into existence an organization in trade that is altogether lacking at present, and in so doing they effect economies by avoiding overlapping and the wasteful competition of rival promoters. German banks can be truly said to finance men with brains. In this country, if such men (or women) write books—books, that is, which are deemed worth reading—we buy them by the million, and yet if in other lines of thought, as of trade, invention, and agriculture, a man equally gifted, perhaps far more so, were to plead for a little financial help, the public, and especially the bankers, would turn their backs on him and retire home to read their six-shilling or seven-penny novel by the fireside, glad to be quit of the "importunate idiot." Thus it comes about "that the Germans should build Zeppelins and we should not ; that we should invent aniline dyes and the Germans exploit them ; that the German and American steel industries should increase by leaps and bounds and ours should remain stagnant," that we should produce palm-kernels and copra, should possess land rich in little-known (to the Englishman) but valuable minerals and chemicals, and that the Germans should scour our possessions and rout these out, like pigs hunt out truffles, to send to Germany to be exploited and manufactured into everyday necessities of life and sold to us (whose lands produced the raw materials) at huge profits with which to fight and worry us, as we deserve to be.

This War, people say, is a hell. Well, that more or less mythical spot may have a nearer and more palpable existence than some of us have hitherto bargained for. It was originally called into existence, we have always imagined, in order that those who have failed to do their duty may be punished, and there is no doubt that all classes in this country, rich and poor, but especially the lower and lower-middle classes, in spite of the millions spent annually to educate them, have woefully failed in their duty to appreciate and make the most of the riches that Nature has showered on us through the Tropics. On the contrary, they have shown, and are still showing, the most callous and incorrigible indifference as to where these gifts come from, how long they will last, and to whom we are directly indebted for their production. We deserve punishment, therefore, and are getting it with a vengeance. but unfortunately the ones who are most to blame are the heads of our Government for not forcing us to do our duty, and they are just those who do not go and fight and so escape the torments of the battlefield. But have they escaped them ? Perhaps a few have, but it must be very few, since most of us will agree that those who remain behind sometimes, and possibly very often, are the hardest hit and most sorely wounded by the bullets that killed their nearest and dearest.

And so the War metes out equal justice to all. Since this is so, let us hope that when peace comes all classes will consider more attentively and think more forcibly of how deeply this country is indebted to the Tropics and our overseas possessions, and what we owe them. If we do this, then the criminal foolishness of which we have been guilty in the past in not encouraging and financing our own men to exploit British products instead of allowing them to go to Germany to be turned into bullets to kill the flower of our land will not occur again, and we shall not have to blame ourselves as much, when the next war comes, for having helped our enemies to kill our men, women and children, as we may have to do perhaps in' connection with the present outbreak.

Going back to German banking methods, we would, in conclusion, ask our readers to refer to what we said in November about the banking machine : " We need, with two big banks a discount bank and many smaller ones, entirely independent of each other but working in unison, to help our trade pioneers and to finance the small pushing man as well as the merchant prince and millionaire contractor." In Germany, we are told, "there is first, what may be called the permanent group of banks round each leading bank. The Deutsche Bank group consists, for instance, of about twenty banks with a combined share capital of something like £50,000,000. . . . Most of the large banks and private banking houses have combined to form, in the case of China, the Deutsche Asiatische Bank, thus assuring united action, not only with reference to Chinese, but also to all Asiatic financial operations, the new powerful syndicate, led by the Disconto-Gesellschaft, undertaking the common planning and managing of loans and advances to the central Governments, provinces, and railroad companies in China, Japan, and Korea, and the organizing of railroad and mining companies in China."

This is the class of institution or banking machine that we need not only in China to cover the East, but also, and especially in Argentine and Brazil, in the West. Such institutions, influentially supported and ably managed, will do as much to push our political and financial influence throughout the world as will our ability to stamp out the blighting effects of Prussian militarism in Europe. We have the capital to carry out such ideas, but are the trained men there to do the work?—we fear not, that is, not to the extent that we shall need. They can, however, be trained fairly quickly if we have the educational machinery ready and waiting for them as soon as they return from the War. This, therefore, brings us to the question of education dealt with in Section V.

SECTION IV.

LABOUR.

CHAPTER XIII.

Will the White Race Lose the Supremacy of the World through their Treatment of the Coloured Races?

Tropical Life, December, 1912.

THE year now fast drawing to a close, and which will, indeed, have run its course by the time the bulk of our readers peruse these lines, has been an important and busy one for *Tropical Life*, and for those engaged in tropical development generally. To use an Americanism, we have often been "hustled" along more quickly than even we cared about, but as the movement has all through been entirely in the right direction, so far as the trade and commerce of our own Empire have been concerned, we do not complain; we are, on the contrary, only too pleased that such has been the case. Unfortunately, we cannot say the same for the Tropics generally. Already labour supplies are restricted in comparison to the demand, but instead of doing all one can to increase them, the leading European countries will still further reduce the number available, unless they speedily mend their ways.

For this reason we hope that the report on the Putumayo scandal, and the Commission[1] now sitting to consider the responsibility of the ill-treatment of the Barbadian negroes and Peruvian Indians in the Putumayo district, will call the lasting attention of the public to the need of serious and immediate reform to stop the way the natives are still being exploited and done to death for the benefit of absentee

---

[1] To the Chairman of which, Mr. C. H. Roberts, M.P., we sent a copy of our August number, calling his attention to the cartoon and leading article on the subject. This was duly acknowledged. We might add that the *Review of Reviews* and at least one other paper reproduced the cartoon.

whites, just as they were four centuries ago under the Spaniards. This state of affairs was driven home to us still more forcibly by the almost simultaneous publication of three books, written by leading authorities on the subjects treated, viz., on South America and Tropical Africa.[1]

Of the authors, we have had the pleasure of meeting both Lord Bryce and Mr. J. H. Harris, the latter fairly often. We were introduced to Lord Bryce at the House of Commons one night and met him on two occasions since. We have seen enough of both men to realize how capable they are of guiding us by their opinions, and also of forming trustworthy opinions on the subjects about which they have written, through the important journeys each undertook—Lord Bryce in Latin America, and Mr. and Mrs. Harris through West Africa and the adjacent islands.

All these books should be read by every one interested in tropical agriculture and commerce, since they deal largely with the native races, without whose help nothing can be done, especially in Africa. The various chapters show how things have become as they are ; what both conquerors and conquered have had to put up with and contend against ;[2] how abuses have crept in, how and where they still exist, and why it has proved extremely difficult and often quite impossible to eradicate them, at any rate up

---

[1] "South America : Observations and Impressions," by the Right Hon. James Bryce, O.M., &c., H.M. Minister at Washington, U.S.A., author of "The Holy Roman Empire" and "The American Commonwealth." 611 pp., including maps and index. Macmillan and Co., Ltd., London and New York. Price 8s. 6d. net.

"Dawn in Darkest Africa," by John H. Harris, Organizing Secretary of the Anti-Slavery and Aborigines Protection Society. With an introduction by the Right Hon. the Earl of Cromer, O.M., P.C., G.C.B. With 40 pp. of illustrations, and a map. Small royal 8vo, 10s. 6d. net. Smith, Elder and Co., 15, Waterloo Place, London, S.W.

"The Putumayo : the Devil's Paradise ; being an account of Travels in the Peruvian Amazon region, and of the Atrocities committed upon the Indians therein," by W. E. Hardenburg, C.E. Edited, and with an introduction, by C. Reginald Enock, F.R.G.S., with illustrations, and a map. Demy 8vo, cloth, 10s. 6d., net. T. Fisher Unwin, Adelphi Terrace, London, W.C.

[2] There is one Indian tribe (the San Blas Indians in Panama, noted for the fine coconuts they produce), Mr. Bryce tells us on p. 13, which "has kept itself quite apart, having maintained a complete independence both of Spanish Viceroys and Republican Presidents of Colombia." To this day they are "so jealous of their freedom and their own ways that they will not suffer a white stranger to spend the night in one of their villages."

6

to the present. Lord Bryce's description of the Teutonic objection to forming legal alliances with pure natives or coloured people, in contrast to the willingness of the Latin races, especially the Portuguese, to intermarry with them, continues a much-discussed, but always important controversy, as to which race this willingness to intermarry is most beneficial to—

(1) The European, his country, and his trade.

(2) The native and the cross-breeds (mulattos, mestizos, quadroons, and even the octoroons), and the tropical country they inhabit.

We are afraid, when looking backwards, that whilst the Spaniards and Portuguese (that is, the Latins) can claim the honour, thanks partly to Columbus (an Italian, and therefore also a Latin), of discovering and Europeanizing South America, other natons (i.e., the English, Germans, and Americans) are the leading countries to-day, and likely to remain so for many years to come. Would it not therefore be right to deduce from this, that for sound, practical, commercial, and empire-building reasons, the intermarriage between white and coloured races is not to be recommended, however freely the not doing so may cause the white men to cohabit with native women when in the Tropics. The " top-dog " alone can cry out the terms on which he is willing to live with the others ; and whatever policy we would like, from a sentimental or moral point of view, to see carried out, after carefully studying both Lord Bryce's book on South America, and Mr. Harris's on Equatorial Africa, one is bound to own that the Teuton, possibly because he never has freely intermarried with the native races, and been willing to live down to their level, has come out, and is always likely to remain, " top-dog " over the Latin races who have always lived on the fringe of " coloured " countries, and even at times been overrun and temporarily conquered by their inhabitants.[1]

----

[1] The following extract from the paper read by Sir Bamfylde Fuller, K.C.S.I., &c., on " The Purpose of Life in the East and in the West," before the Royal Colonial Institute, is worth noting here, for he told his audience that " the habits of the European peoples of the Mediterranean appear to show that they owe their material civilization rather to imitation than to their own initiative. They accept with contentedness conditions which to us appear repulsive ; they can enjoy life independently of comfort and think more of their status than of their possessions. Bound to Northern Europe by a similarity of religion, and influenced in great measure by immigration from the North, they have been drawn towards a similar set of material conditions. At the present

Whether the purer Teuton (i.e., the German) will finally do better than the Anglo-Saxon Englishman or the polygenous American, as regards profits from trading with tropical America and Africa, remains to be seen.

We have, however, both in this journal and when lecturing, always warned our own people that Latin America is the country of the future, for white planters and traders attracted hence from over-populated Europe, and that the country desirous of leading cannot ignore the way in which the commercial German and agricultural Italian are exploiting that continent, which, by the way, this country has done so much to finance, pouring in hundreds of millions of pounds (nearly £300,000,000 in Argentina alone), to open South America up on all sides for the others to benefit from, since Englishmen are far slower than these other races to go to South America as traders or planters. We were glad, therefore, to see that Lord Bryce, on p. 510, calls attention to a remark on this same matter made by Mr. Hiram Bingham, the American, in his book, " Across South America," published in 1911, viz. : " The number of North Americans in Buenos Ayres is very small. While we have been slowly waking up to the fact that South America is something more than a land of revolutions and fevers, our German cousins have entered the field on all sides.[1]   The Germans in Southern Brazil are

---

day one finds so little trace of the energetic originality of either Romans or Greeks as to be inclined to surmise that these nations owed their greatness to immigrant colonists from the North whose exotic energy could only outlast a certain number of centuries." Evidently the East Indian has deteriorated as regards energy in the same way, for Sir Bamfylde Fuller goes on to say : " There is high authority for believing that the Aryan tribes, to whom India owes so much of the greatness of her past, had their origin in the cold regions of Northern Europe ; the modern languages that are nearest akin to Sanskrit are spoken on the shores of the Baltic ; references in Sanskrit literature to snow, and to pine and birch trees may testify to the recollections of a northern home. It is a fact of much interest that, according to the Sanskrit epics, the Aryan women were free, showed themselves in public, and even chose their husbands. But the practical energy of these northern tribesmen evaporated under the Indian sun."

[1] Blumenau, be it remembered, was founded by a German, Dr. Herman Blumenau, some sixty or more years ago. Dr. Blumenau, we understand, obtained a grant of land in Sta. Catharina from the Brazilian Government, and with practically no capital (from all accounts) he went there with a number of German farmers and their families, and established the colony, which was named after him. It seems to have prospered and is now flourishing. Dr. Blumenau returned to Germany in 1864, and died fifteen years later, regretting, it is reported, that he did not die in Brazil.

a negligible factor in international affairs, but the well-educated young German who is being sent out to capture South America commercially is a power to be reckoned with. *He is going to damage England more truly than Dreadnoughts or gigantic airships."* [1]

Mr. Bingham was quite right when he made the above statement and is doubly and trebly right to-day, but it is not too late. If fathers and sons, be they Jingoes or peace-at-any-price advocates, would only read and digest· Lord Bryce's book, they would at once see how true it is that a country's greatest and most dangerous opponents are not always those they encounter on the field of battle.

Leaving Lord Bryce and South America, and coming to Mr. Harris and Tropical Africa, the question of the preservation from extermination of native labour supplies looms prominent right through the book. When one thinks of what the people of Europe, knowingly or unknowingly have caused to be done in Equatorial Africa, it is almost a relief to go back to Lord Bryce's book, and read about Pizarro and the Spanish battues, the slaughter of Atahuallpa, and the Peruvians in the square of Caxamarca, under the sanctity of the Church in the person of Valverde, who absolved the Spaniards and then urged them to massacre the heretics, or to the atrocious slaughter of the same Peruvian Indians when their miseries goaded them to revolt under Tupac Amaru, in 1781 to 1783. Although Tupac was torn to pieces by horses driven in opposite directions, these murders were quickly passed over, whilst the tortures of the red-rubber gatherers leave their mark and their memory up to now.

Two blacks, however, do not make one white, but we cannot help owning that we closed Lord Bryce's book with a far more hopeful feeling as regards the future of the continent with which he deals, on account of the numbers of Latin peasants and European commercial men who are flocking there, than we could possibly own to experiencing after reading Mr. Harris's views on re-marking the map of Africa. The Germans may for a time put money into the pockets of their friends at home, as Pizarro and the *conquistadores* did for Spain ; but as surely as the Spanish labour policy which killed off millions in the past, and (as Lord Bryce shows) has rendered the South American Indian practically useless to-day for development work,

---

[1] Italics ours.—Ed., *T. L.*

even for his own benefit alone, so will the German policy, by its severity and the persistent strenuous effort that it demands of the native, either exterminate him altogether or reduce him to a degree of hopeless, sullen, passiveness that will cause future generations to do as little with him as one can do to-day with the Indians around Titicaca or elsewhere on the Montana of Peru. It is not only that the German is so cruel, but that he is not in Africa for the sake of the Africans, nor solely and purely for the sake of the shareholders in Germany. He is there for political and military reasons, and such a policy as they wish to see in force is bound to crush and kill out the natives altogether in time.

If Equatorial Africa is to continue to pour out its shiploads of raw material for European and American factories. thereby enabling their people to be employed, and to make and send to Africa manufactured goods in return, there is one policy, and one only to follow, and that is to let Africa be opened out and planted up by the African for his own benefit, and not for the sake of shareholders or individual holders in Europe. If the German, Frenchman, or Belgian persists in any other policy, they will find in a hundred years or less that the territories they own will become as useless to them as the vine-rubber areas, or even as the planted centres, rapidly dying out, already are to Belgium.

To work Indians or negroes as they must be worked to put out the produce they do in certain areas, can only be done by inflicting severe, if not downright cruel punishments on them. Such a life quickly reduces their numbers—first, because it removes the wish to breed, or causes excessive mortality among the children that do come along ; and, secondly, because the misery and suffering it entails on the natives kills them off far more rapidly than they can be replaced.

We sincerely hope, therefore, that every one who wishes to see the trade of the Tropics maintained and increased will study all these books. With whatever object they were written, they show that if the Tropics, especially Africa, are to continue to put forth the increased exports that Europe and America are certain to demand of them twenty-five, fifty, and a hundred years hence, a radical and immediate change must be effected in the way the natives are being treated and exploited for the sole benefit of others. We say this quite as much for the benefit of the inhabitants of Europe and America as of the natives themselves.

The whole question makes one ask, How long will the present rate at which primitive races are being exterminated be allowed to continue? Will it go on, and even increase, until it brings about the economic and commercial doom of the Tropics and with that a permanent check to the prosperity and prestige of the white race? And, then, will such a check to the white race induce and enable the yellow and tinted races, owing to their ability to work the Tropics, to be placed at an advantage over the whites and so be able to assume the military and economic domination of the world?

These are great queries and since they are so no thinking man can allow the book mentioned in the footnote [1] to pass him by because no thinking man can deny that the Tropics to-day are a stern necessity to the reputedly civilized nations of the temperate zone, or that an abundant native population, a far larger one than exists at present, is an equally stern necessity if the so-called civilized nations are to continue to satisfy their ever-increasing demands upon the foodstuffs and raw materials that the Tropics can alone produce for consumption and manufacture in Europe, America, or Australia.

Going back to the old, old story of the goose that laid golden eggs, one is apt to compare the black and brown natives of the Tropics to the goose, as without their help we can no more expect to obtain from the Tropics that which we need, than we can expect to obtain even an ordinary goose's egg if these useful though noisy birds should cease to exist. In spite of this, whilst wise men and women have, from time immemorial, taken care of the geese and seen to it that their numbers increased in proportion to the local demand for their eggs and flesh, nothing has ever been done to assure a continuous and increasing supply of native labour for the Tropics. It must be owned, on the contrary, that much has been done to kill off the supplies that already existed, this, too, in spite of the fact that the Tropics, through these persecuted people, have always truly given us eggs of gold, or their equivalent,

---

[1] "Savage Man in Central Africa." A Study of Primitive Races in the French Congo, by Adolphe Louis Cureau, Gouverneur Honoraire des Colonies. Translated by E. Andrews. 351 pages. 18 plates. 9 illustrations in text. Price 12s. 6d. net. Weight 32 oz. *Tropical Life* Publishing Department. Also see p. 16.

whilst the well-cared-for goose can, at the most, but provide us with a simple meal.

This being so, we anxiously turned over the pages of M. Cureau's book, where he describes these typical primitive races, the Fans, the Pawan, and other Congo tribes, hoping to learn something as to how we can preserve these people, since the author tells us at the start that : " For more than twenty years I studied their every phase in all the districts of that vast territory which comprises the French Congo. I spoke their dialects, I lived their lives, and was accordingly able to train myself to think their thoughts, as far as could be done by a mind so very different from their own."

Such an experienced authority therefore deserves the closest attention, and we trust that what he has to tell us will be listened to, especially as he starts the book with a sentence that hits out straight from the shoulder and strikes us, *i.e.*, anyone anxious to see the Tropics prosperous and populous, right between the eyes, leaving us stunned and doubtful as to whether we shall ever win in this fight to secure " the Tropics for the tropical races" and their products for the white race.

" The last savage races are disappearing from the world's stage," are the opening words of M. Cureau's introduction and of the book, and we all know that this is true. But why is it so, since we know that we cannot do without the Tropics, and that the Tropics cannot continue to· be prosperous and productive without the natives ; not the half-educated and half or quarter white native, for such are no better, if as good, as the pure white. What we cannot do without is the pure, primitive, unadulterated native ; black, brown, or red. The cause of our inability to stave off this wastage of labour in the past has been due, we consider, to the needless ignorance on the part of our rulers and their representatives in the Tropics of anthropology. This science teaches us what to look for in those with whom we come into contact, when their peculiarities will help and when they will hinder us in our endeavours to rule them. Without such knowledge black and white will never be able to understand each other in the future any better than they have done in the past ; the result being that the coloured race has had to suffer hitherto. Unless, however, we can stem this tide of ignorance and indifference that is surely, but none too slowly, washing away our supplies of coloured labour, our day of suffering will also come later on, and when it does it will be unpleasantly severe. We say this because with regard to the black lives now being washed out on these tides and lost beyond recovery, their sufferings and anguish has been, and are being, short and sharp compared with what ours will be if future generations are starved out or have "to go under" to tinted superiors. If they do so the fault will be ours. Such a catastrophe will be entirely due to the fact that, in this, the Twentieth Century of the Christian Era, the White Race was too brutal, too selfish, and too indifferent as to the wellbeing of those to follow, to take serious steps to increase and not decrease the coloured races of Africa and elsewhere.

M. Cureau calls attention to this (p. 26) when he tells us " The ethnography of our subject appears to be all disorder and confusion. The races, nations, tribes and families which share the soil of the Dark Continent are innumerable. There is nothing to aid us [1] in untangling the skein, for we find here neither monuments nor traditions, and the science of anthropology [2]—which has never, as a matter of fact, been made the object of serious and generalized investigation—is swamped in an ocean of types which differ from one another by imperceptible gradings, from the individual to the entire black race."

Those who have had to do with natives, and especially those who have watched the white and coloured men when actually handling them, kindly or otherwise, and too often (through not understanding the men, through impatience, over-fatigue, and, let us say, at times through brutal indifference to the sufferings of others) it has been a case of otherwise, will agree with M. Cureau when he tells us on p. 37 (when about to discuss those who consider that the natives are hopelessly depraved and stupid), that we must remember that " Passing judgment upon other people is

---

[1] Up to the present.—ED., *T.L.*

[2] In *Tropical Life* for March, 1912, when discussing the work carried out by Major and Mrs. Tremearne in connection with the tailed head hunters of Nigeria, the Hausa and other tribes (see " Hausa Superstitions and Customs," price 21s., which we published for Major Tremearne), we concluded our plea for more attention to the anthropological study of native races under the British flag, by expressing the hope that "this country, governors and governed alike, will give more encouragement to those who study race-history and see that anthropology is placed at least on the same level as entomology, mycology, &c., and that those carrying it out are paid at the same handsome rates for studying the history of man as their fellow-scientists receive for studying trees, bugs and beetles."

an act of presumption from which the general run ot mankind does not shrink but which is, nevertheless, fraught with peril. . . . Every man has in front of his judgment something which is like a bit of coloured glass, and which represents an aggregate of inherited or acquired ideas, prejudices, interests, desires and sensations that are derived from tradition, physiological or pathological peculiarities and surrounding influences." Thus it is that when the untrained white man tries to understand and fix the ideas of the black on his own mind that he fails, because, as with a kaleidoscope, every time he looks into it, the ideas take on new shapes and colours even as one watches them, and he is unprepared for the unexpected which often happens.[1]

Meanwhile the primitive races are being exterminated and so one wonders how it will all end, and when that end will come. Are the Tropics to go back and back to the prehistoric days, that is, to such a pitch that the jungle and the swamp, the beasts of prey and the snakes, the heat and miasma, the mosquito and tsetse-fly, make it untenable for the white man, since there will then be only a Noah's Ark proportion of the primitive people left, not enough to keep Nature at bay even under the guidance and direction of the white superman.

Peoples and races, we are told, rise and fall; the Inca and Maya kingdoms, Egypt, Persia, Greece, Rome, and so on, and their cycles last about a thousand to twelve hundred years. Has it been that, thanks to the discovery of the New World, the white race has enjoyed a double. spell, first in Europe and then abroad. Look back 1,500 years and then think of five hundred or seven hundred years ahead, and ask yourself if, as we are fast allowing matters to tend in the Tropics, whether it is beyond the range of possibility for Nature, pure and primitive, to come into her own again, owing to the white man being physically incapable, under the heat of the tropical sun, of driving her back, and to there being only a handful of natives left, a number altogether insufficient to help him do so. We would not only maintain that such a thing is fully possible, but that it is certain to happen unless[2] we can devise a

---

[1] All of which is as a closed book to all but the well-trained anthropologist.—ED., *T.L.*

[2] "There is a tide in the affairs of Man,
　　Which, taken at the flood, leads on to fortune.
　　Omitted, &c., &c."

means to save what of the primitive races is left, and tending these, gradually improve, house, look, after and inter-breed them, one kind with another, until we have learnt how to increase their numbers and improve the breed, as has been done in Europe by raising the level of comfort and through that the standard of intellect in the lowest classes. We must mate a primitive with one a shade better (but only a shade, for big jumps up are a mistake) in the social scale, and so, like that wizard, Luther Burbank, has done with plants, gradually raise up a new and improved type of a still purely tropical race, indigenous to the soil, just as we have done and are doing by very slow stages with birds, beasts and plants.

We apologize to our readers for having devoted so much space to this question of the preservation and improvement of the primitive races, but do so because we feel that, handsome and imposing as may be the agricultural and commercial palace that the super-scientist and the super-financier shows us on paper, it can still only be a " Castle in Spain." We say this because, when the building is completed, it will never stand, but always remain rotten and sinking in its foundations if the native labour on which it can alone be erected is not equal to and in everywise worthy of the building itself.

CHAPTER XIV.

Lord Leverhulme on the Natives in Africa.

Tropical Life, April, 1917.

SPEAKING at a meeting of the Colonial Section of the Royal Society of Arts, after a most interesting paper on the economic development of the Belgian Congo, by Monsieur Horn, LL.D. (Brussels), with Sir Arthur Steel-Maitland, M.P., Under Secretary of State for the Colonies, in the chair, Lord Leverhulme (then Sir W. H. Lever) said that, as one who had travelled with M. Horn through the Belgian Congo, he was of opinion that the author had not overstated the prospects of the country or the great work that the Belgian Government carried on there; in fact, he had understated and underestimated whenever he had ventured either to make a statement or a prophecy. Personally, he wished the author had drawn the picture a little nearer those sanguine lines which he was sure in his heart of hearts he thought was correct. The Congo was offered by Stanley in succession to the United States, England, France, and Germany—but they all refused it. Belgium possessed a far-seeing king, who saw the immense possibilities of the country ; he took an early train to Marseilles, met Stanley on his arrival there, and secured for his country what had been refused by the great nations of the world. It was right, therefore, that Belgium should enjoy the benefit of the foresight of its king. With regard to the attitude taken by this country to native races, whenever he went into English colonies he always found an outcry against what was called " Exeter Hall." It was a curious fact that in the House of Commons the same people stamped, and stormed, and raved about the iniquity of dukes, who held their land for their own comfort and kudos and not for the service of their fellow-men, and it was considered wise that statutes should be enacted to compel dukes to use their broad acres for the general benefit of the public. But the same men said in regard to a black man, who might or might not be a prince, that this country had no right to interfere with his land, and that he must use it or not use it as he liked ; that there might be countless millions in Europe starving for oils and fats and for all the produce that generous Nature could pour forth under tropical suns and tropical showers, but the black man must not be interfered with. He did not consider that that was good government. There were good black men and bad black men, and good white men and bad white men ; but he did not see why we should have a sentiment for a man because of his colour. Nevertheless, that was the case in British colonies all over the world. In his opinion the world was meant for the use of the people who were at present living in it, and the man who could make use of the tools, whether the hammer, the chisel, or the broad acres, for the benefit of the general public had a right to them. The only title of every white man or black man was to make the best use of them for the public. He believed the black man could be spoiled as much by sentiment as by brutality, and he understood the latter better than the former. But neither of them need enter into the question of the government of the black man. The main thing was the education of the native, and the Belgian Government were showing the English the way in that respect. If the black boy was educated from an early age, great use could be made of him. It was absolutely necessary to remember that the country would never be developed unless the black men who lived in it were educated. White men were nòt necessary there. The black man could get on without the white man, as he always had done, but the black man was necessary to the white man. It was impossible for progress to be made in the Tropics without the aid of the black man. If the black man disappeared, as he had in some parts, the whole place would become a desert. Having educated him, the next subject that must be dealt with was transportation, and that was being dealt with by the Belgian Government through the building of railways and the making of rivers navigable. Boats must be put on the rivers, and produce carried for the smallest traders at equal rates obtained by the largest, so that all were placed on one level of equality in competition. That policy, in his opinion, would do more for the black man than sentiment. He must be educated, trained, and disciplined; but, above all, it was necessary to be firm with him and let him understand that the land that he might call his own or not had to be developed and exploited and made to produce the fruits of the soil. On those lines, which the Belgian Government were following with great ability, the Tropics would yield their full and abundant harvest for the benefit of the white man in the temperate countries.

SECTION V.

EDUCATION.

CHAPTER XV.

The Demand for British Agricultural Colleges in the Tropics if our Resources are to be developed.

Tropical Life, July, 1916.

THE publication last year of the discussions that followed the various papers read at the Third International Congress of Tropical Agriculture, which, it will be remembered, took place in London at the Imperial Institute, just before war broke out,[1] goes to prove more convincingly than ever how great is the need in the Tropics for at least one agricultural college to be established in their midst, and how unanimously and eloquently the leading authorities on tropical agriculture throughout the world have pleaded for such an institution at an early date. We say this without taking into account the part taken in the agitation by Professor Wyndham Dunstan, President of the Congress, and father of the idea, and the Editor of *Tropical Life*, who have pleaded for the colleges for many years past.

Going elsewhere, however, the book of the Congress, in reporting discussions on the papers read, tells us that

---

[1] See also *Transactions of the Third International Congress on Tropical Agriculture*, for a full report of the papers themselves (Vol. i, pp. 1-56) as compared with the reports of the discussions that followed as given on pp. 62-80 in the *Proceedings of the Congress*, which appeared first. There are now three volumes of these reports, viz. : (a) The *Proceedings*, with abstracts of Papers, and the Discussions in full. 407 pages. Weight 24 oz. 10s. net. (b) The *Transactions*, without discussions, Vol. i, dealing with Technical education (in the Tropics), Cotton, Fibres and Rubber. Pp. 728. 10s. net. Weight 40 oz. (c) *Transactions*, Vol. ii, dealing with Cereals, Sugar, Cacao, Tobacco, Vegetable Oils, Soil Fertility and "Miscellaneous." Pp. 710. 10s. net. Weight 40 oz. Published by John Bale, Sons and Danielsson, Ltd., London.

Mr. Gerald Dudgeon, F.E.S., Consulting Agriculturist
to the Ministry of Agriculture, Egypt, and a Vice-President
of the Congress, explained to those present how the rapid
growth of plantation work in the Tropics demanded the
services of qualified technical men in order to obtain the
best results whilst the supply of such men available is
limited. This was entirely true when Dr. Gough read
the paper in Mr. Dudgeon's absence through illness, but
it is trebly true to-day, when the supply of men suitable·
for tropical work has been further curtailed, whilst the
need of obtaining the best results from the estates has
been greatly increased already, and will be still more so
for several years after the War is over. Dr. Gioli,
Director and Founder of the Colonial Agricultural Institute
at Florence, described in his paper how the people in his
country had been devoting themselves to the scientific
study of the production and marketing of crops from
their colonies. What our Editor had to say on the
subject is already known, but following him comes the
paper contributed by Dr. Francis Watts, Imperial Commissioner of Agriculture for the West Indies, who
vigorously urged the establishment of the colleges, and
indicated the lines along which they should be conducted,
claiming, as do all the supporters of the movement,
that an institute for agricultural research should be
associated with the college, and could well be regarded as
the main affair to be aimed at. The endowment of an
institution to carry on tropical agricultural research and
education, concluded this authority, would, there is reason
to believe, yield a rich harvest to the country providing for
such a need. We now come to the discussion, which was
preceded by the President's (Professor Dunstan) summary
of the papers, in which he described our Editor's paper as
being an "exceedingly interesting and, I think, weighty
plea for the establishment of an agricultural college in
the Western Hemisphere, for which he adduces evidence
not merely based upon the importance of such a college
to the West Indian Islands, but goes further and points
to the importance of establishing it as a means of training
the numerous young men who go out to Latin America to
engage in agricultural pursuits."

"What is mostly occupying our minds to-day," pointed
out Mr. Lyne, Director of Agriculture for Ceylon, who
opened the discussion, "is a plan for higher training in
connection with tropical agriculture. . . . A student
in England can become a fully equipped farmer, but there

is no man living who can say that he is a fully equipped tropical agriculturist because, to be so, he must be a specialist. . . . Not only do we require specialists for the various crops, but in the case of certain ones like sugar (and we are coming to the same thing in regard to rubber) we require specialists for the field and specialists for the factory." Mr. Lyne could well have added : can such specialists in sugar, rubber, tea, cacao, cinchona, &c., be trained in England ? An answer to such a question is ' superfluous. In these days of war economies it would be waste of printer's ink to include it.

"It seems to me," said Professor Ainsworth-Davis, Principal of the Royal Agricultural College, Cirencester, where Mr. Kelway Bamber, Mr. James Mollison, Sir J. Muir Mackenzie, and others were students, "that instead of debating whether it is better to go to the East or to the West, we should have as many colleges as we want—as many as are indicated as necessary."

" I will begin at once," were the words with which Professor Carmody, Director of Agriculture at Trinidad, B.W.I., started his remarks, " by allowing that the East may have a college, and I will mention a few reasons why I think we should have a second college in the West Indies. . . . Having certain advantages (named), the estimate of cost which Mr. Hamel Smith has quoted will be very much less in our case." Meanwhile, all interested in tropical agriculture will be glad to learn from Professor Carmody that " the improvement in cacao cultivation and estate sanitation since the introduction of the prize system introduced in Trinidad, has been very marked and most gratifying to the Board of Agriculture providing the prizes."

Then came M. Edmond Leplae, Director-General of Agriculture in Belgium, who said that he and his Department had read with great interest all that had been said by the President, and all that had been written in *Tropical Life* on the necessity of establishing agricultural colleges in the Tropics. " A school of agriculture," he went on to say, "established in the Tropics, and in touch with up-to-date tropical plantations, would offer such advantages from a practical point of view, that the high expense should be considered only with the purpose of finding a way to reduce it as much as possible. . . . I venture to express my opinion that two schools, one in the East and one in the West, would meet the requirements better than a single school, the natural conditions being quite

different. I should add that if a school is established,
either in the East or in the West, the Belgian Congo will
certainly wish to send some students to learn from the
experience of the older countries."

"Wherever the tropical agricultural college may be
located," said Dr. Tempany, at that time attached to
the Agricultural Department, Leeward Islands, but now
Director of Agriculture at Mauritius, "we can never hope
to realize within any one locality the broad range of conditions which prevail throughout the Tropics, but the men
who attend the colleges will realize what after all is the
main thing, the atmosphere permeating the whole of the
Tropics, and the college will provide a focus and a centre
for those tropical countries where research work is being
done, and will serve as a stimulus and a guide to many
of us who are attempting to do, in the intervals of our
other occupations, a certain amount of purely scientific
work under our isolated conditions."

Truly had the father of the idea reason to be pleased
with the results of the discussion, to which he had also
contributed in the morning by incorporating in the important presidential address that he delivered at the opening of
the Congress, a splendid appeal for providing the necessary
technical and scientific education needed by those who
desire to make tropical agriculture the work of their lives.
To-day this is a subject which is claiming the consideration of all nations interested in the Tropics, it being too
well known that the training of those men who are destined
to fill important berths in the various Departments of
Agriculture in the Tropics is not, at present, definitely
provided for, but is left to chance.

"The subject is bound to come up at other meetings,"
said Professor Dunstan, when closing the discussion with
palpable regret, "but since the opening of the Congress
the question of an Imperial Agricultural College in the
Tropics has assumed an international character," and the
President was right. Much has happened since then, and
more is bound to happen still before the question of
establishing British agricultural colleges in the Tropics
can once more occupy the important position in practical
politics that it occupied in 1914, but it is time, however,
that we started to gather together the lost threads again—
some of them, we fear, broken beyond repair, but these
can be replaced by others—and we must see to it that,
as soon as the time is ripe, no further delay occurs in
establishing these much-needed colleges, and let us make

up our minds to have two at least, one in Ceylon and one in Trinidad or elsewhere in the West Indies.

"If this Government," our Editor pointed out in the paper that he read at the International Congress just referred to, and therefore before the war when the present demand for organizing and making use of the nation's man-power has rendered a conscription of the Empire's man-power and wealth possible along lines that would have been incredulous in 1913, "or, shall I say, any Government that rules this country and its dependencies, were as keen on wringing out the labour and Empire-building capacity that is latent within us all (although some are very loth to make use of it), as they are of squeezing out our money for taxes, I reckon that the development of the resources of the Tropics and Sub-Tropics would go ahead at a much more rapid rate than it is doing at present. Why not adopt the idea of con-scription to compel everyone to do his (or her) share of the work of the country, so as to develop the resources of the Empire by the united effort of all as well as for the benefit of all, either driving away the slackers or reforming their ways on a tramp farm or labour-colony?

"I say this because I think the bulk of those who at present work at half or quarter pressure only would be much more healthy, as they would be more useful, if they worked at full pressure, and their help is certainly needed. Standing next to me at a meeting held at the Mansion House in support of the British Dominions Exhibition which was to have been held in 1917, was Mr. Will Crooks, the well-known Labour M.P., who, in the course of his speech, claimed, and rightly claimed, that the lower classes, because they are used to roughing it, were often the very ones who got on best when they went forth into the world to make their way. This being so, surely it must follow that, once educated men with capital who have had the advantage of being trained at an agricul-tural college in the Tropics are induced through this training to go thence to increase our supplies of food-stuffs and raw materials, these others will follow, especially if slackers are discouraged, if not coerced, at home, and every workman compelled to do at least an equal mini-mum share of his country's work in the same way as these same men are so very keen just now to compel their employers to pay them all—good, bad, or indifferent —an equal minimum wage. One day, perhaps, our Government will find that it is their duty to round us all up once a year, as the ranchers do their cattle, take stock of all, asking each what he is doing, ascertain what he can do, and then see that it is done. This may sound autocratic, but it will be at least fair—far fairer than the world is to-day, when a minority of us work, and work hard, to pay the major portion of the taxes and help slackers to have an easy time.

" Since the Government of to-day has found the money necessary to ensure the health of the workers in this country, and to keep the aged from having to depend on charity, so also is it their duty—that is to say, the duty of ourselves—to spend an amount that is far less than 1 per cent. of the total of this year's Budget to ensure this country receiving those regular and increasing supplies of food-stuffs and raw materials without which we cannot continue to be one of the leading—if not the leading— countries of the world. If on a Budget of £200,000,000 we cannot squeeze out a one-thousandth part to secure our enjoying the lead in the world's commerce, then I would maintain that we should be signally failing in our duty, both to the present generation and those who are to come hereafter."

CHAPTER XVI.

British Agricultural Colleges in the Tropics. The Question of their Establishment as discussed in 1914:

Tropical Life, July, 1914.

THOSE who, like ourselves, have been strenuously endeavouring to induce the Government to establish at least two Agricultural Colleges in the tropical zone, say in Ceylon and Trinidad, will do well to study the published account of the important Tropical Congress that took place at the Imperial Institute under the presidency of Professor Wyndham Dunstan, C.M.G., M.A., LL.D., F.R.S., Director of the Institute, during the last seven days of June. We say this as we believe, thanks to the speeches made by and to the leading men who took a personal interest in the proceedings, that if we still have plenty of work in front of us before we can hope to see the colleges established, that (to some folks) hopeless uphill pull we have hitherto had "all on our own" is now being shared with others. With such help if the goal is not yet in sight, it will henceforth be more a matter of diplomacy than hard fighting, and of pulling together, East and West in friendly unison, along a fairly level road, taking care only to avoid any pitfalls. This will, however, be easier than the uphill work we have had during the past four or five years. This opinion was considerably strengthened when we were told that the King, who is patron both of the International Congress of Tropical Agriculture as well as of the Rubber Exhibition and Congress, sent the following message of welcome to the delegates gathered together at the Imperial Institute:—

"It is with much pleasure that I welcome to London the delegates of the International Congress of Tropical Agriculture. The importance of their deliberations and the number and variety of subjects to be discussed are of especial interest to me. I trust that their discussions will contribute to the advancement of agriculture in the Tropics.—GEORGE, R.I."

Taking the President's speech first, Professor Dunstan in his address of welcome [1] to the delegates taking part in the Congress very truly said that there was no subject at the present time in the whole field of human activity which demanded greater attention than the organization of those agencies which made for the agricultural productivity of the tropical regions of the world. The subject was of importance to the native races of the Tropics, who were coming more and more under European control and influence, and who looked to the example of European knowledge and experience for guidance in increasing the productivity of the soil. It was of no less importance to

---

[1] Delivered, be it remembered, before such men as Lord Emmott when Under Secretary for the Colonies, Lord Sudeley, Sir George Reid, who was at that time High Commissioner for Australia, Sir Sydney Olivier (ex-Governor of Jamaica and later on Permanent Secretary to our Board of Agriculture), Sir Horace Plunkett, Sir Hugh Clifford (Governor of the Gold Coast), Sir H. Hesketh Bell (Governor of the Leeward Islands), Sir Henry Blake, Sir George Denton, Sir Frank Swettenham, Sir Frederic M. Hodgson, Sir James Wilson, Sir William Schlich, the Hon. Gideon Murray (Administrator of St. Vincent), Sir E. Rosling, Mr. Arno Schmidt (International Federation of Cotton Spinners), Mr. J. Arthur Hutton (Chairman of the British Cotton Growing Association), Mr. Wilson Fox (British South Africa Company), and others.

all governments of tropical countries. Moreover, the temperate world has to depend on the Tropics for the supply of numerous materials which have become necessaries of life and the basis of some of the most important manufacturing industries of modern times. With these remarks we cordially agree, because we believe that the best, and, in fact, the only way to help the natives to help themselves is to train up white planters, managers and Government experts to go out and plant and make their estates pay well, for once the native, be he in the East or West, sees that the new-fangled ideas have wisdom in them, *i.e.*, that they give bigger profits, he will then follow the example set and proved by practical results, whilst he will not budge an inch when the teaching is only by theory. "With this material progress made of late years," Professor Dunstan went on to say, "had come, somewhat slowly, the recognition of the fact that tropical agriculture was an applied science, and the reflection that progress would have been more rapid and less costly had it been effected more generally under that enlightened direction which depends on the considered application of scientific principles. No one who had studied this question in its many aspects could doubt that a great need existed for the establishment within the British tropics of at least one agricultural college, properly equipped with all the facilities for instruction and research in the several branches of tropical agriculture. The college should be Imperial in its educational character and open to properly qualified candidates from all parts of the Empire without distinction of race, and whilst having close relations with Government Departments of Agriculture in the country in which it is established, should, as an educational institution, be separately organized under the management of a board on which all·agricultural interests were represented."

A remark of Professor Dunstan that it "cannot be doubted that well-trained men with the diploma of a (tropical agricultural) college will readily find remunerative employment," still points to the idea that the bulk of the students would train to work under others. Besides the above the class of men we also want to see come as students, and who we believe will frequent the colleges, East and West, when established, are those who mean to plant for themselves either alone or in pairs. These are the men we want to see spread over the Tropics, and they are just the class of men that are *not* going at present in such numbers as the requirements of this country call for.

The reason for their not doing so is, we believe, due to this being an age of cold reasoning, and lack of initiative compared to what prevailed fifty, a hundred, or a hundred and fifty years ago, when men did not look before they leapt; and though their temerity cost some of them their lives, in the aggregate the results exceeded all expectations, and it is to these bold spirits we owe our present-day prosperity and supplies of food and raw materials. To-day those who might go out to plant, not only look where they are going but take a telescope and microscope to examine the soil, and would like to ask the Government or some one to indemnify them against loss if they come to grief. Since it is no use kicking against the pricks, and since people will be cautious and are no longer willing to risk their money, health or lives, we must let them see ahead where their way tends, and how best to get to their destination with the least risk—in fact with none at all. The father wants to know that the son will not "go slack" whilst learning his profession; and the son, if about to invest his own patrimony, wants to make sure that he is going the right way to work. Both, therefore, we take it, need agricultural colleges to help them, and until we get the colleges such men will not send their sons, nor go out themselves to plant. Those who wish to train to work under others will form class two, then there will be Government officials and consulting experts, whilst America, France, Belgium, and other countries all promise us students, whose presence we should welcome, for the same as we like to see young Englishmen go to foreign colleges, in the same way we must welcome their sons to ours. Once established, therefore, no doubt need exist that the colleges, the *two* or more colleges, will be well patronized, and that the benefits they will confer on the Empire will be immense.

Those taking part in the discussion included the then Director of Agriculture in Ceylon, who told us what they were doing in that island as regards plans, a site, &c., and then Professor Carmody, at that time Director in Trinidad, who went one better, saying that not only had they plans, site, &c., but had the building ready and waiting for the staff to instruct the students as soon as the money is forthcoming to pay the professors, &c. Referring to the abstract of the paper prepared by our Editor, we are glad to say that the £500,000 spoken of as being necessary to establish a college in Ceylon is now said to be a mistake, it should have been only one-tenth that amount, viz., £50,000. On hearing this we rewrote our paper and went back to our own figures. "As I wrote to the *Times*, on April 14 of last year," urged our Editor, " 10 per cent. of the cost of a Dreadnought, which would, from all accounts, amount to £2,250,000, would supply ample funds for two fully equipped colleges at £100,000 each, three at £75,000 each, or four at £55,000."

In order to dispel any idea that the West may be antagonistic to the East having the first college, instead of being, on the contrary, willing to assist the East to get hers first, we call attention to the following portion of our Editor's paper. This paragraph came immediately after the opening one explaining why he had chosen the question of agricultural colleges in the Tropics as the subject of his debate, and in it he told the Congress :—

" Before I go on to say one word in support, not so much of the claims of the West Indies for an agricultural college, as to show the absolute necessity of this country, if it means to enjoy that share to which it is entitled of the ever-increasing commerce of Latin America, to establish such a college in the Western Hemisphere, I want it to be clearly understood that I am not urging the claim of the West Indies in competition with Ceylon, for such is in no wise my desire. On the contrary, if, *pro tem.*, there is to be only one college, then I agree that Ceylon should have it."

We were glad to see that the Congress generally and our paper in particular received prominent notice in the Press, and it is this which leads us to hope that we have reached the brow of the hill leading to success, and so can look forward to an easier time before us. The *Financier* discussed Professor Dunstan's address very fully, and gave striking headlines to the " Proposed Establishment of Colleges." The *Financial Times* gave our paper two half columns next to the big head-lines reporting the opening of the Rubber Exhibition. " Mr. Hamel Smith dwelt strongly on the necessity of establishing a British Agricultural College in the Western Hemisphere," was the comment of the *Daily Telegraph*, whilst the *Morning Post*, the *Financial News* and other leading newspapers all gave prominence to the plea for agricultural colleges in the Tropics, and seemed pleased that the matter was being so influentially supported.

CHAPTER XVII.

British Agricultural Colleges in the Tropics. Their Establishment discussed in the House of Commons and in India.

Tropical Life, September, 1917.

THOSE who read the leaders in our May and June issues, when we discussed two of the several plans now before the public to increase the resources of the Empire, will agree, we feel sure, that we, as an Empire, cannot · be too deeply and genuinely interested in the matter, and since this is so, we trust sincerely that the man or men with the best plan, i.e., the plan that will be to the greatest ultimate and lasting benefit to the Empire and its people, will come up top and be allowed full scope to put that plan into practice to serve as a basis on which to mould similar schemes, but with variations to suit each and all centres.

Favoured with a seat under the gallery of the House of Commons, so that he was on a level with the floor of the House, and thus able to follow the debate closely whilst the Colonial Office vote was being discussed, our Editor heard as clearly as any Member of the House itself what was said, and we, therefore, have much pleasure in reproducing a portion of the speeches, together with our own comments on same.

First of all the Secretary of State for the Colonies (Mr. Walter Long) practically devoted the whole of his remarks to informing the House how magnificently the Overseas Dominions, from the Australian Continent and the Dominion of Canada down to invisible islets in the Southern Seas, as Marakeis in the Gilbert Islands, or on the Mainland, the Liwali or Chief of Vanga in British East Africa, were · continuing to support the War, each in their own way, but all to a degree and in a manner that was equally valuable and praiseworthy, and thus entitled them to the eloquent earnest tribute paid them in the House.

Having spoken of these Dominions and Colonies, Mr. Long was equally emphatic in his tribute to those officials, in the various departments that governed Greater Britain, for the way they had remained at their posts (not without vigorous protests, and often, as he explained, vigorous personal attempts, either directly or through friend sat home to be allowed to enlist), " eating their hearts out in their desire to come away and serve in France," instead of "remaining at their posts under the orders of the Colonial Office in all parts of our Crown Colonies and Protectorates, doing dull and dreary work, very often wholly unknown even to their immediate chiefs, never talked of in this House or in the newspapers ; doing work that is essential if the British Empire and our Government is to be maintained." We were very pleased to hear the Secretary of State for the Colonies speak in this way. He did not exaggerate the case and the great importance of the work being done, for the simple reason that it is impossible to do so, but we can and do say that he spoke as forcibly as he could on the matter, and spoke with knowledge and conviction that what he said was the truth, so that the statements made carried far more conviction, we feel sure, to those who heard the speech than any printed report could do. Finally, Mr. Long discussed the magnificent resources of the Empire and how they could be developed to the full. It only remains for us to see that these resources are developed by those who own them, and not, as has too often been the case, by those who are now the enemies of the entire world, civilized and uncivilized, alike.

Following the Colonial Secretary came Lord Henry Bentinck, who confirmed all Mr. Long had urged as to the need of developing the resources of the Empire, and then proceeded to point out the only real way to do so, viz., by educating the natives and, indeed, all races of planters to adopt scientific methods, together with time and labour-saving appliances, and to follow the example of those who bring science and knowledge to bear on their work in order to increase the output. These two important speeches, and also those of Mr. Molteno and Mr. Wilson-Fox, should be studied by every well-wisher of the Tropics, and by all who realize what the Tropics and sub-Tropics can do for the Empire if properly developed. On this one point, i.e., what they can do, we are all agreed, the point of difference comes in when we discuss the words, " properly developed." How are the Tropics and sub-Tropics to be properly developed, and who is to undertake the work ?

Lord Henry Bentinck, after carefully explaining to the House in detail the splendid work that has been done, and the excellent results achieved on the West Coast of Africa, then went on to say (after suggesting the appointment of a Commission to inquire into the resources of the Crown

Colonies and our Protectorates and Dependencies with a view to increasing their output of raw materials and food-stuffs), " I would put to my Right Honourable friend (the Colonial Secretary) the necessity of this Royal Commission inquiry into whether the capacity of our Dependencies to produce could not be enormously increased by further provision for research. I do not for a moment deny that very good work is being done both in East Africa and West Africa, and also in the West Indies by their Agricultural Departments, but it would be of enormous benefit to our Colonial Empire if we were to spend more money on research. *We want two agricultural colleges—one in the West and one in the East*[1]—first of all for the stimulation of research ; secondly, to train young Englishmen to go out to our Crown Colonies and to settle down as producers themselves ; and thirdly, to train a large staff of young Englishmen who could go out and act as agricultural instructors, and who could in turn educate the natives. I do most strongly urge that research is the basis of all progress in agriculture, whether it is at home or in Africa or India. The House will be interested to hear of the enormous progress that has been made, for instance, in India in this respect. In 1901 Lord Curzon established a college of research, and it is interesting to note that he was enabled to do so by the aid of Mr. Phipps, a citizen of Chicago, who gave £30,000 towards it. Already the official report says that the value of the agricultural products of India has been thereby increased by over £3,000,000. A great scientist, Mr. Howard, and his wife discovered a new wheat which was rust-proof and strong in its strain, with the consequence that the production per acre has increased by Rs. 16, and it is estimated that the agricultural wealth of India will be increased through this by £5,000,000 a year.[2] It is the same with regard to cotton. Wonderful work has been done in fixing seeds of native kinds and producing cotton for the use of the Lancashire market. If we are going to develop our resources properly, the first thing we should do is to spend money upon research. I have given proof of the wonderful increase of production

---

[1] The italics are ours. This is, we believe, the first time that a request for these two colleges has been made in the House of Commons—at any rate, that their foundation has been asked for so plainly and emphatically.

[2] And yet we wonder how many people in the United Kingdom have even heard of Albert and Gabrielle Howard, and know that Pusa, when we speak of it, is in India.

that has been brought about in India, and I suggest that a similar increase could be brought about in Africa and the West Indies by the same means."

It is interesting to remember that whilst Lord Henry Bentinck, half-brother of the Duke of Portland, was so earnestly pleading for these colleges and all that they stand for in the way of scientific agriculture and research, the Indian mail arrived in London bringing reports of the Budget speech made by Sir Claude Archer Hill, K.C.S.I., &c., the member in charge of the Department of Revenue and Agriculture of India, at the meeting of the Imperial Legislative Council on March 10 last, when that gentleman also mentioned Pusa, and Mr. and Mrs. Howard's work especially in connection with the No. 12 Wheat. During the course of his remarks Sir Claude said (quoting the Supplement of the *Agricultural Journal of India* for July, which published it in full) : " Turning now to agriculture, the first subject to which I propose to refer is agricultural education . . . . and I propose to convene a conference on agricultural education to assemble in Simla some time during the ensuing summer, to be composed of expert agriculturists and educationists together with, I hope, additional members interested in the subject."

This important conference duly took place at Simla on June 18, at the Committee Room, Orton Castle, and a very full report of the proceedings has been published in the *Madras Weekly Mail* on June 22, pp. 383-384, and from this report we are able to give quotations from Sir Claude Hill's speech, but those interested in the matter, and we trust everyone is so, should turn to the full account of the proceedings. Speaking of agricultural colleges in general, but especially of one for Upper India, Sir Claude said that it should be possible to arrange that students taking the degree course should be able to qualify by an intermediate examination for employment in the lower ranks of the department. Continuing, he said : " I would first of all reiterate the remark I made at the outset of our deliberations at Pusa (February, 1916), viz., that our needs are first and for all time to improve the agricultural methods of India, and to secure this end we must have : (1) scientific investigation, (2) courses of instruction to ·fit Indians to help in these investigations, (3) practical instruction on· agriculture, (4) courses of practical and theoretical instruction to fit men to give instruction in practical agriculture as well as to qualify for service in the Department of Agriculture, and (5) instruction for agriculturists . . .

I am going to venture to propose that . . . we should commence this work at the foundation [that is, among the lower classes of agriculturists—Ed. *Tropical Life*] . . . . because we have felt that unless we can see our way to create widespread developments of interest in better tillage on the part of the mass of the people who do not, as a rule, proceed to the higher branches of education, we.must inevitably fail to achieve the great result I have ventured to lay before you, viz., the improvement of the agricultural · methods of the country at large."

This, of course, refers to India with its millions of *ryots*, and an overcrowded population. Elsewhere in the Empire it will be best to begin at the top, and train the future planters, scientists and plant-doctors at the agricultural colleges so generally asked for—" one in the West, say Trinidad, and one in the East, say Ceylon," and through their successful example induce the small proprietors to adopt up-to-date methods, by being able to show them how it pays to do so. Even with India Sir Claude Hill emphasized the great and pressing need for properly trained teachers, and these can never be forthcoming without agricultural colleges in the Tropics as we have in India. " We shall," Sir Claude urged, " have to consider whether we cannot, in conjunction with the agricultural educational institutions, organize arrangements analogous to the normal schools of educational departments for the training of teachers to take charge of agricultural schools. . . . The ultimate goal I put before myself is one agricultural high school," &c., &c. . . . and so the tale goes on, but we must stop. At the same time our readers will note that the whole of this programme hangs on the existence of a more advanced system of scientific education and of its being carried out " in conjunction with the agricultural educational institutions," i.e., agricultural colleges.

One word in conclusion about the agricultural colleges, and it is this : Cinderella went to the ball three times, and on each occasion, we are told, in a more attractive dress than before, and in the end, &c., she married the Prince and lived happily ever after. We trust that it will be the same with the agricultural colleges in Ceylon and Trinidad. Three times now has the matter been given prominence. Firstly, by the suggestion of Professor Wyndham Dunstan at the late Mr. John Ferguson's lecture in December, 1910, before the Royal Colonial Institute, followed by our article on the subject ; secondly, by a petition sent home

THE NEED OF BRITISH AGRICULTURAL COLLEGES IN THE TROPICS.

to the Colonial Office from the West Indies, following our plea for the college or colleges as a memorial worthy of King Edward, and followed in its turn by the meeting at Sir Robert Perks's, when speakers both for Ceylon and the West Indies addressed leaders of thought in London ; and now, thirdly and lastly, Cinderella, i.e., the question of the establishment of these colleges and institutes of research, has turned up again in a still more attractive and prominent garb, and been introduced within the walls of· St. Stephen's itself by Lord Henry Bentinck. Surely after this the Prince, i.e., Ceylon, and Cinderella, i.e., Trinidad, should· be married and left to guide the destinies of our tropical dependencies, as they are well capable of doing, by training men willing and able to take charge of the other colleges that will be established in the F.M.S., Australia, and elsewhere. As Professor Ainsworth-Davis (Principal, Royal Agricultural College, Cirencester) told the delegates at the meeting of the Third International Congress of Tropical Agriculture, held, it will be remembered, in 1914, just before the War started, it is not a question of " whether it is better to go to the East or to go to the West, we should have as many colleges as we want—as many as are indicated as necessary. Furthermore, I do not know that all of them need be so extremely expensive," and the Professor was right. In comparison to the wealth that they will cause to be produced towards paying the expenses of this War, the cost of the first two agricultural colleges in the Tropics will not be noticeable, whilst the results, as proved by one item alone (that of wheat), out of many dozens obtained by one institution already established, viz., Pusa, shows that the cost will be only like an acorn, compared with the giant oak of wealth that is certain to spring from it if care is bestowed on the acorn.

This discussion in the House of Commons on the need of increasing the Empire's trade and productive resources calls to mind the fact that the *Daily Graphic* of August 13, 1917, published an excellent cartoon by Mr. Jack Walker, which, thanks to that paper, we have much pleasure in reproducing on the following page. It upholds our theory that we shall do far better in the near future, but especially later on, if we encourage individual producers, black, white, or tinted, to come forward and help feed the Empire and send our factories the raw materials they need. By such means we shall discover the easiest and most certain way to discourage any attempts to " hold up " areas and to

WITH A LITTLE PATIENCE
WE 'SHALL GET THERE
WITHOUT THE WHIP.
INCREASED
UTPUT OF
IMPERIAL
RESOURCES
State Exploitation
J. BULL
NATIVE
LABOUR

allow lands to lie idle. Meanwhile, it is to be hoped, we shall by then be doing all we can to educate every class and colour of man *both here and in the Tropics* to help increase the output of raw materials and food supplies for the Empire and its Allies, as without this no one will prosper as fully as they otherwise can do. Belgium knows only too well what the Congo means to her just now, and it is to be hoped that the natives of West and Central Africa will, on their own initiative, be as anxious and active to increase their crops as the Basutos and other tribes lower down south have shown themselves to be. Then, as the cartoon shows, the horse whose name is Native Labour will be far quicker and more ready to carry John Bull, urged only by the reins (of Agricultural Education), to the land of increased Imperial resources, without the need of the whip of State exploitation to drive him to work, as has been used on him far too often in the past.

Urging on the natives by the reins only, and establishing agricultural colleges in the Tropics for those who are to lead them by their example of how estates should be managed and pests, &c., kept at a distance is bound to be the best policy in the end. By such a course we shall turn out experts of all classes, but equally useful each in their own way, whether as planters, plant-doctors, or agricultural chemists, and the great strength of such a movement will be (as with men in an army at war) that the best men who come out top will be drawn from all ranks and conditions of men. This would give everyone an equal chance, as each (under the scheme we want to see established of granting agricultural scholarships from the lower schools to the secondary ones, and then up to the agricultural colleges at home or in the Tropics) will have an equal chance with his fellows, for the Empire needs such help, and must therefore see that all those under training live healthy lives whilst being taught. Steady work, strong limbs, sound health, tenacity of purpose, keenness to seize every opportunity to push yourself and your country ahead, these are the monopoly of no single class, or, if they are, such qualities are perhaps more frequently found in those who have never had all that money could buy, and have done their best to " make good " with whatever tools or chances comes their way. In our Imperial development scheme of the future, every man that means to get on shall get on, no matter what his colour is, for, like the warriors under Napoleon, each one must be allowed to start with his marshal's bâton in his knapsack. No more

8

romantic figures ever loomed across the horizon of a nation's advancement than did the forbears of the Dumas, *père et fils*. The father of Dumas *père* especially, mulatto as he is reported to have been, must have been a man in every sense of the word, and when one remembers that he is supposed to have been the original of the brawny Porthos in the "Three Musketeers," one feels that the brawn as well as the brain of such a man must have been a great asset to France in those days. We are pleased to think that such men are still with us, and are as ready and anxious to help in the economic aggrandizement of the British Empire as the original Porthos was to advance the political aggrandizement of Richelieu.

CHAPTER XVIII.

The Viceroy (Lord Chelmsford) discusses Agriculture and Agricultural Colleges in India and the Tropics.

Tropical Life, November, 1916.

IN the course of the carefully worded and very instructive address of welcome that H. E. The Viceroy delivered to those present in the Council Chamber of the Viceregal Lodge at Simla on September 5, on the occasion of the opening meeting of the Imperial Legislative Council, His Excellency (Lord Chelmsford), according to the *Madras Mail*, discussed agricultural education in India as follows:—

"The recommendations of the Conference on Agricultural Education, over which the Hon. Mr. Hill presided last February, have been considered by the Government, and have recently been referred for the opinions of the local Governments. The Conference dealt, among other matters, with the question of reforming the system of education in agricultural colleges. One of the chief needs of these colleges is to attract suitable students. The development of agricultural farms should tend to effect this object, but more farms can only be opened as men become available to manage them. Agricultural education and development are thus inter-dependent. I should like, from my personal experience in Australia, to lay stress on this. Agricultural Colleges and demonstration farms have played a great part in the development of the agricultural industry in that country, and though the farming community is notoriously conservative, it has, through these means, been awakened to the possibilities opened out by science. I should like to impress this further fact on Indian parents when they are planning the future of their sons. They might well pause to consider whether, instead of sending them to join the overstocked market of the legal and literary professions, it would not be better to turn their attention to the possibilities of employment in scientific agriculture. As the department expands it will afford greater opportunities of advancement, and the man who elects this service may work for himself and at the same time contribute to the prosperity of his country. The Indian cultivator has shown himself quite ready to adopt improved methods as soon as he is convinced of their utility, and I look forward to a time when demonstration farms will be spread all over the country bringing the practical results of scientific research within the reach of the agricultural masses. The improvement of agriculture, besides bringing prosperity and contentment to the majority of the population of India, will provide a worthy career for the young educated Indian who desires to serve his country, but does not always find the best way of doing it."

A great deal in Lord Chelmsford's remarks is equally applicable to the question of the *lack* of agricultural education in the Tropics outside India, as in plantation rubber centres, in the coconut belt, in the West Indies, &c.

We have long tried to impress on English (not Indian) parents, when they are planning the future of their sons, to consider whether, instead of training them to join the already overstocked market of commercial, banking, and insurance clerks over here (whose work is being ably carried on by their sisters so as to enable the boys to fight on the field of battle, as, we hope, later on they will remain fighting, but this time to protect our interests on British-owned estates and in banks and offices in the Tropics), it would not be better to turn their sons' attention, even when still at school, to the great future that lies before them, and with their help, before the country at large, in scientific agriculture—a profession still in its infancy. A profession, which, as it grows and develops, and as the educated community learns to know and to realize its value, will expand on all sides, and call into being immense riches which it can and will distribute lavishly among those who prove themselves worthy of such gifts. Agriculture does honestly add to the riches of the world, for it calls into being crops, and therefore national wealth, which did not exist before and will never exist without its help. With its assistance, however, especially as conducted on the modern scientific and labour-saving scale, half a dozen men and women can raise and gather in quite a large area of foodstuffs, and so, when you make the six into sixty thousand or six million willing workers, the output increases accordingly.

To-day we need this increase, next year we shall need it still more urgently than we do to-day, and this is why the scientific agriculturist must be placed second to no one but the Army man, for without the agriculturist no army, not even the British Army, could last a week.

This is why we have always pleaded so forcibly to have British Agricultural Colleges established in the East (Ceylon or Malaya) and in the West (Trinidad or elsewhere), as we realized that, sooner or later, we should need their help to " munition " the men on the field o battle, as we need explosives and steel, rubber and vegetable oils, &c., to munition the guns. Let us see to it, therefore, that we are as carefully organized to turn out the first to keep our men alive, as we have become with gun-food to kill those who are against us. Remember that agriculture is the mother of commerce as well as of all trades and professions, not their sister or dependent. She came first and from her sprang in the past, and from her are still springing all those many sources of wealth which have made nations so powerful and terrible to-day. Kill or even starve and neglect agriculture and what will become of us? Nourish and develop her, on the other hand, as she deserves to be nourished and developed, and she will repay those who do so a hundred and a thousand fold in the course of years. Let us, therefore, give her a more prominent position in the household of the Empire and not push her into the background as we are a little inclined to do.

CHAPTER XIX.

Agricultural Education in the Dutch and British Tropics compared.

Tropical Life, April, 1915.

THE late Dr. Melchior Treub, who, as everyone knows, was Director of the Government Botanic Gardens until 1905, and then occupied practically the same post under a different name as Director of Agriculture until 1909, always regarded it as part of his duty to stimulate general interest in the botanical problems of the Tropics. It was at his suggestion that the old question of agricultural education (dropped about 1884) was again taken up at the beginning of this century. The Agricultural School founded by Scheffer in 1876 (Dr. R. H. C. Scheffer, who was in Java from 1868 until he died in 1880 at the Sindanglaya Sanatorium, not far from the Mountain Garden at Tjibodas, regretting that his illness had hindered his work in connection with what he called "his children," viz., the Economic Garden and Agricultural School), having been allowed to fall into disuse, the Dutch Indies was without agricultural education for some fifteen years. Unlike this country, however, Holland evidently realized the mistake of· such a policy, for we understand that Dr. Trenb, deeply impressed with the need, even then, for education under tropical conditions, gave the authorities no peace until in 1903, just two years before the appearance of the first issue of *Tropical Life*, he eventually succeeded in achieving the establishment of this school, his idea being (and we believe that idea has been fulfilled) to have a school that would assist both the European estates and also (most wise of directors) native agriculture as well, since he reckoned that the young Europeans trained there as estate assistants could, in their turn, impart the knowledge that they have acquired, both theoretical and practical, to some of the future native chiefs, and by such means they would be able, later on, to effect improvements generally in the work of the native landowners and agriculturists.

His, moreover, was no narrow horizon, bounded by the limits of Holland's and her overseas possessions, but his views and wish to help included everyone, native as well as white, genuinely interested in tropical botany, economic or scientific, his great. idea being to induce botanists to come to Buitenzorg, as we described in our March issue, in order to investigate the problems connected with botany on the spot.   It was as a first step in this direction that he succeeded in persuading the Government to erect a special laboratory for the benefit of foreigners, until in 1885 the " Foreigners' Laboratory " was officially inaugurated.

The importance of this to the Laboratory was very marked ; importance that is both to Buitenzorg as the second Mecca of tropical botanists (Peradeniya, of course, being first, though probably our Dutch friends will not agree with this), and also to the scientific botanical world in general.   From 1885 until the present day, reported a recent publication emanating from the Java Department of Agriculture (No. viii, on " Scientific Information issued in connection with the San Francisco Committee "), no less than 150 foreigners have already made use of the laboratory, including many famous scientists, although we do not see the names of any Englishmen among them, an omission which we regret.

Meanwhile, however, Treub was not satisfied, as he quickly saw (after 1885) that the great majority of botanists could not afford the expense of the journey to Java, and even if they could manage that, the stay there was still too often an insurmountable obstacle to their devoting their energies, as he wished to see them doing, in the Foreigners' Laboratory that he had called into being.

Nothing daunted, this new difficulty was immediately tackled and overcome by the indomitable Dutchman, and as a result of his own personal.influence, a fund was established in Holland which, with the aid of the Government subsidy, enabled a botanist to proceed to Buitenzorg to study every two years.   Later on Treub also succeeded in inducing the establishment of similar funds in various other countries.

In addition to this, Treub also provided facilities for botanists to carry on work in the Mountain. Garden at Tjibodas by erecting a small building there as well.

Surely, therefore, what Treub and, through his persuasive powers, Holland have done for this country as a foreigner, our own Government will one day, " when the War is over " (equivalent to *mañana* in Spanish), wake up and do for us.   No one can deny that the institution, i.e., the Tropical Agricultural College and Institute of Research, was needed before the War, but when peace is declared and we all glide into smooth waters again, that want will have increased tenfold.

Who is going to do for England and the British Empire what Treub did for Holland and for us?

Will this country repeat, in connection with the scientific development of the economic potentialities of the Tropics, the same glaring mistake, now recognized by all, that was made when, by ignoring the crying need for first-class chemists in England, we allowed that most remunerative industry, the chemical one, including the manufacture of aniline dyes, to pass over to Germany? If steps are not taken soon to place tropical agriculture on the same deservedly lofty basis that Germany has all along placed the organic chemical industry, we run a very good chance of cutting as sorry a figure in connection with the production and preparation of tropical crops as we have cut ever since the War broke out in connection with drugs, dyes, and a host of prime necessities to the War Office and the nation generally because they were all " Made in Germany." We believe that all these could and would have been made here if those in whose hands the fate of our educational system laid in the past had not failed to recognize the importance of organic chemistry to such a degree that many of our universities, and particularly those of Oxford and Cambridge and in Scotland, contributed practically nothing to its advancement, whilst in Germany schools were specially devoted to the subject, where the leading experts taught and directed the efforts of willing and clever students.[1]   Having once failed to train our young scientists to best advantage in connection with chemistry, are we to sit up and see the same mull repeated in connection with tropical agriculture?   With the organic chemistry industry we can never recall the past ; the scientific basis of tropical agriculture is still within our grasp, so we trust that those who wish well for the Empire's progress in the future will see that, for the sake of £100,000, this country does not have another black mark put against it, as it has got, and always will have, in connection with the millions that our folly enabled Germany to pocket since 1870, and with which they are now financing the War that is costing us so dear.   Foolish enough to allow Germany to fleece

---

[1] See the Presidential Address delivered by Dr. W. H. Perkin (son of the late Sir William Perkin, F.R.S., the discoverer of aniline dyes) before the Chemical Society at the end of March, 1915.

us of our chemical industry, let us now wake up, whilst there is still time, and teach our young men scientific agricultural methods *in* the Tropics before the wily Teuton collars that industry also, to go with the manufacture of aniline dyes, of drugs, and of chemicals that he already possesses. If the Government has given £100,000 to those interested in organic chemistry, to make amends for a mull in the past, so can it vote a similar amount to avoid making an even worse mull in connection with the development of our tropical dependencies in the future.

SECTION VI.

DEVELOP INDIA.

CHAPTER XX.

India—a Neglected Heritage.

Tropical Life, June, 1916.

An important paper was read at the invitation of the Indian Section of the Royal Society of Arts on June 1, by Professor Wyndham Dunstan, C.M.G., on the work donè by the Imperial Institute in the interest of India during the last twenty years. Published in full in the pages of the *Journal of the Society of Arts*, it clearly proved by the lecturer's statements how very blind the people of this country have been to the value of their own possessions, although we have had such men as the Director of the Imperial Institute and a long line of equally scientific and practical workers standing with lighted torches in their hands, pointing the way to that Aladdin's cave of riches that has been ours for so long.

Instead of following the direction pointed out, however, this country has rather been contented to sit by the wayside, and beckon to strangers without our gates to come in, exploit, and carry off our treasures to manufacture or otherwise turn into articles of commerce, and then re-sell them to us at a huge profit—a profit which, in the aggregate, has gone a long way to help these enemies keep up the incessant rain of projectiles and bullets for nearly two years with which they have been assailing us as if it were a just reward for our stupidity and indolence. We say this, as there is no doubt that indolence is very largely at the bottom of our indifference and inability to utilize the raw materials with which the British Empire abound, as was shown in numberless cases by Professor Dunstan. It was these defects that have caused us to allow and almost to invite the Germans to develop our resources until we learnt, too late to a certain degree, how much we needed the manufactured products from our own raw materials, both on the field of battle, in the military hospitals, and at home.

Beside this, almost criminal indifference to and ignorance of the value of our own possessions, as proved by the low amounts of grants hitherto devoted to the scientific exploitation of them, as the Imperial Institute, Kew, and similar institutions know to their cost, this country has also suffered from a lack of organization in carrying out such investigations even when they have been set afoot. " It was suggested to the Government of India," Professor Dunstan told his audience, " that a special search should be made in India for thorium minerals, since the existence of these minerals in Ceylon rendered it probable that they would also be found in India. The reply of the Government of India was that no special search was necessary as the Geological Survey were already alive to the importance of the subject. There the matter rested until 1909, when a German prospector, Schomburg, discovered deposits of monazite sand on the coast of Travancore. Specimens examined at the Imperial Institute showed that the sand was rich in monazite, whilst the monazite contained nearly twice as much thoria as the monazite of Brazil. A company, the Travancore Minerals Company, was subsequently formed under German control, and Travancore monazite was worked in German interests. Since the War this company has been reconstructed, with Sir John Hewett as Chairman, and it may therefore be hoped that its valuable produce may be secured for the British gas-mantle industry. In addition to the area worked by this company, other areas of the Travancore sands are to be worked by other British companies, so that in future it is to be expected that the gas-mantle industry in this country will be able to pursue a course of untrammelled development." How very differently has Germany and the Germans behaved in such matters for many years past !

It is a true saying that what is everyone's business is no one's business, and we honestly believe one important reason, if not the main cause of this country's neglect of its overseas riches, has been due to its having hitherto been nobody's business to attend to it. Germany not only drained her own colonies, and the inhabitants thereof, of everything worth having, alive or dead, but overran the surface of the earth, including that covered by the British Empire, with the same tactics, and thereby obtained similar results to our loss. The Imperial Institute, as a centre of learning, has helped to counteract this evil to a considerable extent, and would have done so to a much larger degree had the funds placed at Professor Dunstan's disposal been on the scale that Germany would have given him to carry on the work in which he and his staff has been so strenuously engaged. Now that the Institute has passed under the control of the Colonial Office, it is to be hoped that money, both during and after the War, will flow more freely into its coffers to help on the good work. If this does not turn out to be the case, we shall suffer again in the future as we have done in the past, and the great lesson of the War will have been lost. It is not only that the Imperial Institute has done much work at home as well as having trained a goodly-sized army of enthusiastic men to carry it on throughout the Empire, but it is the example and atmosphere of sound, useful work that the Institute offers, and which has gone so far to encourage others to join in the movement. It is the same with an art school or hospital, the surroundings in which urge the students by the mere spirit of rivalry and by the interest generated by watching each other's work, not only to do likewise, but to go one and even two or three times better; and, when this occurs, who is more pleased when one student scores a big success than his fellow-workers? Far from feeling jealous, they are the first to blazen forth to the world that Jones or Smith of " Ours " has " licked creation." Every student is encouraged to go and do likewise either at home or abroad, and the country and Empire at large, benefits immeasurably, far beyond the cost of causing such results to be called into being. Without the training colleges or centres of training such an atmosphere and the emulation it engenders is non-existent. To call it into being, to bring about and encourage scientific research in connection with the Empire's economic resources, is but one of several more reasons why the work of the Imperial Institute, its Director, and staff should be much better known and appreciated by the public, especially at home, and much more liberally supported from the public funds in the future, the near future especially, than has been the case in the past.

———

Since the previous chapter was written I have had the advantage, on March 13, 1918, of hearing Mr. Octavius Beale, ex-President of the Associated Chambers of Manufacturers, Australia, read his paper on " The Production and Financing of Prime (or Raw) Materials," before the

Fellows of ·the Royal Colonial Institute in which that authority on international and inter-Imperial trade, told his audience that " A recent article in the *Muenchener Neueste Nachrichten*, written by Professor Foerster, of Munich, pointed out that :—

" ' Even if the continuation of the struggle for years were to end in our retaining Belgium, and possessing the great economic resources of the country, what could all that profit us, if the rest of the civilized world were stubbornly to shut itself against us and to refuse all moral and economic community with us ?

" ' Assuming even that we conquered all Italy and all Russia, and, in addition to Belgium, held the whole of the North of France as an economic indemnity and as a base against England, how would all that help us to rebuild our great world industry, which is entirely dependent upon the enormous markets of Pan-America and of the British World-Empire ?

" ' *It is by being carried upon the back of the British Empire that we Germans have acquired our greatest riches.* Only by the help of that gigantic export could we pay for our indispensable raw materials—for example, for the wool which we imported from the British Empire to the value of 17½ million pounds sterling a year.' And so forth.

" Fix in your minds this noble phrase, exquisite in its candour, inexpugnable in its truth : ' It is by being carried upon the back of the British Empire that we Germans have acquired our greatest riches,' for I shall have occasion to ask later, Do you propose to resume the obsession of the Old Man of the Sea, the grinning ogre whose inner essence you now know so well ?

" In the *Hamburger Nachrichten*," Mr. Beale continued, " fire-eating von Tirpitz" thus counselled his compatriots a few weeks ago :

" ' Not only has England taken our colonies and Mesopotamia, but everywhere she has made deeper and firmer bases for her maritime and colonial supremacy. She has abolished German competition in almost all parts of the earth, and has tarnished and trodden down the prestige and honour of Germany by unprecedented calumnies. In the whole Overseas world we are considered as conquered and done for. . . .

" ' Imagine the position if we simultaneously have to bear the burden of the taxation which must fall on every German and, despite the fallen value of German money, we have still to buy the most necessary raw material and

food supplies from abroad! Can anyone in his heart of
hearts really believe that in these circumstances, without
an increase of power, with no indemnity, and without
security, we could avoid Germany's ruin?'

"The way, we were told, by which our enemies hope to
avoid such troubles was for manufacturers in Germany
to associate themselves, respectively, according to their
various departments of production. Each trade thus
syndicated is to prepare estimates of their future requirements of prime materials, which will be duly checked by
the appointed authority. A State department will be
charged with the buying abroad of the metals, wool, jute,
cotton, foodstuffs, hides, tanwares and the thousand
diversities that make up the schedule of prime materials.
This Ministerial department will—if according to present
example—constitute itself, for reasons of convenience and
camouflage, a joint-stock company by name and external
appearance, 'eine juristische Person.' On the well-
proved pattern this juristic person, in the fraudulent legal
jargon, can form as many subsidiary 'companies' as may
be found desirable so as to disguise the fact of the scheme
of working being precisely a 'knock-out' when it comes
in the usual way to purchase goods at auction.

"Competition is thus charmingly eliminated whilst, for
instance, the unorganized British producers of wool,
meats, or hides and skins, mere unconnected pastoralists,
are left exposed. For convenience just this one illustration
is adduced. Up to the present it applies to producers
generally. And our beautiful British legal fictions lend
themselves admirably to the German procedure as planned.
It is essential to remember how a British High Court
decided that a German company established in England
for the purpose of distributing manufactures from Hanover,
the company and its business being owned by the Hanover
manufacturer, was an English company because registra-
tion had been allowed in England. But a still higher
Court put aside that contention by the dictum that a
practice cannot lawfully be carried on indirectly that
could not lawfully be carried on directly. Yet a man may
lawfully avoid his unlimited liability by duly forming
himself into a limited liability company.

"Priority of importance need not here be considered,"
continued the lecturer. "It is a question of preservation
of industry, and once that principle be recognized, nothing
that is produced or producible by honest human effort
when well remunerated is too small to provide for. A

minor glass industry may mean success or failure to our
armies.[1]   The whole year's value of Burma tungsten
(' Handbook of India ') was only £150,000.   Yet the steel
and machinery of the world largely depended upon it.
Let the illustrations suffice.   Despise not the day of small
things.   Contempt of the efforts of their fellow-citizens has
ever been a chief weapon of British political economists.
What India, Australasia, South Africa, and Canada well
know is this : were Germany finally sunk for ever beneath
the ocean, they would be commercially and industrially
no whit the worse off.   The two ruling factors are : to
produce as much and as diversely as possible, and at the
same time to obtain just values for the products.   Towards
neither factor did Germany contribute.

" Basic, again, to most industries are hides and skins, as
being the raw material of leather.   The great resources of
India in this connection were exploited to the advantage
chiefly of Germany.   Seventy per cent. went there direct.
Indeed, one of the chief officers of the Indian Civil Service
said to me, ' For years we have been running India for
the benefit of Germany.'   Allowing for hyperbole, there
was too much truth in the remark, and it would have been
better for Germany had she been less hasty in grasping at
the still unripe fruit, for her grip of the reins was tightened
with each year.   High officers of State in England, chosen
for office during a generation because of their views,
favourable or unfavourable, as to Ireland, were anyhow
favourable to Germans in India and Further India.   So
Germans were firm in the saddle, and could even use the
spur.

" So, too, the rice-milling trade passed out of British
hands, for British banks financed more than willingly the
German banks and trading firms by discounting their bills
without question, on the great scale, as to whether or not
they were merely accommodation bills.   British rice was
bought for Germans with British money, taken to the
Continent to be milled—Germany getting the benefit of
the offal—whilst German steamers were supported by the
freights also financed by British money.   Certainly the
British trade and the British mills went to ruin, but the
political economist had at most a sneer for the misfortune.
As aforesaid, all transactions are conducted for the sake of
a margin, extremely narrow in rice and steel and other

---

[1] Thus confirming what I say on p. 131, on the advisability of establishing
a trade in optical goods in India and elsewhere within the Empire.

great staples, so that not much fiscal intervention by way
of bonus or customs duties, or secret parallel concessions,
suffices to ruin the exposed individual and to armour-plate
his antagonist.   The German statesmen had their eyes
skinned, where the English statesmen suffered from the
cataract of Cobdenite casuistry.   We want arrangements
with India for the hides and skins and with Burma for
the rice.   Everything else—tanneries, mills, and all—is
ready.

" British copra, crushed in Germany, the oilcake remaining there that ought to feed British cattle, to give our people
meat and milk, must come to England, by arrangement
with the producers, through the respective Governments.
I do not mean that Government officials shall interfere
with things they know nothing about—tanning, boot-
making, rice-milling, metal-refining, cattle-feeding, and
all the rest.   It is true that with long practice customs
officials are extremely efficient, conspicuously so in the
United States and Canada, in receiving, checking, valuing,
and controlling imports and exports of all kinds.   Yet they
have nothing to do with procuring, handling, manufacture,
or ultimate disposition of the goods.   Through the Department of Trade and Customs in each Oversea state all
arrangements can be made."

Concluding this section of his paper, which I hope
everyone will study in the original, Mr. Beale went on to
sum up in these words :—

" The proposal to carry Germany again on our back after
the War, plus her Allies, no matter under what guise, or
impulse, or form of words that proposal be made, must be
rejected.   A favourite phrase is, ' There must be no
boycott of the enemy.'   Lord Lansdowne goes so far as to
propose that materials should flow freely in their former
channels !   It will not be a question of boycott, but simply
whether we shall exclude our suffering friends in order to
restore and enrich their cruel foes.   In the midst of their
rapine, carnage, lust, and perfidy, are British hands to be
held out to the Huns with promises of conciliation and
level treatment ?"

It is also as well to remember, as a Japanese writer
reminded us as recently as March 24, 1918, in the London
Observer, that German agents have been working in India
from the very beginning of the War, in order, as is well
known, to create sedition.   Such a menace, and all these
dangers, will be warded off if there were to arise a
reconstructed Russia, able to give resistance to German

aggression, before its rushing tides overflow the boundaries of European Russia.

Having studied the above carefully, I would be glad if everyone interested in developing our Anglo-Indian-Russian trade connections would turn to the report issued by Messrs. Chadwick and Black on the desirability and possibility of increasing the trade between Russia and India, and more particularly to promote direct commercial relations between Southern India and that country. Copies of this report can be ordered through any news-agent or Government agency and should be carefully studied. Mr. Chadwick has been for years a director of agriculture in Southern India, and Mr. Black is connected with the Bank of Madras. Both men, therefore, were in a position to "tackle" any queries that arose *en route*, whether in connection with agriculture, commerce or finance, and this is shown in the careful way in which they have drawn up the report and the exhaustive manner in which they have anticipated any query that might arise and needs answering before the would-be Anglo-Indian-Russian trader feels able to make a start. The report discusses the present economic difficulties, the great need that existed in Russia at all times for tropical products, naming those especially in demand, and what causes them to be so. It is shown how Germany has hitherto enjoyed the bulk of this trade, except perhaps in tea, and the means that enabled her to secure such advantages. All this and much more is explained to us in a way that I cannot even outline in this book.

I will, however, reproduce the view of the position generally as outlined by Messrs. Chadwick and Black, after their tour through Russia in July, 1917. How far these views hold good now, no one can say; all the same everyone should bear them in mind. "If the views detailed in this report are at all correct," we are told, the position is this:—

(1) Russia was steadily taking in the course of her development more and more Indian produce. (2) She was needing and taking a varied list of products. (3) Few efforts had been made to foster or develop this trade or to open out or develop new lines. (4) *Germany had done the bulk of this trade* [1]—except in tea. (5) Russia will continue to need these products and possibly others, and her needs will probably develop more rapidly than in the past. (6) In

---

[1] The italics are my own.—II. H. S.

view of eventual competition it should be India's advantage to establish direct relationships with what promises to be a large and developing market. (7) India is not badly placed geographically in regard to Russia and Siberia in view of future possibilities. (8) The Russians have the reputation of loyalty to a connection, but demand personal intercourse. (9) The expressed desire in Russia is to get into close relationship with producing countries. (10) The prospect of return trade to India, though remote, still exists.

The immediate question to be considered and answered would therefore seem to be " whether Indian firms consider it worth while to endeavour to cater direct for the opening now (July, 1917) existing and for future possibilities, or whether they will be content to leave their trade the step-child of some other country, i.e., Germany, who has studied Russia, and has had trade relations with her in the past. Germany, who sits at one gate whilst Japan, who is becoming more and more active in India, who is developing a mercantile marine, and who is now sending her commercial emissaries and information agencies in large numbers to Russia, sits at another."

CHAPTER XXI.

India—Her Duty towards the Empire, and the Empire's Duty towards India.[1]

THE many proposals for developing the latent resources of the Empire and India that have recently been brought before the notice of the public to be criticized, blamed, or praised, all have one thought-compelling point in common, no matter how diverse the policies of those who make or who criticize the proposals may be. All agree emphatically that such development is needed and that it must

---

[1] This article is not, as I hoped would be the case, a reprint of what I wrote for the *Mysore Economic Journal*, but is based on the same notes, and has the advantage of being more up to date on one or two points. As the December issue of the Bangalore Monthly did not include my article, I have had to do what I could from my notes. What I now say is, however, very similar to what I wrote last year.

be brought into action at once, and that the sooner it is in
working order and going "full steam ahead," the better
for all of us.   However much men may differ in their
opinions as to how the work can best be carried out, and
whatever hopes and fears each may have for his own or
his neighbour's scheme, all vote solid on the one point—
let it be done and done at once.   Many of us, meanwhile,
are probably amazed that so important a work should
have been left in abeyance for so long, even when it was
known, as explained in the previous chapter, that our
neglect has proved our enemy's opportunity; for whilst
we have allowed our immense riches to remain latent and
buried so far as we are concerned, we took no steps,
previous to the War, to prevent our present enemy from
seeking out the land and discovering what we had and he
wanted.   This ascertained, Fritz then extracted our wealth
and, sending it to Germany, either resold it to us at a big
profit or turned it into war supplies; but in either case,
utilized our wealth to supply him with the sinews of war
to fight our Allies and ourselves.

It is not only the undeveloped riches in India and our
Colonies that, hitherto, have been neglected in the manner
described.   One splendid industry, at least, that could and
should well have been carried on in England, where the
raw material for the work is produced, has also been
allowed to go to those who live in Germany or who,
by birth or descent, come from that country, but have
migrated to increase the wealth and power of the Fatherland in other countries, and this time it is America and
not England or in British territory.   The industry I am
referring to is, of course, the optical industry, the glass
for which comes, I believe, from a well-known firm in
Birmingham, from where it is exported to the United
States.   Over there the glass is, or was until recently, cut
up, ground and polished principally by those with German
names, under the guidance of the well-known firm of
Zeiss, of Jena.   As Mr. Octavius Beale very properly
pointed out in the paper that he read before the Fellows
of the Royal Colonial Institute on March 13, this playing
into Germany's hands and filling her pockets with our
money must stop.   We must remember that, as Professor
Foerster, of Munich, openly stated in a recent article
that was published in the *Muenchener Neueste Nachrichten*,
Germany would not have been so well off as she was
previous to this War, if we had taken life as seriously and
had worked as industriously as Fritz and Michael have

been trained to do, and as we still *must* do if we want to bring about a clean "wipe out" of Prussian militarism and of the would-be junker domination of the world.[1]

"You will be foolish to forget," Mr. Octavius Beale told us, "that Professor Foerster owned that '*It is by being carried upon the back of the British Empire that we Germans have acquired our greatest riches.*'" Those who have watched the development and trade routes of our tropical and over-seas dominions know that this statement is perfectly true. We subdue, organize and develop the colonies, and the Germans, and not our own men, have immediately followed in our wake, and suck out the profits which should have come to London and sent them to Berlin. All the more foolish of us to allow them to do so; but it will be worse than foolish if we allow such a thing to continue after the War.

The glass having been turned into "optics" is then shipped back to us by the "ton," and so much valuable space has, all along, been required first to take the glass to America and afterwards to bring back the manufactured article to this side, an article too that could just as well be produced in this country or elsewhere within the Empire, especially now that we have so many men who could sit and grind and polish when other vocations are denied them owing to their honourable scars. As it is, I believe, the lack of space on board the trans-Atlantic boats has caused us to go without much that we have really needed, and would have used with advantage, had the industry been established partially on this side.

Millions of capital must be invested, from start to finish, in one form or another, in this German-controlled industry of optical goods, microscopes, telescopes, field glasses, &c.,

---

[1] If there is anyone who still imagines that America as a nation is not being urged to do the same, I would suggest that they took note of the following "quote" borrowed from a recent (March, 1918) booklet entitled "Steps to Victory," sent out by the Mechanics and Metals National Bank of the City of New York, on the subject of the War and the need for Economy, Saving and *Hard Work :*—

"The War is not a side issue. It is the biggest and most serious thing America has ever faced, and in the crisis we must keep that thought constantly before us. The cost of the War to the United States is calculated at more than a billion dollars a month. This means that in turning our energies to the manufacture of war indispensables, a billion dollars' worth of labour and materials must be diverted regularly, every month, away from the gratification of our personal needs and desires. A billion dollars equals 30 per cent. of the American people's monthly income.

"Can we effectively divert so large a percentage of our income to war purpose without application of every possible ounce of effort and self-denial ? Hardly."

as those who are used to handle such goods in bulk will tell you. Our demands alone, taking the Empire as a whole, are immense and yet, like so many other leading lines, the trade in them went to Germany—and so did the profits, whilst we had almost to beg and pray for field glasses with which to supply our officers, and to cripple important work over here through having to commandeer lenses for Government use. All this, however, I trust, is a thing of the past. In future, with the help of our overseas workers, added to the assistance that will be forthcoming on this side we shall be able to produce not only all the lenses and optical goods that we need within the Empire but should also be able to produce a large surplus of better grade goods to sell to others against Germany. I say better grade goods, because I take it that, if the glass from Birmingham was not the best procurable, a more suitable quality from elsewhere would have gone to America and not our own. I am making these suggestions in no harping or mean spirit, or out of petty spite against Germany for carrying on her war in such an un-cultured way, but on account of the pressing need that exists to develop such latent industries in our own midst and to cause life to be instilled into them to enable the glass and optical goods trade to take its place among so many other industries, that we have hitherto neglected, to " Help pay for the War."

And this brings me to India, for our Eastern Empire could do valuable work in the cutting, grinding and polishing of optical goods, as it offers a class of work which is very suitable for a large proportion of her millions of patient, plodding, industrious and painstaking people, who will need help to pay their share of the cost of freedom from the yoke of Prussia, just as we shall, if we are wise, do equally useful work in India with regard to the output of sugar.

The other day His Excellency, Sir Hugh Clifford, the Governor of the Gold Coast, told that Colony through his speech to the members of the Legislative Council that the Gold Coast had advantages over other centres in connection with the production of cocoa, advantages which the native producers (the whole industry is in the hands of the natives) would be wise to note and make use of, and not to spoil or cast on one side through neglecting their estates. It was a good speech, well delivered, so I would ask to be excused if I introduce the following words from it in this article on the production of optical goods and sugar in

India. " If the price of cocoa ever fell, to an unremunerative level," His Excellency pointed out, " the Gold Coast is almost certain to be still able to go on selling at a profit, whilst other centres have already well exceeded the border line of cost price,[1] . . . for cocoa is capable of being produced in the Gold Coast at a phenomenally cheap price, and were a slump in the market to occur, the farmers in this colony and in Ashanti could still sell their produce at a profit long after the rates have fallen so low, that practically every other cocoa-growing country had been reduced to disposing of its crop at a loss.

" On the other hand," His Excellency went on to say, "there is no blinking the fact that the cocoa gardens of this colony are cultivated in a more slovenly and perfunctory manner than any areas of approximately similar value in the West Indies or the Eastern Crown Colonies. . . . In the opinion of my technical advisers it is all too probable that the farmers of the Gold Coast and Ashanti will, sooner or later, have to buy their experience at a heavy price through the failure of their crops, brought about by the persistent neglect of elementary agricultural principles."

Every word of this should be read and digested by the sugar-cane growers in India, for there is much in common between the slip-shod ways and old-fashioned methods in which the production of sugar-cane is carried on in India, and the cultivation of cacao on the West Coast of Africa. Both countries and industries must modernize their methods and organize their industries, the one in connection with cacao and the other with sugar. Until they do so, they cannot expect to enjoy the goodwill or confidence of their fellow-men, because they are not justifying their existence as useful members of the Empire by making the most of their chances. The Empire to-day cannot afford to have millstones hung round its neck in the shape of large masses of inefficient and half-fed people who have not, apparently so far, been able to raise the level of their own comfort or their share of the national wealth as high as it should be.

As I am urging elsewhere, in my own paper *Tropical Life*, the time has come when it is necessary for the Empire as a whole to see that every acre of land and each unit of the population on that land contributes, year by year, its full quota of money, food, raw materials, &c., for

---

[1] See *Tropical Life* for December, 1916, p. 198.

the public good, and the land and the individual that fails to do so will have to receive attention, and be levelled up to the required standard or otherwise dealt with. All ranks, colours and creeds within the Empire must be treated in the same way—English duke, Indian prince, or African chief owning or holding sway over vast areas of land. And a similar treatment must be meted out to the workmen and workwomen in this country, the *ryots* in India or the native labourers in Africa, the West Indies and the South Sea Islands. Each and all, if they wish to continue to enjoy their independence and freedom from the iron heel of bureaucratic and arisocratic thraldom which the subjects of some of the European powers have to put up with, must in future agree to put forth a larger percentage of that which they produce (food-crops, manu-factured goods, machinery, structural works, &c.) than they have done in the past. We must tune up our own standard of national efficiency to Germany's concert pitch, for if we do not do so we shall not be able to maintain our supremacy either in the world of politics or of commerce; and one of the first industries needing attention is the production of sugar within the Empire and especially in India.

As I state on p. 37 of " The High Price of Sugar," it is not too much to ask India, if she stops or restricts the emigration of her surplus population, to rouse herself and produce far more sugar in future in order to make up the deficiency elsewhere that the absence of her labourers may bring about.

Even India, in spite of her (so-called) surplus millions, which are, or rather which would be, no surplus if her economic resources were more fully developed, must go in for a more intensive system of cultivation, in order to cheapen costs and to increase the output per man and per acre. In transport alone the saving would be consider-able, as even Cuba, the home of huge areas, is beginning to find out. Everyone can understand also that it would take fewer men and implements, and less time and culti-vation (hence less money) to produce three tons of sugar, and dry sugar—not semi-molasses—to the acre instead of one ton or less as at present. Better cultivation and in-creased supplies of manure will help here, and if the *ryots* cannot afford to adopt such improvements, local committees or authorities ought to be formed to see that they are financed at a fair rate of interest, and, when the crop is sold, that they receive promptly and in full, the balance of the proceeds due to them. Patience will be required at first, also pressure at times from headquarters, to get the local committees formed, but once a start is made and the natives see more money, quickly paid, coming in, surely the wish to do likewise will become infectious and spread over the country.

No one can sit up and say what is best to do in any particular area in such a vast country as India. One can only broadly outline a scheme and leave it to local experts' to arrange the details. If no local experts exist, they must be found or trained and put there, otherwise nothing can be done. With so many schools and training colleges, such men should soon be forthcoming, especially if steps be taken at once to start the ball rolling.

I believe that I am right in saying that the sugar world generally has always been ready and eager to give India full credit for what she had done in the way of trying to place her sugar industry on a higher plane generally than she has hitherto been able to claim, and they will be equally ready to praise her as she further progresses step by step. " In Southern India," reported the *Louisiana Planter*, " the sugar-cane grows to splendid proportions, showing as it does, the adaptation of such crops to the land, thanks to the fertility of the soil and the suitability of the climate for the industry." If this is true of Southern India, the lands up north seem still more promising for, continues this leading American authority, " The more northerly provinces in India are said to produce far more sugar as a total production than is done in Southern India. This leads us to believe that not many years hence there will be a speedy interest excited in the production of cane sugar in India."

Our Eastern Empire cannot therefore pretend that she has not the eye of the outer world on her, and by no means a jealous or envious eye, but one that expresses nothing but goodwill and anxiety to see her go ahead and prosper. All the more shame to her, therefore, both to rulers and ruled, if she cannot find a way out of her present morass of difficulties and indifference, and giving herself a good shake, wake up and start putting the whole industry in order. A thorough reorganization based on carefully thought out plans must be evolved, and those working out the scheme must ever keep their *eyes* on the best centres, not only in India but elsewhere. Having done so they must then arrange to copy their plans, make trials with their most successful varieties of canes, and above all adopt their systems for draining, cultivating, irrigating and manuring their lands, so that the districts under their control can do as well, and perhaps even better than the model centres which they have set up as their ideal.

All this, you will be told, will need money, and a great deal of it. Well, has not India as a nation got sufficient wealth to invest in such an undertaking. Will not the capitalists, even the Government itself, have excellent security for any advances made since land well cultivated and looked after is of greater value than neglected areas. We are told that it is very difficult, almost impossible to wean the native from his land, if so that should render the task the easier for achievement. All we have to remember is that the land is not there to be wasted, and if the ryot wishes to keep his property and not have it taken over by the State, until some heir more capable than himself can inherit it, he must bestir himself and prove himself worthy to own the land, in the same way as the ruling princes and the highest officials have to prove themselves worthy to carry out the tasks and occupy the high positions they enjoy. Such men, if they make mistakes ask for no mercy, but recognizing their errors resign their positions. If this is the case with the highest in the land, since all are equal in the eye of the law and of practical politics, why should not an idle, stupid, or self-willed land owner, who cannot or will not mend his ways, have his land taken from him to be utilized by others for the good of the general community, and handed back when the next heir to the property is able to prove himself worthy to inherit it.

Having discussed the possible future of the optical (and also in the same way of diamond and gem cutting and polishing) industries for India as well as the development of her present sugar industry, I would like to call attention to the following, written in March, 1910, just after the first excitement of the rubber boom was over.

Armchair critics and wiseacres, I urged, may say what they like, and may wag their warning fingers as vigorously as they please at the millions now being poured into the Tropics to plant rubber, and develop estates already laid down, but this broadening of the basis of the nation's investments is the very best thing that could happen at the present critical state of our trade to stimulate and increase the commerce of the Empire. Pessimists on both sides of the House of Commons are complaining, probably maybe for party purposes, of the national wealth going abroad for investment, but whatever the reason of its doing so may be, the sooner these truly Little Englanders and anti-Imperialists learn that the trade of this country can never be properly developed if capital is not sent abroad freely to be invested in real estate or commercial enterprises, the better for everyone within the Empire, for if we do not send our capital abroad to increase our trade, other nations will send theirs. Even if everyone of the rubber companies now being floated by the dozen are not all they should be, with none of them will the money be actually wasted. With the most unsatisfactory company yet floated the money will be used to some extent in opening up the Tropics and paving the way for a more practical or genuine planter to come along and complete its development. Every penny invested in the Tropics is a penny to the good, for it forces those who have given the money to take an interest in the locality where the estate is located, or said to be located, and so teaches the stay-at-home a little geography, which most of them sadly need. If, perchance, the investor, in his hurry, puts his money on the "wrong horse" and finds that rubber cannot be produced in that locality, he cannot say that the home Press has not warned him, and, at the worst, he will have learnt a valuable lesson in economic geography that he would have known long ago if he had taken the real interest in the potentialities of the Tropics and our colonies that every Englishman really proud of his country should do. It is all very well to stop in London and reap big dividends, and watch Jubilee processions with troops from every nook and corner of the world—civilized and uncivilized—but someone *not* in London has had to work, and often to die of illness or disease contracted to secure these splendid dividends, and to develop those lands that need the native police and soldiers that were sent to swell our late Queen's Jubilee, over which the ordinary Londoner was, on the whole, more anxious to claim the glory than his share in obtaining it warranted him to be entitled to. Unless young London shows itself more willing to go abroad to the Tropics, where so much money is being made out of rubber, cacao, and other produce, and help to increase the output, and to send a larger portion to the United Kingdom, they may find that the next Jubilee procession in London will lack representatives from some of those centres which were prominent in 1887 or 1897, instead of having fresh contingents to be added.

Every industry that tends to open up and develop the Tropics and our Colonies should be encouraged and pushed on just as vigorously as we are pushing on the building of our warships and the expansion of our Army. For this reason, therefore, we welcome every fresh rubber company that appears, as we feel that, even if not in our own colony, it tends to increase our trade and the demand for machinery from this side, whilst at the same time it forces the nation to take more interest in the Tropics, which the bulk of the public have neglected most shame-fully. It only remains for the Tropics, and especially the rubber company promoter to see that they do not abuse the trust put in them by the public, for if they do, if even one black sheep turns up among them, it may serve to prejudice and put back the investor's interest in the Tropics, which, if encouraged by adequate remuneration, will prove of great value to the public, to the Tropics, and, above all, to the Empire at large. Most, if not all, of the companies at first were floated on a conservative basis, but they must continue to be so. Care must also be taken to teach the investor that rubber cannot be above 8s. a lb. for ever, but that the sooner it drops to 4s. or 5s. the better for the trade and themselves. The home Press has sounded several warning notes, even going so far as to call attention to the way in which "insect pests and labour difficulties are scouted." If, therefore, the public are caught by one or two bad flotations, or pay too high for the good ones, it will be, to a great extent, their own fault.

————

With regard to labour supplies and their even distribu-tion, as required throughout the Empire I attended a dinner in November, 1910 (when the question was quite as burning a one as it is to-day), given by the Liberal Colonial Club to Sir George Reid, who, at the time, was still High Commissioner for Australia. As a result of what we were told in the speeches that followed the dinner, I published the following notes on the subject in *Tropical Life* for December (1910).

As usual, Sir George Reid made a most diverting speech, intermingling kindly jokes with solid advice and useful facts, getting in sly little home-thrusts now and again in a way that is peculiarly his own. Certainly, he is a man well worth listening to; so far as our knowledge goes, he has never been known to say the wrong thing, but very often says the right one ; and it was the right things he had to say, and said so pleasantly, that we went to hear.

The remarks that left the greatest impression on my mind, however, were those connected with the question of inter-colonial labour supplies, coloured or white. ˙ Several speakers warmly supported the cause of a white Australia, but not one seemed able to show, wisely they did not attempt to show, how Australia was to be kept white, however much they desired it, if the continent is to be opened up and developed as she is capable of being ; because, in spite of all the efforts to draw " whites " out there, its development, especially as regards an excess of population, progresses at a very slow rate.

Sir George Reid referred to the establishment of an Imperial Parliament, where matters concerning the Empire at large could be discussed as is done in the German Reichstag,[1] leaving more local matters to be dealt with by each section of the Empire in a separate assembly, as in the Prussian Diet. When that much-to-be-desired day arrives, it is to be hoped that one of the subjects to be freely discussed and properly organized on an Imperial basis will be the question of inter-imperial labour. Until something on these lines is done, extensive areas and fertile corners of the Empire, particularly in Australasia, cannot be brought into cultivation as rapidly as they are capable of being, and ought to be, if the most is to be made of their resources. By such means alone will this country be able to assist its self-governing colonies to do their uttermost to increase the trade of the mother country, by attracting the labour and capital they need on the one hand, and, by ordering our goods, to give employment to the less fortunate ones left at home on the other. This, however, cannot be achieved until the lower classes at home are trained to acquire some agricultural knowledge,[2] instead of being forced, as a rule, to drag out a miserable existence as casual labourers and low-class factory hands in the cities.

Since the Home Government has established labour bureaux to regulate and equalize the distribution of the

---

[1] Also we take it in the French Senate ; our old friend, Mr. L. T. Knight, of Martinique, having been a representative there ever since we first made his acquaintance, some twenty years ago.

[2] See *Tropical Life* for September, 1910, p. 175, with footnote showing articles that we have published on this subject.

home labour supply, why not extend the principle (without waiting for an Imperial Parliament to do so, since I fear that this will not come during the next session of Parliament) to inter-colonial and inter-imperial labour generally ; whites for Australia and Canada ; negroes for Africa, West Indies, and elsewhere ; coolies for Malaya, West Indies, Mauritius, British Guiana, &c. ? The idea has already been put in use in the shape of the Emigration Agents in India, and the Protector of Immigrants at the planting centres, or the Planters' Labour Bureau in the Federated Malay States. The results, however, do not seem altogether satisfactory. The planters (the same as African mine-owners) ask for more, whilst the House of Commons, 'or influential opinion behind it, protests and threatens to give less. The other day an important Commission sat to consider the question of Oriental labour in Mauritius, the West Indies, Natal, and elsewhere, and money was spent in getting over witnesses to give evidence against the purely planting financier, who tends to dominate London opinion on the subject when it comes up for discussion on this side. The report issued was, I believe, in favour of continuing the system at present in vogue ; at least, several planting organs in the colonies employing the coolies, indulged in retorts, more noted for smartness than tact, at the expense of their opponents, which lead one to feel that they at least were satisfied with the results of the inquiry. But laugh as these supporters of Oriental Immigration may, at the expense of their opponents who have the courage of their opinions (which, locally, are very unpopular among the moneyed classes) and are not afraid to express them, it would be as well to notice the growing attention being given to the matter at home,[1] and the increasing objection to all forms of tied labour. Evidently the opponents here see only the harsher and more or less unfair treatment meted out to the less able-bodied immigrants by the " task " system, or other matters gathered from local knowledge, or Government reports, and are unable to realize the advantages. If the planters, therefore, wish to see the system continued they will have to see that their backsliders and the over-grasping element are either refused supplies or forced to mend their ways, for once let the public on this side

---

[1] As, for instance, the articles running in the *Daily Chronicle* of London, October 26, November 2, 1910, &c., on " Coolie Labour in British Colonies, and its Evils, which calls for Redress," by Mr. John H. Harris, and since republished in pamphlet form.

become really prejudiced against Coolie labour as it is against Chinese labour, or San Thomé labour, indentured Coolies will go the way of the Chinese, and then, when it is too late, the planters will have discovered their mistakes.[1]

The *Madras Mail* pointed out a little time back that planters in India have more than a passing interest in the labour troubles of their brethren in the Straits Settlements and the Federated Malay States. For one reason the yearly output of rubber from that part of the world, which will probably be the determining factor as regards rubber prices in years to come, will depend on the supply of labour there ; and in the probable event of the Dutch Government prohibiting the emigration to the Straits from Java of indentured labourers, following the example of the Government of India, the Rubber Companies will have to choose between free labour from India and the Chinaman. At present, fortunately for planters in India, the latter seems most in favour, in spite of his independence, the high scale of wages he demands, and the language difficulty, which is likely to prove a serious drawback. The first batch of Chinese emigrants to Malayan rubber estates reached Singapore from Hong Kong a short time ago. Only about sixty coolies arrived, but, owing to scarcity in parts of Southern China, there are said to be plenty more available. The *South China Morning Post* suggests that the Government of Hong Kong should take an interest in procuring the 1,000,000 coolies who will be required, it estimates, for the Malayan rubber estates, and in directing a constant stream of others to make up for vacancies. If this scheme means that Southern India is to be freed from the attention of the Straits recruiter, the agriculturist on this side will wish it every success. It is also stated that when arrangements are made for Chinese coolies to be repatriated at the end of their contract, a better class of labourer can be obtained, and, in accordance with this dictum, the Planters' Association of Malaya recently passed a resolution favouring the principle

---

[1] A great deal depends on the Protector of Immigrants, indentured or free ; see *Tropical Life* for June, 1909, when we said : " If the East Indians have a real friend in their Protector of Immigrants . . . the system, on the whole, does good."

Now, of course, in March, 1918, it is too late to try and mend matters. The indenture system has been condemned and is to cease. Whether so drastic a step could have been avoided I cannot say. As things appear to have been, however, I am not surprised (but very sorry as the labour is badly needed) that is has been necessary to put an end to the system.

of repatriating Chinese coolies, provided the indenture entered into makes the importer, and not the employer, liable for the cost thereof. See also the rather sharp controversy now raging between South India and Ceylon, because the latter persists in recruiting Indian labourers from districts which the South of India planters maintain not only require the men for themselves, but could well do, in their turn, with an increased supply—" Lots of lands were lying idle in the Tanjore district," we are told, " because of coolies emigrating." On the other hand, Mr. Couchman, I.C.S., Director of Agriculture, Madras, draws attention, in his Report for 1909-10, to the present prosperity of the Madras cultivator, for which the high price of cotton is largely responsible. It would seem, he adds, that the labourers have not participated to a proportionate extent in the increased prosperity of their employers, but an advance of agricultural wages is necessary in the near future. The Board of Revenue has little doubt that if employers of agricultural labour would only allow their landless employees to participate much more largely in their increased profits due to the high prices of produce, by raising the wages of labourers, and in other ways ameliorating their condition, much difficulty connected with labour would disappear (in India).

The whole question of cheap labour for the Tropics and the Colonies, to be dealt with properly, must be handled, pending the arrival of the Imperial Parliament, by an Imperial Labour Board or Bureau, and the sooner such a body is called into being the better for everyone, planters and labourers, shipowners and shippers, governments and governed. It should be arranged that, so far as the labourers were concerned, the Board should see that :—

(1) The labourers are well received on landing.

(2) That they receive a living wage, based on a daily rate, and not by the "task."

(3) That "task" labour be done away with, since it is too often based on the endurance of the strongest, rather than that of the weakest, units.

(4) That the planters' responsibility to the colony or the immigrant does not cease, through the ill-health or misconduct of the latter, or through estates being abandoned, causing the coolies to be thrown on their own resources.

There has been, in the past, a tendency with some men to regard indentured labourers in the light of automatic chattels; to be thrown aside when worn out or done with. It is not to the interest of the colony importing the labourers, nor to the coolies, nor to the Empire at large, that this tendency be allowed, as each unit profitably employed is a trade stimulator, but an idler, whether through habit or ill-health, is a drag on the wheel of prosperity and a hindrance to the welfare of others as well as to himself. The men, cast aside as being undesirable, or because the planters abandon portions of their estates, must therefore be followed up and profitably employed, and not left to drift into prisons or hospitals to be kept at the expense of the general public.

SECTION VII.

UTILIZE SEMI-ARID ZONES.

CHAPTER XXII.

Increased Food Supplies during and after the War can be raised by Dry-Farming Methods.[1]

ONE result of the European War will be, in fact, one can well say that one result of the War has been to make the world at large take stock of its larders and to note, with dismay, how the cost of replenishing them tends to increase just when we are least able to afford the money, and owing to the stoppage or curtailment of trade (outside the requirements of the combatants) throughout the world : worst of all is the prospect, or rather the certainty that the expense of feeding the families, is bound to increase whilst the incomes of the buyers, at any rate in Europe, are equally certain to decrease for some time to come.

Ask a butcher what effect the War has had on his trade now that the cost of meat is between 40 and 50 per cent. dearer than it was before the War (beef now is nominally 1s. 6d. per lb.), but when you go to buy any, the butcher either has none to sell, or assures you that what you see is already bespoken, and he will tell you, at least those I have asked did, that the public spend as much money on meat as before but are unwilling to spend any more, and therefore the higher the cost the less the weight delivered, and so, although the cash paid and received may not alter much, the amount of meat consumed must be very much less. This, if it continues, may exceed the limit of public good for, if in the past the man who works in the city has tended to eat more meat than was necessary or even good for him, that does not say that his dependents at home did, and nowadays, in these times of stress and anxiety all of

---

[1] Written in July, 1915, and reproduced from the Report of the Eleventh International Dry-Farming Congress.

us want to keep up our stamina to be able to throw off the trials and troubles of this wicked world—young people most of all. It is the young people I am chiefly thinking of whilst writing these notes, for they have to carry on the work of the world, and repopulate it when peace comes, and so, if we want a healthy people in the future it behoves us to look round and keep some food in the larder for those of to-day with such a task before them.

Therefore as one of the direct victims of the high prices caused by the War, placed as I am in this city of London where all are consumers and none of us can produce, although you in America, Canada and elsewhere have not escaped altogether, judging by the cartoons I have seen of " the innocent onlooker " being hit by the cannon-ball of the increased cost of living, I would like to take this opportunity of discussing with you (unfortunately not in person) how you can help to fill our larders for us in exchange for goods from this side, at a fair profit to yourselves, without having to pinch us too severely as to the cost during the next two or three years.

This discussion is well placed in such an assembly as there is no doubt that many semi-arid districts can greatly increase their output with the help of a little capital from agricultural, co-operative or other banks, a little encouragement and guidance from the authorities, and much care and experience on the part of the farmers.

The head of the office ot the U. S. Department of Agriculture, Mr. C. V. Piper, when discussing a possible increase last year in the output of forage crops for four-legged animals put a question [1] which can be applied with even greater force to-day to the output of foodstuffs for us two-legged beings when he asked " How much of the dry lands of the West can be brought into permanent and profitable cultivation?" Mr. Piper, of course, referred only to the Western States of North America, but I am asking myself the same question of the dry areas in Brazil and elsewhere in South America, in Ceylon, Canada, Russia, Australia—in Spain, in China, in fact I suppose in all countries nearly, and since it is so, all the better for us in the cities as goodness knows we shall need the food badly enough. Even I, a man, cannot look into the future without some anxiety as to ways and means, and this being so, how will it go, I ask you, with the dependents of

---

[1] Page 138 of the Proceedings of the Wichita Congress.

10

those four or five millions of men that have been killed or injured in the War, and whose numbers are mounting up at such a terrible rate, hour by hour, day by day? It is more than mere selfishness therefore that causes you and I to-day to ask how can we assure the output of the largest amount of food possible to sell to those who have none, and who, unless they can secure their supplies at rates lower than those ruling, even before the War (when the world as a whole was prosperous and had savings in the bank), will feel the pinch of poverty due to the high prices very keenly, if, indeed, they do not go under altogether, the women especially.

At present, money is being doled out as army pay with a comparatively free hand, but directly the men are disbanded this will cease and the women and their men folk (maimed or well) will in thousands of cases stand up and say, what can we do to get food as the cities are over-crowded with people like ourselves, i.e., non-producers of food, of whom there is a glut on the labour market, so we must turn to the land first to feed ourselves, and in the aggregate, to sell the balance of our crops to send to others in exchange for clothes, &c.

Roughly speaking, I hope therefore that the experienced dry-farmer will push more out into the open and plant up new areas, as they have the knowledge of how to do so which these future recruits to the agricultural world will altogether lack. Fertile lands elsewhere will be broken up and laid down in wheat, and everywhere we are urged to increase the number of cattle, pigs, poultry, rabbits, &c., to bring grist to the mill. The big man must become bigger, and fresh recruits must come in at the other end, to add their " mites " to the general store.

I am afraid the foregoing savours more of politics than dry-farming; if so, I apologize, but I have included them to show that never has there been the need that exists to-day, to go ahead with dry-farming methods so as to produce more on some areas than has hitherto been done and, more important still, to urge you all to open up fresh sections and bring them under cultivation as well. If, before the War, the increase in the population of the world tended to outrun the increase of its food supply by two or three to one, it certainly will do so when the War comes to an end, and, in fact, it is doing so to-day—doing so very rapidly too. I therefore as a man of the town— a non-producer of food of any kind—may be excused if for once I stop discussing how to plant, and only talk of where to plant, viz., in every nook and corner you can come across, wet or dry, drained or irrigated, up on the hills or down in the valley. In spite of the horrible depopulation that the War is bringing about, those that remain will still continue to outstrip the supplies obtained by those that are left, unless you come to our aid and utilize lands at present of little or no value to increase the output.

Dr. Durand last year, you will remember, touched upon the subject (see Wichita Proceedings, p. 113) and the case to-day is much worse than it was when he addressed you. At that time the War had only recently started and yet he told us that to increase the production of food more land must be used, or more must be got out of the land. Either of these may be accomplished in two ways, by more labour or by more science. Necessity I believe will produce the labour : for we will have to go back to the beginning in many things, and the beginning means agriculture; city life and factories came long after; for trade and commerce are the daughters of agriculture, not her parents.

Dr. Durand then went on to say that taking the world over, there is still much unused but usable land. It will be necessary for us to use more and more of those lands where moisture is somewhat deficient. Some of the land will be better adapted to grazing and to forestry than to tillage. In arid and semi-arid sections, there are large areas capable of cultivation. . . . It is a familiar fact that Western Europe produces far more food per acre than the United States, which can, however, support many times its present population and obtain far larger yields of each particular crops. In the long run, the man who devises means of producing food where none was produced before, or of increasing the yield of the land, will be looked upon as a greater benefactor than any other discoverer or inventor. To Canada and America therefore I would say : Obtain yields similar in size to what Europe can turn out as shown in the following table, thereby taking steps to support many times your present population and send your surplus crops to us to buy, for we need them now, and shall need them still more in the near future.

So much for science and now in conclusion a word as to labour, and in these remarks I would perhaps address myself more particularly to my fellow-Britishers and say : You should arrange with the mother-country to train a large proportion of her children as agriculturists, including dry-farming methods. In England our Educationists seem to forget that an agriculturist, like a doctor or engineer, is welcomed everywhere and for this reason that whilst a handy agriculturist is equally able to earn his living in town or country, a townsman is no use in the country. I say this because, whilst they leave no stone unturned to keep us well, or cure us if we fall ill, they are altogether out of date as regards training us up to earn our living; they *will* only teach us townsmen's work, and so force us to become consumers and not producers, whilst the world needs producers rather than consumers.

PRODUCTION OF WHEAT PER ACRE IN THE UNDERMENTIONED COUNTRIES.

	Bushels		Bushels
(1) Denmark	44·90	(16) Hungary	18·44
(2) Belgium	36·43	(17) Chile	17·55
(3) Holland	35·53	(18) Bulgaria	15·46
(4) Great Britain and Ireland	32·41	(19) United States ..	14·72
(5) Switzerland	31·81	(20) Italy	14·42
(6) Germany	30·63	(21) Serbia...	13·53
(7) Sweden	30·63	(22) Spain	12·94
(8) New Zealand... ...	29·88	(23) India	11·44
(9) Egypt...	26·32	(24) Australia	11·30
(10) Norway	24·53	(25) Argentina	10·26
(11) France	22·22	(26) Russia in Europe ...	9·81
(12) Luxemburg	22·15	(27) Algeria	9·52
(13) Austria	19·92	(28) Russia in Asia ...	9·36
(14) Japan	19·33	(29) Uruguay	8·33
(15) Canada	19·03	(30) Tunis	4·46

It is interesting to note what a comparatively poor yield per acre America taken as a whole also shows. It is the same with potatoes. Evidently the farmer element in the U.S.A. has yet to learn how it pays to cultivate and manure the crop adequately and wisely.

So much for the children, now for the grown-ups. Long ago, my friend, Mr. Reginald Enock, who has written many books on many lands, urged the Home Government and local authorities to secure parcels of lands abroad on which their own people could go to, and so have " friends from home " to work with, whilst others would train them to become farmers. Remembering this, I published the following appeal in the August issue of my paper (*Tropical Life* of London) and sent copies to some 300 leading men in all parts of the world. I did so as wars are common to all people, and those yet to come will prove as murderous, and probably still more wasteful of life and limb than the one now being waged. All nations, therefore, may be interested in what I said, and when their day of trouble comes they can do for their men and those dependent on them what I now urge my government to do with ours, both in England and her dominions overseas, viz. :—

BACK TO THE LAND IN INDIA AND ELSEWHERE—
EX-SOLDIERS AS AGRICULTURISTS.

It is significant of the times that in the House of Lords, on July 22, Lord Sydenham asked whether the Government of India were preparing a scheme for giving grants of land after the War to officers and men of the Indian Army who had distinguished themselves in the field, and whether government posts would be made available for those who were not agriculturists.

Lord Islington, after paying a well-deserved tribute to the valour of the Indian troops, replied that the Government of India had already approached the local authorities with a view to ascertaining what land was available, but there were many intricate and difficult questions to be considered before any decision could be arrived at.

Whether these intricate and difficult questions may cause so excellent a scheme to be abandoned I cannot say, but sincerely hope that such will not be the case. Meanwhile the whole matter touched upon by Lord Sydenham, namely, the placing of ex-warriors on the land, must not, in any case, be lost sight of, whether the men be Indian or British-born subjects, both for the sake of the men as well as of those who are dependent on them for a living. In Russia the ex-Tsar and Tsarina, we were told, had established agricultural settlements where the orphans and other victims of the War could be trained to earn a good living under healthy and happy conditions. This excellent example can well be followed by this Empire.

With the serious reduction in the output of foodstuffs with which we are faced in all parts of the world, and the need that there will be to feed and find employment for thousands of men with the wives and children, what better work could be found for a large number of them than that of an agriculturist, first to feed themselves, and then as their output increases to help feed others ; the sale of their produce and the purchase of their supplies for the farm and home to be organized on a co-operative basis. Municipal and local bodies can help by securing land here or in the Colonies (as Mr. Reginald Enock has long urged shall be done) to send their own townsfolk to, if work cannot be found for them at home.

Above all, let us remember what a benefit agricultural pursuits could and should prove if run on such lines as those adopted by the U.S. Bureau of Plant Industry when it established boys' corn clubs and girls' canning clubs to teach the members what was best to grow and how to cultivate the crop chosen. Quoting the *Bulletin of the Pan-American Union* for July, and the little work by Mr. W. W. Tracy, of the Bureau of Plant Industry, on "Tomato Culture," I can report that the first girls' canning club was organized in 1910, and by 1914, in the fifteen Southern States known as the "Cotton Belt," the total enrolment numbered 33,173 girls, of whom 7,793 put up 6,091,237 lb. of vegetables, mostly tomatoes, all grown on the small, one-tenth acre gardens allotted to each girl and which she cultivated. The estimated value of this up-put was placed at $284,880 against the cost to the girls of about $85,000 only, thus giving a magnificent but well earned and thoroughly deserved profit of practically $200,000 or $25 each. If two or three hundred such returns could be registered throughout the British Empire and America, think what an advantage it would be both to the producers and consumers alike, as the activities of the girls were not exhausted on earning this $25 for they did the routine orchard and farm work as usual; this was a little by-play and there is no doubt that the larger the number of members (boys and girls) and the greater the output, the cheaper will be the cost and the larger the profits, whilst the risks are so spread out, that even a total loss through frost or hurricane need not ruin the producers. Replying to the address of welcome offered to him after his victorious campaign in German South West Africa, General Botha referred in a prominent manner to the part that women had played in the campaign, especially in maintaining the farms whilst their men folk were at the Front. So they have done and are doing over here, in the offices and in the factories, to keep the homes going and the Empire's needs supplied. If they can do this whilst a trying campaign is on, how much better could they help when the campaign is over, if put in the way of doing so. Hard as it will be for many men to come back halt, maimed, and blind, their lot can be greatly ameliorated by being engaged in a form of work in which they and their women folk can both discuss plans and help each other by their companionship and advice when difficulties have to be overcome. Also, I take it, that such men will always be able to command the ear of their more fortunate and experienced fellow men, and so, even in the worst cases of disablement, thus prove a source of comfort and help to their dependents through their very helplessness causing others to be willing to help them. To do this, however, large numbers must go back to the land, as the towns will not be able to offer them a living, and it is therefore only right that the Imperial Government and also the local bodies should start discussing among themselves where these good and useful servants can go and how they can most satisfactorily and inexpensively be placed there, with the necessary implements, seed, live stock, and, above all, the house to live in, so as to make a start first to feed themselves and then later on to repay the advances that they have received.

Judging from what one sees of some of the hospitals, especially those with playgrounds attached (as is the case in front of the building in which I am writing these notes), the men, although wounded, could at least help with chickens, rabbits, and other live stock, and even do a little vegetable raising, whereby they and those who are too ill to come out would immediately benefit by having such healthy and nourishing food brought in " free from the farm." Meanwhile, experience would be gained when, if necessary, later on, the men are put on a homestead or plot of land of their own. As matters now stand the convalescent (wounded) soldiers seem to have nothing to do to kill time and the land is wasted, whilst we are all being told to eat less and produce more. I feel that there is a screw loose somewhere in this department that could, with a little organization, very easily and advantageously be tightened up.

SECTION VIII.

EXPAND THROUGHOUT LATIN AMERICA.

CHAPTER XXIII.

After the War, which Country will Dominate the Commercial World in South America?

Tropical Life, February, 1916.

DISCUSSING the methods of the German banks in Chile, the *Bulletin of the French Chamber of Commerce* at Santiago, Chile, tells us that, although the War has naturally hindered the operations of the German banks in that Republic, their excellent organization enables them to find an important market in North America, and the United States are, at present, making great efforts to promote their commerce in South America, and as they do not possess banks of their own there, they are working with the German banks, all of which have branches in New York.

Such tactics on the part of Germany are, of course, not confined to Chile, and we would claim they are being carried on still more vigorously in Brazil. This is why we were so anxious to bring the suggestions included in our book on " The Rubber Industry of the Amazon " before the authorities, so that they can either adopt them or, better still, cast them aside as being less suitable than other plans which shall be put in force without loss of time. Otherwise, do what we like to Germany in Europe, Germany in South America will flourish and prosper in the future even more than it has done in the past, and so undo the good we are striving so strenuously to achieve over here.

The intelligence departments of the South American (German) houses, as of the German banks in Chile, are very well organized and render great service to German manufacturers and merchants, and the (German) banks in conjunction with their shipping companies complete a magnificent organization for promoting the export trade of the Fatherland, so much so that it will always be a difficult matter to gauge how much Germany's ability to stand up against the Allies as she has done, has been strengthened by the support, moral and financial, that the German banks and commercial establishments in Latin' America have been able to give her. When will the rising generation (and even our rulers) learn to appreciate the importance of urging a large number of our younger men to go abroad to push the financial and commercial interests of our Empire in English-controlled banks and merchants' offices in the same way as they so willingly go to push its prestige and military glory on the field of battle? Not only is Germany doing so in the matter already described, but the U.S.A. also, as shown by the Consular and other reports, are now waking up and realizing the need there is for Uncle Sam to greatly " speed up " his commercial activity in Latin America instead of being, as his own cartoons showed him to have been, the " Rip Van Winkle " among nations to appreciate the value of the Latin American trade.

Meanwhile the enormous wealth that the United States are accumulating over this War, and the fact also that a large proportion of her most pushing commercial men are also Germans, or of German extraction and working on the same relentless lines, make it therefore a double necessity for the British to get more out in the world, and be more widely represented over there by our kith and kin in the future than we have been in the past. Now that even banks and insurance offices have been invaded by the girls, let them remain there and send the boys and younger men abroad, where their presence will be of far greater value to the nation than if they stayed at home. In the old days the girls' labour was wasted, and several sections of the labour unions seem to want it to be so always, as if they are afraid of the competition of the women. Such conduct is not only cowardly but most unpatriotic, and will in the end do more to " dragoon " labour of all classes in England on the lines along which it is organized in Prussia than anything else. Such a course must follow if we have a selfish, unorganized democracy which cannot expect to prevail permanently against the autocratic iron walls that the Teutonic race have brought to such perfection ; and we take it that this country has no idea of playing second fiddle in the European concert to please the Labour Congress men who have remained at home to vote, leaving others to do the fighting.

We say this because strenuous times are ahead of us, and the nation who goes even a shade slacker than the pacemaker will get ridden down, and all chances of his winning the race to gain the commercial supremacy of the world will be lost to the best organized and most strenuous people. From what we can gather from the speeches of some of the stay-at-homes, if their advice is followed we shall become very parochial in our ideas. This will never do. As every man who is not a slacker is to-day in the field fighting his country's battles, so should the majority of the same men continue the fight for the commercial supremacy of the Empire after peace is proclaimed. If the girls have done so well in the few months they have been at work, how much better will they become, those who do not marry, some years ahead. Again, when the men come back a little later on, as they will be doing, just when living will be so costly, they will want to push the women out from the work they have been so loyally performing, and then what chance will they (the women) have, since about two million of them are unlikely to marry and they will have to earn their living the same as the men ? Going back to the Germanization of Latin America, either directly or through the United States, our Consul at Pernambuco (Mr. H. E. Dickie) pointed out the other day, when calling attention to the United States commercial activity in the southern continent, that the establishment of American banks " down south " is only the thin end of the wedge, and it is significant also to note the natural sequence to the first step, viz., the systematic training by the banks of young men for the express purpose of exploiting the Brazilian and Argentine (our own pet Argentina) markets. Therefore we say, *Wake up, England, and do likewise.*

CHAPTER XXIV.

If Germany had a Free Hand in Latin America.

Tropical Life, February, 1917.

IN the London *Financier* of January 2, in *Tropical Life* for December and January, and elsewhere in our own as well as in other papers, we have called attention, as forcibly as circumstances *plus* the Censor permitted, to what Germany has done and what she means to do to retrieve her fortunes by " peaceful penetration," since she has failed utterly to do so by force of arms.[1]

In no part of the world is she carrying out this policy more vigorously than in the two Americas. Leaving the United States to look after themselves, we would warn our own folks, as well as our friends throughout Latin America, to keep their eyes open as to what is taking place south of the United States territory. We believe that one of our readers sent between twenty and thirty copies of the *Financier* with our article to leading men overseas known to be interested in South American affairs in order to let them see our views. Attention was specially called to the following sentence : " During the entire course of this War, and for some time before the outbreak of hostilities, the Germans in Germany, but especially in the United States, have been fighting as strenuously to secure a commercial and financial grip on Latin America, especially over the A.B.C. Republics (Argentina, Brazil and Chile), as the one they strove for and expected to obtain from a military and political standpoint in Europe. . . . True to his character, the German loses no chance of getting his blows home, whether he hits above or below the belt. A hit is a hit to him—that is all. Whether, therefore, he comes in fair and square as a German, or under the cover of the Monroe doctrine, as a hyphenated American, the danger to us is not lessened but increased."

Following this came the January issue of *Current Opinion* of New York, which tells us, under the heading of " An

---

[1] See also the remarks by Lord Denbigh, p. xxxii, on this War being brought on by Germany on account of the slowness or failure of her scheme to penetrate peacefully wherever she wanted to go.

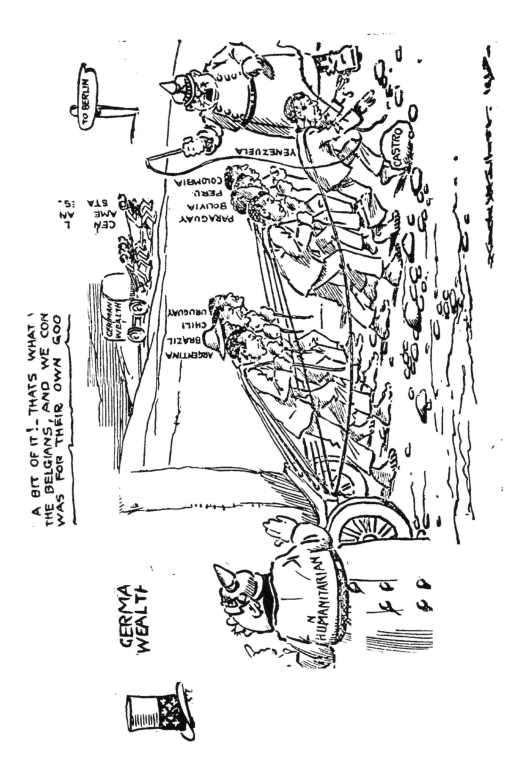

Alleged German Effort to Buy Peace at our Expense," · that: "Not very long before the peace suggestion of last month came to Washington from Berlin, Germany offered to end the War upon the terms of the Allies, with one condition: Germany was to be given a free hand in Central and South America. The offer is still open. The Allies rejected it; but the Wilhelmstrasse considers this chapter of diplomatic history still incomplete. . . . The records of the Department of State show," adds the London *Spectator*, "that Germany has long wished to have a 'free hand' in Central and South America. It has not been convenient to the United States Government to make any public protest about it, that is all. During the acquisition of the Panama Canal zone and the subsequent construction of the Canal, to follow the account in the English periodical, Germany tried in every possible way to induce the United States to agree to her being allowed to exercise an influence in South America as the price of her acquiescence in these changes. Our Department of State refused to recognize Germany's right to claim a *quid pro quo* because America was acting in the Caribbean or in Central America."

Truly our New York contemporary is wise to suggest that Germany, in asking for a free hand in Latin America, is striving to buy peace from Europe, whom she has outraged and wronged, at the expense of the United States. At the expense also, we would add, of *everything* that makes life bearable, much less happy, to the Latin American, which people, had the Allies agreed to Germany's terms, would have been as much at Germany's mercy to-day as the Alsatians and Lorrainers, the Poles, the Wends, and other nations have been in the past, and still are at the present moment.

Meanwhile, let no one forget, Northern and Southern America, or allied nationalities over here, that the disease has got a firm grip on the two Americas, and is running through their veins as a fever or cancer does in a patient. To what extent they are attacked, however, no man can tell until trouble comes, say between America and another nation, and the patient wants all her strength and energies with which to fight—wants them, only to find that they are missing, owing to the virulence and taint of Teutonic blood running throughout her system from Canada to Cape Horn.

CHAPTER XXV.

The Woman in the Case. — Miss Edith A. Browne on " British Trade Prospects in South America after the War."

Tropical Life, January, 1917.

IT is typical of the times that in the third year during which this stupendous War has been raging, and thereby taking up the time and attention of every man but the most unconscionable slacker, a woman stood up in the rostrum of the Royal Colonial Institute (at the Hotel Cecil) to tell us how we were losing ground in Latin America, and how we can regain it. Told them, too, from first-hand knowledge of the subject, and in a clear, practical way, that will go home to every man and woman who takes a real interest in their country and its welfare, as will be seen when the next issue of *United Empire* (the organ of the Royal Colonial Institute) appears with a full report of the paper read and the discussion that followed.

Typical also was it of the Royal Colonial Institute to have given .Miss Edith Browne the opportunity of addressing the Fellows, both those who faced her on December 19, as well as those who will read the paper in *United Empire*, to which we refer our readers, trusting that they will all secure a copy.

The lecturer's remarks confirmed our opinion as to the need of publishing " The Rubber Industry of the Amazon," viz., to show how suicidal it would be for these two giants, the old and the young, in the rubber world, i.e., Brazil in the West, and Ceylon and Malaya in the East, to grow up with the idea that they must fight a fight to the death until one of the two sinks from exhaustion. When giants fight, the winner suffers as well as the loser, and in this case, whilst it is impossible for the plantation rubber industry to go under, it would be extremely harmful to our interests in the East to see it emerge from the encounter, victorious maybe, but badly winded and battered in the fray, as it certainly would be in a fight to the finish with Brazil, where, be it remembered, we have far more capital at stake than we have invested in plantation rubber in the East.

Miss Browne also confirmed our views that there is room in the world for both centres, whilst she further emphasized the fact that the Amazonas rubber industry is largely dominated by the German element, and therefore, we would add, that those who buy this rubber through America are often helping the enemy.

All this led the lecturer, as it is always leading us, to the question, What is an American? Are the Schulzes, Muellers, and thousands of others in the United States. Americans or Germans? They are, of course, Germans heart and soul, and so are their children and great-grand-children, since we are told that the sins of the fathers are visited (and reproduced) in the children unto the third and fourth generation, and this is especially the case with the German race in the United States. It behoves us, there-fore, as we pointed out last month, to be very careful to ascertain the history and reputation of those with whom we are trading and entering into friendly relations, whether as planters in Malaya or as dealers in rubber from Amazonas.

One day perhaps the last section of " The Rubber Industry," which deals with the Monroe Doctrine, will be dis-cussed in the columns of the leading London and provincial papers in the manner that its importance entitles it to be, and as it would have been had it not been for the War. There never has been any doubt in our opinion (and a remark that fell from Miss Browne supports our contention) that Germany and the hyphenated reproduction in the United States is gripping hold of Latin America to the utmost extent possible, even to actual possession, under the cloak of the Monroe Doctrine, supported by a widespread system of peaceful penetration, and of establishing German settle-ments out there, in a way that has been going on for many years, and was never so vigorous as it is to-day.

One of the speakers who took part in the discussion remarked on the need of finding employment again in South America for the 7,000 or more men that he knew had come over from there to join up for the War. We should certainly say that this must be done, and further, hope that when the War is over the wise men of this country, taking no notice of old-established interests here, will give every encouragement to pushing, restless, but reliable men to spread themselves out over Latin America. When there, such men must be supported with money and prestige, and above all with marks of approval in return for services rendered, which to many, and perhaps to most, such prodigal sons counts for more than the money itself. As these sons grow older, perhaps the romance of Empire, whilst losing none of its force and impelling power, will not prevent its worshipper from being practical and glad to receive payment whilst still being able to realize that there is romance even in the most prosaic business, that leaves mere wealth-earning far behind, although, be it remembered, the very doing so urges on the laggard to further effort in order to get his share.   Romance, because he has not entered into the competition himself can, therefore, well be described as the pacemaker for those who race to grow rich, and this is why men who try to do without her seldom succeed in the long run.   These good knights, therefore, fighting for their country, might just as well receive their share of the profits, for big profits are bound to be made, and if they do not take their share it will only go elsewhere, probably to one who has done far less to deserve it.   We have been willing too long to do the fighting and pioneer work, and having opened up the country and made trade possible, to leave others (and as often as not it is a German) to scoop in the profit.   Our future knights of the Empire, therefore, must be both practical as well as romantic, and not allow the trade routes we cut out to lead to anywhere and everywhere but London.

During the lecture we were told that our policy should be, as it was when we laid the foundations of our commercial supremacy in South America, viz., *Help South America to help herself, to the mutual advantage of both sides.*

" Since the beginning of the War, Germany," Miss Browne urged, " has published a ' Prophetic ' Map of South America, with most of the Republics re-allocated as German territory.   That is equivalent to a prophetic robbery of British railways, banking and mining interests in South America, and we should take it as a warning to use every means in our power to prevent Germany from further developing belligerent machinations under the name of ' trade.'   We must put our commercial supremacy in South America on a footing that is considerably more secure than is the case now.

" It is often argued that when peace has been declared we cannot continue to treat Germany as an enemy.   Is it not equally moral and logical to argue that we must help to keep Germany out of temptation's reach and give her a chance to win back her honour ?   For Germany, there can be no ' peace with honour ' ; that hardest of all tasks, to win honour after being dishonoured before the whole

civilized world, will be the retribution for her barbarous
interlude of running amok. Is it not our duty, not only
to ourselves but to all civilization, to see that our trade
is never again conducted in any way that might tempt
Germany to fling aside a treaty as a ' scrap of paper ' ? ''

Miss Edith Browne, judging by her paper, evidently
agrees with much that we have just said, and therefore we
hope that her lecture will be widely distributed and read—
then those who have done so will, if they have the good of
the Empire at heart, go out to Latin-America and hunt the
Hun out of our preserves (that is, out of the centres
developed with our capital), as he is slowly but surely
being hunted by the Allies out of France and Belgium.

In a portrait sketch of Miss Browne, published on p. 8
of the same issue of *Tropical Life*, we pointed out how
genuinely anxious Miss Edith Browne was and still is to
push the interests of the Empire in whatever position and
sphere that she believes she can be of the greatest use.
To do this she can well be described as having chosen the
calling of a Peter the Hermit in favour of a crusade against
the ignorance and indifference of the people of the Empire,
and especially of this country, to the wealth that lies in our
Colonies, and to the romance and world-power that awaits
us if we lead in the development of Latin America, instead
of letting it fall into the hands of the Huns and infidels.
Not only is she carrying on the campaign described, but
in doing so she offers an excellent example of what we have
always maintained to be quite possible, viz., that healthy,
energetic women from this country can go to Latin
America and to the full Tropics without harm, and that
they can become the stronger and more vigorous by their
sojourn there, instead of only the other way round. But
to do so you must be interested in life and Nature for itself,
not for the sensations and excitement that are obtainable
from them in great cities, above all you must be healthy in
mind, body and disposition, as then, and then only, will the
world appear to be healthy to you.

Since, therefore, Miss Browne has proved beyond a doubt
that an English woman, not yet acclimatized to the full
Tropics, can lead a strenuous life out there, always on the
move, often undertaking long journeys under rough conditions in order to attain her ends, and as, when doing so,
she has always found, thanks to her disposition, that all
races on all the rungs in their social ladder were equally
anxious to help her achieve her object, we were glad when
we heard that the Royal Colonial Institute had invited her

11

to express her views on " The Possibilities of British Trade in South America after the War." We say this because, not only is what she told us of great use, as will be seen by the above, but also those who heard her lecture and noted the force, clearness and shrewdness with which Miss Browne expressed her views could not but realize that the lecturer was not only in excellent health and spirits on that date, but must also have been so when travelling through Brazil and the other Latin-American Republics. During this trip Miss Browne visited all the principal Republics of South America, made several journeys into the interior (into the rubber lands of the Amazon, to La Paz, in Bolivia, the highest capital city in the world, to Bogota, in Colombia, &c.), and was the first white woman to go alone into the interior of British Guiana, our only Colony on the South American mainland. She has also been in close contact with business conditions in many other parts of the world, having toured the Middle and Far East, &c., on business connected with the London Rubber and Tropical Exhibitions of 1911 and 1914.

SECTION IX.

TRUST RUSSIA.

CHAPTER XXVI.

The Outlook before Lenin's Supremacy.

WRITING in *Twentieth Century Russia*, as far back as September, 1915, on "The Future of Russia as a Trade Centre," I then claimed that Russia and Latin America have two points in common, viz. : that to the ordinary Englishman, or Britisher, and his cousin in America, both countries—one could well say both continents—are an almost unknown quantity so far as their history, people and trade possibilities are concerned. Yet both the ex-Empire of the Slavs and the Republics of the Latin-American people undeniably offer inexhaustible opportunities for trade, for the export of almost everything made in the British Empire and America, and the import of many of the foodstuffs, raw material, and indeed, many other things, of which we are badly in need.

The possibilities of expanding the trade between the English-speaking people and Russia were emphasized by the principal speakers at the inaugural meeting of the Russia Society in London which I had the pleasure .of attending. This was held on March 10, at the Speaker's House in the Houses of Parliament, and since then the Speaker (Rt. Hon. J. W. Lowther, M.P.) has consented to become the first President of the Society. Among those present who spoke was the late Mr. Neil Primrose, M.P., who told us that "You cannot expect a great country like Russia, with unlimited wealth which as yet has hardly been touched, to feel satisfied with her present arrangements for the circulation of her products throughout the world. We must, then, learn to sympathize with and understand her legitimate aspirations." It is agreed that Russia's rupture with Germany will leave an enormous gap in her trade connections which we Englishmen are well able to fill if we will only take the trouble to study what Russia wants, as our Teutonic rivals have done so carefully and thoroughly. " I was over in Russia some three years ago," Lord Charles Beresford told us, after Mr. Primrose had spoken, " and saw all classes of society. What struck me most was their distrust of the German nation; and their trust, sympathy, and, I may say, affection for the people of these islands. If we examine Russia we might without exaggeration say that her resources are illimitable. We, I think, could aid her a great deal if we were to help develop her industries and agriculture by means of our capital; we would thus benefit the two great Empires." " Russia," urged Mr. T. P. O'Connor, M.P., who followed, " has not yet reached its full and possible heights as an industrial manufacturing country; for the moment it must be regarded mainly as an agricultural centre like my own country (Ireland) " and, Mr. O'Connor might well have added, like Latin America " Russia," said her very good friend, Mr. Stephen Graham, " stands with her arms full of gifts for us, full of blessings like, perhaps, the goddess of agriculture. . . . Russia needs people who know Russian, and if the English go to the provincial towns they cannot get into real touch with the people without a knowledge of the language." This is as true of Russia and her people and trade, as it is of Latin America; and I am told that, once you can decipher the letters, Russian is easier to learn than German.

Meanwhile both Russia and Latin America—i.e., from Mexico in the Northern Continent, through the smaller States in Central America, right south to Tierra del Fuego —are, at present, to the " man˜ in the street," like 'an apparently bottomless pit into which the many can look but only the few can see anything but dust and disorder, turmoil and trouble. Yet it is not really so; those who know and understand the heterogeneous mass of races that go to make up these countries realize that existence is not one long round of trouble for them, but that life still goes on and is almost as bearable as it is here in England, where we have our labour strikes and " peaceful picketing " that no one but the magistrate believes is peaceful.

All nations have much good and a little evil in them; Russia and Latin America are no exceptions to this rule, but, in their case, I firmly believe that what is good in them can be greatly developed by outside influence and financial assistance, provided care is taken that the money is spent in the right way. I understand that this Review hopes to point out how this outside influence and money can be best utilized for the advantage both of Russia and ourselves, and to prove that, instead of a bottomless pit, Russia at least (leaving Latin-America for others to take care of) is more like a gold mine or, better still, like a cornu-copia, for, hidden far away in her recesses, are vast and as yet undeveloped stores of health-giving and valuable foodstuffs to be had—of Dame Nature—for the asking. Applicants, must, however, learn to ask properly, and that is what the Editor of this Review has undertaken to teach them. I am quite sure that he will prove a capable master and will find among his readers many apt pupils.

In Russia, at present, there are only seeds growing; here and there, perhaps, a sapling or even a young tree may be found, but none are yet fully developed and all of them need appreciative care and skilled attention if they are to expand and grow vigorously so as to be able to yield the bumper crops which each of the various trees of industry could do if given a chance; these bumper crops would mean great gain to England, to our Allies the French who have invested so many millions in Russia and, especially to our American cousins, as well as to Canada. I say this because Russia has huge tracts of cultivatable lands. She has thousands of square miles which, like the everglades of Florida, only need to be dyked and drained to become a sea of wheat, flax, sugar and other crops. Such a huge area cannot be ploughed like our English fields. At first, therefore, we shall have to look to Canada and America for those magnificent labour-saving appliances that can pull twelve plough-shares at once with harrows and clod-breakers in the rear of them. These modern machines which have been used to break up the old hunting-grounds of the Redskins and on the great farms in Alberta and Saskatchewan will again do good work in the lesser known Canadian prairie region of Assiniboia, Yukon, Athabasca and Ungarac, and in Russia. In the Russian steppes these monster machines will be required to "break" the land and render it fit for peasant cultivation; when this first "break-up" has been done, then the peasants can use the ordinary plough drawn by horse or ox—(or perhaps, by the handy gasoline or other tractor)—which will mean a great demand for English ploughs and tractors; in fact they will be needed by the shipload.

As the date (1915) in the second line of this Chapter shows, these remarks were published three years before Count Ilya Tolstoy said the same thing in America as can be seen further on (p. 180).

CHAPTER XXVII.

Russia at the Parting of the Ways.

The Duel between Autocracy and Democracy to Dominate the World and the Tropics.

Tropical Life, March, 1918.

THE evening of Friday, March 1, found one of the reception rooms of the Piccadilly Hotel crowded to overflowing with a distinguished company anxious to welcome as their guests our Ambassador at Petrograd, Sir George Buchanan, G.C.B., together with Lady and Miss Buchanan, who had recently arrived from Russia.

The occasion was a dinner given by the United Russia Societies' Association in honour of the new arrivals, and as this was the first occasion which had offered itself to "the uncrowned King of Russia" to lay his views on the situation in that country before an English audience, it was little wonder that all who had the chance of thus bidding the world-famous Ambassador welcome were also on the tip-toe of expectation to hear what he had to tell us.

The Speaker of the House of Commons (Rt. Hon. James Lowther, M.P.), President of the Association (of Russian Societies), was in the chair, and among those present I noticed Mrs. and Miss Lowther; Colonel Yate, M.P.; Lord Sanderson, who proposed the health of the President and Chairman for the evening; Sir Robert Perks; Lord Blyth; Mr. A. E. Brayley Hodgetts (the Hon. Sec.); Sir Bernard Mallet; Sir Henry and Lady Primrose; Mr. Alexander Onou, the new Consul-General for Russia in London; Mr. James A. Malcolm, the founder of The Russia Society, now merged in the Association; Mr. Zinovy Preev, Editor of *Twentieth Century Russia;* Lord Carnock; Dr. Ronald Burrows, Principal of King's College; Sir J. T. Agg-Gardner, M.P.; Sir Donald Mackenzie Wallace; and Sir Albert Spicer, M.P.

As the Chairman reminded us, in the course of his opening remarks, Sir George Buchanan, whilst in Russia, won the confidence of everyone—of the British Government, of successive Russian Governments, and, he believed, of the Russian people. Whilst at Petrograd he had maintained British interests with discretion, with great knowledge, and with extreme ability. We knew that shortly before the War the German newspapers had dubbed him "the uncrowned King of Russia," a title which should command our confidence as well.

" The lesson we had learned," Mr. Lowther went on to say, "was that Prussianism was not to be met by proclamations, nor militarism counted by manifestoes. The Russians had been seized with a passing frenzy. The storm cloud is dark over that great country. The thunders were rolling and re-echoing from north to south and from east to west. Lightning was flashing, and everything looked black. Destruction and havoc were being wrought in many quarters. Notwithstanding all this, I for one believed that that cloud had a silver lining, and that, though the time might be long, yet it would come when the clouds would roll away."

The guest of the evening, of course, spoke guardedly, but those who know a little of Russia and its disease learned much if only by having their views confirmed by so eminent an authority. "Perhaps some day," Sir George Buchanan told us, " I may be able to tell you what I know and what I have seen in Petrograd. It was such a sad tale that it almost breaks my heart to think of it. I told the Czar that the Army and the people were one, that he had come to the parting of the ways and had to make a choice between two paths, one of which would lead to victory and the other to revolution and disease. The Czar chose the path of reaction and the revolution followed, and was fraught at the time with serious consequences to the cause of the Allies. It was always risky for a great country to make a plunge from extreme autocracy to extreme democracy.[1] . . . There was not a word of truth, I am convinced, in the report that the Czar had ever contemplated concluding a separate peace with the Central Powers. The Emperor of Russia, no doubt, had much to answer for, but he was no traitor, and never would have betrayed the cause of the Allies. He was always the true and loyal friend of this country.

" The Bolsheviks were Internationalists first and Russians after, and in order to form a brotherhood for the

---

[1] And one can well ask, *cui bono* when done so recklessly without thought or consideration. What else could Russia expect than her present fate? Let us hope that she will soon recover herself and, with the help of her Allies, be able to expel her autocratic and reactionary enemies. Is it an exaggeration to say, when looking backwards that the most exacting autocrats have sprung from out of the midst of the most ardent democracy?

maintenance of peace they had sacrificed many of Russia's most vital interests. Whatever sympathy might be felt for Bolshevist ideas, the methods by which they had tried to obtain them had been attended with such disastrous con-sequences to the whole country that they were not likely to commend themselves to British democracy. Instead of a democratic peace based on the principle of self-determination, Russia would appear to be on the point of accepting a peace determined by German Imperialism. She was rent by civil war, in which class was fighting against class, and, like a house divided against itself, she could not stand against the onslaught of the invader. What an object lesson to other countries and to us at home on the need of presenting a united front to the enemy !

" Russia, however, was not dead. It was for us, who had known and believed in her under happier conditions, to consider what we could do to promote her recovery. She could not herself hope to take up the work of reconstruction in hand without assistance. If the Allies left Russia severely alone, Germany would not be slow to exploit her for her own ends. There was little we could do at the present moment, but we must prepare before-hand to act when the right moment comes. . . . The moral oxygen necessary to restore Russia was education, and the more familiar we could make the masses of the Russian people with British culture, the more we could do to help them to organize a system of technical educa-tion, the more would British ideas and British influence permeate the country."[1]

In face of the above, *Tropical Life* was right when, just ten days before Sir George Buchanan delivered his speech, it published the following words at the beginning of p. 29 of the February issue : " The Stock Exchange and everyone else are watching the triumphs (?) of the disorganized masses in Russia now that it has had the

---

[1] It was to carry out such a scheme that caused us to start *Twentieth Century Russia* in 1915, in the midst of the strenuous work of finishing off and publishing " The Rubber Industry of the Amazon." We felt, however, that there was no time like the present, and although we knew we had set forth on an arduous journey, we felt that the reward was worth striving for even in those days. Now, three years later, the very fact that the journey has become thrice as difficult has enhanced our desire to achieve success fourfold. Those who do not know *Twentieth Century Russia* should write for a specimen copy (enclosing if possible two penny stamps, but in any case write), and if we have one to spare it will be forwarded with pleasure.—H. H. S.

chance of hurling itself against a well-regulated and thoroughly organized force like the Prussian aristocratic military party. Many people will be well advised to watch the finale of this drama ; they will learn much if they do."

Going home in the train after the dinner, and having a somewhat lengthy journey, I opened the *Round Table* for March,[1] and read what it had to say on the *pros* and *cons* of Prussianism as compared with the practical (more often impracticable) ideals of democracy in Russia, in England, and in the United States. It would be well if everyone opposed to Prussianism did the same. Those who place so much trust in Majority Rule must remember that this is what Russia has got, what has hurled her to the ground, and made her lick the boots (*pro tem.*) of the absolute opposite of all that Bolshevism, in the best sense of the term, stands for. And since this is so, and since Minority Rule has done so much for Prussia, and in a lesser degree for Federated Germany, trade unionism, and especially a body like the A.S.E. (Amalgamated Society of Engineers),[2] and all that their ideals stand for, will do well to remember the fate of Russia, even the fate of the Czar of Russia, lest they, too, in striving for an unpractical ideal, play into the hands of those whose views are so diametrically opposed to their own. In making such a remark, I am not saying that the A.S.E. or any other trade union, here or elsewhere, is right or wrong. I simply maintain that we, like Russia, may become as a house divided against itself, and, if we do, nothing but disaster can follow, and with that will come the final triumph of Autocracy and Minority Rule. Those who cannot be relied upon *at all times* to follow a rule, a standard, a guiding central authority as the basis of its social scheme, must

---

[1] No. 30, price 2s. 6d. Macmillan and Co., London, New York, Toronto, Melbourne, Bombay, Calcutta, and Madras. I hope all your readers in these centres will secure a copy.

[2] Speaking on another point in which the question of a "comb out" is not included, Sir Eric Geddes, in the House of Commons on March 5, said : "To reach an ultimate production of ships at the rate of 3,000,000 tons per annum is, I believe, and am advised, well within the present and prospective capacity of our shipbuilding yards and engineering shops, but I wish to make it perfectly clear that those results cannot be obtained unless the maximum output is given in every shipyard and marine engine shop by everyone concerned. If employers hesitate to play their part, or if men anywhere "down tools" or go slow for any reason, they will now do so in the knowledge of the grievous extent to which their action prejudices the vital interests of the community."

and will go down before Prussianism, which does allow
itself to be so guided. Prussianism, bestial as its worse
side must be, will never be overthrown by "gas" or strikes,
or shirking of public duties for conscience' sake. Say
what the idealist will against it, Prussianism, as the history of the last three and a half years has proved, and is
still proving, has the power to call forth and to maintain
at high pressure, whether as a spy or a lying courtier in a
foreign country, or as a (worse than) wild beast in Belgium
and France, an abundance of sacrifice and endurance that
is as amazing as it is pitiable to anyone able to realize the
base uses that such talents are turned to. These talents,
however, are being turned to such base uses simply and
solely to uphold Autocracy within the German Empire,
and to fling Democracy elsewhere, panting and beaten,
to the earth as has happened to Russia. If Democracy in
England and elsewhere does not want to share the fate of
the Bolshevists of Russia to-day, let them see to it that
they do not commit the same mistakes that Russia has.

I say this, partly on account of what is going on
around us, and partly because on p. 267 of the *Round Table*
the following passage caused me to do so: " Were Prussianism purely evil it would have collapsed long ago. It
could not have drawn on the reserves of strength which
have enabled it to maintain such an heroic unequal contest
against hunger, hardship, and superior numbers. Prussianism stands for more than the use of howitzers and
cannon fodder. It is a creed held, with intense conviction,
by men who have had the courage to apply it, logically and
consistently, to every relationship of life." It is all this and
more. It is the one champion of everything that stands for
Autocracy and Rule by Divine Right, against everything that
stands for Democracy and the Rule of the People, for the
People, and by the People. The end of the duel now in
progress may or may not be postponed to some future date,
but whenever the end does come it will only be when one
of the two opponents is as dead as Queen Anne or George
Washington. Truly it is a case of "win or go under,"
and the way some people are working on this side tends
to make one wonder whether they fully realize that it is so.

Again it was interesting to note that in the *Evening
Standard* of March 8 "A Trade Unionist" contributed
a two-columned article, in which he told us, almost at the
beginning, that "quite apart from the immediate dispute
between the A.S.E. and the Ministry of National Service
over the interpretation of the agreement of May, 1917,

there are many other constantly operative causes of unrest. In this article we will confine ourselves to a very brief description of one of these causes.

" During the last two years there has been a recrudescence of Syndicalism. . This has been most noticeable among the skilled workers in the metal, engineering, and shipbuilding trades. The principal leaders of this movement reside in London, Glasgow, Sheffield, Barrow, Coventry, and Manchester. At other centres like Liverpool, Newcastle, Darlington, and Southampton the new ferment is not yet so active.

" The object of this movement is the complete control of the engineering and shipbuilding industry by the workers therein employed. It should be mentioned that in this Syndicalist organization there is no recognition of any distinction between the skilled and unskilled workers in the industry. All workers in the engineering trades are to be enrolled in one union—an Industrial Union similar to the one union scheme of the American I.W.W.,"[1] " irrespective of craft, grade or sex."

" These Syndicalist leaders of the rank and file movement fully endorse the extreme methods and demands of the Russian Bolshevists, and of late they have been most active within and without the workshops of the principal munition centres of this country. During the last two years they have been the cause of many strikes, and they were entirely responsible for the Engineers' strike last May."

On the other hand, those in this country will be very wrong if they continue to look askance at the Russian soldiers and peasantry, and to lose all faith in Russia as a nation because of its fits of frenzy and the outrages committed by the Russian mobs on educated and well-to-do people, especially upon anyone holding an official position or owning manorial rights and lands in the country. Those among us who are inclined to do so would be well advised to closely follow the history and sufferings of these people, before throwing down the sponge and crying out that " Russia is lost to us. Russia is far worse than no good to us, for her German landholders are hand-in-glove with Prussia. They come from a common stock, and have the same brutal instincts of making everyone else slave and suffer in order to serve and satisfy their insatiable appetites for the grosser things of life, money, power, arrogance,

---

[1] Known to most of us as the " Incorrigible Won't-works."—ED., *T.L.*

sexual desires, &c., &c." I would claim, on the contrary, that bad as things are through the revolution, they would have been still worse without one. Germany may boast as much as she likes of her success with Russia, but can she hold it?—I do not think so. Like a religious fanatic in India, she lies over Russia as the fanatic lies over a bed of sharp nails, and with a little patience, and much help from her Allies, the Russian peasantry will recover themselves before it is too late, and, turning the apparent nails into veritable bayonets, thrust them far into the vitals of the fanatic that lies so heavily over her country, but if we do not stand by and help, the nails themselves, instead of turning into bayonets, will disappear and leave modern Germany as well and comfortably embedded in Russia as were the Germanic landowners before the upheaval.

Those doubting this should turn to the March issue of the *Round Table* and read the context of the following notes from the section on " The Peoples of the Baltic Provinces and Lithuania," as on p. 295, where we are told that, " The most westerly Lithuanian tribes, the original Prussians, are now almost extinct—just a few hundred of them are left in East Prussia, in villages on the Kurisches Haff." They have perished in the struggle against the southern branch of the Teutonic Knights of the Cross, the founders and forerunners of the modern Prussian State. And yet we have heard that, "wolf never eats wolf"—the old Prussian tribes know better. Now it remains to be seen to what extent we shall allow the descendent of these wolves of the Cross to have further meals at the expense of Lithuania.

The Germans meanwhile have not had it all their own way, but, the same as to-day, organized might was always bound to win over disconnected and disorganized tribes and races. The *Round Table*, p. 302, points out that " The history of the Ests and Letts has been an endless struggle against the German Baltic Barons. Nowhere in Europe has serfdom been as ruthless as that imposed by the German conquerors in the Baltic Provinces, a fact admitted even by German historians. Only at times did outside interference succeed in lightening a little the burden of the serf population. . . . When in the reign of Alexander I, the German Barons found it necessary to admit a change in the legal position of their peasants, and abolished serfdom in the Baltic Provinces, they declared the entire land their private property, whereas everywhere else in Eastern Europe, on the abolition of serfdom, a part of the land was assigned to the peasants. Moreover, all kinds of feudal rights were maintained, and in parts now under German occupation they survive to the present day, for they were not abolished by Ukase until 1916." If this was the state of affairs when Russia was supposed to rule herself, how much worse would have been the state of this peasantry under its German Barons and the Overlord at Berlin, and this, I would claim, is what they foresaw was coming when they revolted. Like a dog long tied up who is suddenly unleashed, what wonder that it picks up and shakes everything that it comes into contact with before coming to heel, and how can the Russian peasants come to heel when there is no master to call on them to do so? "The average Est or Lett is, by nature and training, a revolutionary and, at the present time they supply the Bolsheviks with the most intelligent, best trained and best disciplined regiments. But more than anything else in politics the Letts and Ests are anti-Germans, for reasons both social and national." Surely with such information before us we need not despair for Russia; we need not fear (if we handle her properly and with understanding), that these people who make such excellent soldiers, who have been so oppressed by the Germans, and who, therefore, detest them so cordially, will wish to go back under the German yoke—and a still heavier yoke—than that from which they have just tasted the joys of freedom. I for one do not think so; the dog, now changed into a horse, is out loose on the steppes, with Germany hard pressing her with a lasso; let us, therefore, hunt down the hunter and drive him off instead of leaving the horse to its fate simply because it did not immediately take its place in the traces and help drag the cause of the Allies in triumph through the streets of Berlin.

It cannot be denied that the opportunities which lie ahead of us to develop much welfare, happiness and wealth throughout Russia both for the Slavs as well as for ourselves, are very great; what a pity therefore, that we have hitherto been so slow to realize this and make the most of such chances. What a still more serious mistake it will be if we continue to allow these opportunities to pass us unheeded and thus leave them to be utilized by others in a way that will not truly benefit Russia and will only prove a menace to ourselves.

CHAPTER XXVIII.

The Outlook in Russia with regard to Post-War Trade.

ENGINEERS and manufacturers of agricultural, dairy, umbering and other implements and appliances, either for power, animal or hand drive, can disregard the present and look forward to having a " bully good time " when the big gun has been exchanged for the power plough and the rifle for the cultivator, and all the fighting to be done will be that with Dame Nature who knows so much better than we do—(or shall I say " we did until this War ")—that to make mankind appreciate a thing you must force him to strive and fight for it. To-day, we are fighting for our prestige and good name and that of our Allies; the next move will be to fight for their happiness and prosperity so as to repair the ravages of their enemies; they will need much help and I feel sure that they will get it.

Think of the wealth that has to be replaced; of the food and prime necessities of life we shall have to grow and manufacture to provide for the destitute and the maimed— the destitute and maimed who have become so that we might be safe and sound!

Mr. Edgar Crammond estimated soon after the War started that its total cost for twelve months would be no less a sum than £9,147,900,000 divided as follows:—

British Empire	...	...	...	£1,258,000,000
Belgium	...	...	...	...	526,500,000
France ...	...	...	...	...	1,686,400,000
Russia ...	...	...	...	...	1,400,000,000
Germany	...	...	...	...	2,775,000,000
Austria ...	...	...	...	...	1,502,000,000

This did not include the losses of Japan, Serbia or Turkey, nor the very considerable loss and expenditure of the Neutral Powers. To-day we are painfully aware how these figures have increased not only with regard to the upkeep of the War on sea and land, but also for the maintenance of the public and of the civil service at home.

Once peace is declared, we can expect an ever increasing demand for English goods from an invigorated Russia and a reunited, revived Poland; then, too, their great trade centres will be able to supply us with oil, beet-sugar, wheat, and the other cereals that hitherto we have imported from Germany and Austria, also with flax, linseed, hides, timber, hemp, tallow, lumber, wood-pulp and the host of other agricultural products which we must always import as we have neither the time nor the land space to produce all we require.

It is far easier to realize in one's mind than to estimate on paper what this increased trade, coupled with cheaper food, will mean to everyone, but especially to the middle and lower middle classes of the United Kingdom. May we very soon be in a position to secure these blessings. The review *Twentieth Century Russia* hopes to take an active share in helping us to attain them by promoting an intimate acquaintance between the Russian and Anglo-Saxon peoples ; by persuading each to take such an interest in the other that an interchange of visits will take place, and by building such a foundation of mutual appreciation and confidence between the countries that the populaces of London, Liverpool and Manchester, &c., will want to know Petrograd, Moscow, Warsaw, and Odessa as well as they now know Paris, Havre, New York, Boston, Chicago and San Francisco.

Personally, I heartily agree with the housewife who told her newly-married neighbour that the surest way to keep a husband happy and good-tempered was " to fill him with good food and assist him to line his pockets with good money, well earned " ! Sound advice, plainly spoken, and advice which we may with advantage follow with regard to Russia, for, in helping her to grow rich and contented, we shall, at the same time, help France, Belgium and Serbia, and secure peace, prosperity and happiness not only for our Allies and Europe, but for the whole world.

In a more recent number of this same magazine, viz., its issue for July, 1917, pointing out the interest that Ex-President Roosevelt had shown in the recently democratized Russia, I included his letter to Count Ilya Tolstoy, in which Colonel Roosevelt congratulated Russia on the change in her Government.

This I obtained because in 1915, when I had reason to communicate with Colonel Roosevelt regarding a book I was then writing on Brazil,[1] and the good-natured answer

---

[1] " The Rubber Industry of the Amazon," to which, as explained in the introduction, I invited Lord Bryce as representing the English view and Colonel Roosevelt as writing for the United States, to contribute a Foreword to the book on the modern interpretation of the Monroe Doctrine.

I received, emboldened me, when I heard that the ex-President of the United States had written to Count Ilya Tolstoy congratulating Russia through him on the overthrow of the old pro-German régime, to again write asking for a copy of that letter as well; having done so I am glad to say, a reply came to hand, which ran as follows:—

METROPOLITAN,
432, Fourth Avenue, New York.
May 27, 1917.

MY DEAR MR. SMITH,—In connection with your request of May 3, I enclose herewith copy of my letter to Count Tolstoy.

Sincerely yours,

J. Roosevelt

Mr. H. Hamel Smith, c/o *Tropical Life,*
Russian Department, 112, Fenchurch Street, E.C.,
London, England.

Here is a copy of the letter :—

May 1, 1917.

MY DEAR COUNT TOLSTOY,—Through you I send my most hearty congratulations and good wishes to the men who have led the Russian people in this great movement for democratic freedom. I speak to them as a fellow-democrat and a fellow-radical, when I urge them, for the sake of the ultimate welfare of the mass of the people of Russia, to see that their striking victory is used with such moderation and wisdom as to prevent all possibility of reaction. I have the keenest sympathy with your programme for religious, political, and industrial freedom for all, and for equality of opportunity for all. It is not a very easy thing to carry through such a programme ; and in any such great movement as yours, the danger, at the point you have reached, comes almost as much from well-meaning, unbalanced extremists who favour the revolution, as from the reactionaries themselves. As you have put it, the torch of enlightenment fired the revolt ; see that the light of the torch is not dimmed by any unwise and extreme action, and above all, not by any such sinister and dreadful deeds as those which a century and a quarter ago in France produced the Red Terror, and then by reaction the White Terror. All of us who love liberty, who believe in political and social and industrial democracy, are now looking with eager hope to Russia ; and not only for your sakes, but for our own sakes, we beg you, exactly as by courage and disinterestedness you have forced through the revolution, so by wisdom and self-control to secure for your country the permanent benefits of the revolution.

Very faithfully yours,
(Signed) Theodore Roosevelt.

Count Ilya Tolstoy, c/o Bernard Sandler,
    261, Broadway, New York.

Probably the letter will have a niche in the history of this War, and of the important changes it has brought and still promises to bring about. Who knows but that a similar letter may still find its way to brave old Liebknecht in Berlin, now languishing in prison (and more recently Herr Dittman, the Independent Socialist Member of the Reichstag, who was arrested and sentenced, it will be remembered, early in February, for alleged high treason, to five years' confinement in a fortress, although mitigating circumstances and absence of dishonourable intentions were admitted), as so many well-wishers of Russia have done in the past, simply because he had the courage to speak out in the hour of danger, and call attention to the " writing on the wall," that is still apparently as inexplic- able to the German Emperor and his clique in Berlin as it was to the Emperor Nicholas in Petrograd.

At the same time, what adds so greatly to the value of this communication is the moderation shown in the word- ing and the kindly note of warning sent by one of the foremost men of the day, and one, too, with great experi- ence in the handling of a widespread and cosmopolitan democratic nation, within the boundaries of which many tongues are spoken, and many conflicting international interests are always threatening to clash the one with the other. If any country can truly judge the task that lies ahead of Russia it should be America ; and since this is so, who is more capable of sending the new democracy a friendly word of congratulation and encouragement than the ex-President of the United States ?

———

Much has happened since the middle of February, but it is well to remember that about that time Count Ilya Tolstoy, to whom ex-President Roosevelt addressed the letter that

12

appears on p. 176, foretold the downfall of the Bolsheviki, in a long article that he wrote on the subject for *Current Opinion*, of New York, and which was published by that enterprising monthly in their March (1918) issue. With the fall of the Bolsheviki element will come, we are told, the rise to power of the social revolutionists under the leadership of Chernov, ex-Minister of Agriculture in the Kerensky Cabinet. At the present time even, the son of the great Russian novelist and humanitarian claims that the social revolutionists are by far the most numerous and their representatives formed the majority of the representatives to the Constitutional Assembly which was broken up by the Bolsheviki, known as the social democrats, since by force alone could such a majority be disposed of. It is the knowledge of the certainty of this majority when it comes to a question of votes, that has all along made the Bolsheviki so antagonistic to the social revolutionists.

Looking ahead, one naturally asks—What has the future in store for us? What are the desires and wishes of the leaders of the social revolutionists who are—no one knows where just now. Count Ilya Tolstoy claims that the overwhelming majority of the Russian nation—who are peasants since they constitute 85 per cent. of the population—has a definite desire and a clear goal in mind. All they ask for is land and liberty and the fact that they are doing so is, I would claim, the great reason why we can still hope to see the German Baltic barons and the German influence, pushed out of Lithuania and elsewhere in Russia and not welcomed as a friend and helpmate, for even the long-suffering Est and Lett is not so foolish as to expect permanent help from their German overlords who have so long held them in serfdom, deprived them of their land and generally tyrannized over them.

This cry for land and liberty can be heard from all corners of Russia—from the Black Sea to the Baltic. "The slavery of our times," wrote the father of Count Ilya, "lies in the existence of big estates and in the lack of land among the peasants." If, therefore, modern Russia submits to the modern Teutonic yoke, the most illiterate of them will soon find, if they do not already realize it but are too indolent to try and shake themselves free of it, that their future state of misery and oppression, nominally under the Bolshevik social democrats, but really under the heel of Berlin, would exceed even that which they had to put up with, and of which Count Leo Tolstoy complained under the Czars.

" As we stand to-day," sums up the editor of *Current Opinion* in his heading to what Count Ilya Tolstoy has to tells us, " it is daily becoming more apparent that Russia under the Bolsheviki, is not to be allowed to govern itself by a parliamentary assembly representing a majority of the people, nor is the minority of non-land workers to have lot or part in the administration. The early days of the French Revolution developed no more positively a Reign of Terror than Bolshevism has done. Count Tolstoy's article is a clear call for American aid, moral rather than material, which, we are assured, will yield an incalculable dividend of gratitude to the oldest from the youngest democracy for which the world is being made safe."

Colonel Roosevelt must have foreseen the possibility of what has happened when he warned Russia, through his letter to Count Ilya not to " run riot and commit excesses" as they have done, but since what is—is, it is as much to the interest of America as of France and ourselves to do all we can to counteract the evil influence and example of the Bolsheviki, and to give the constitution-believing social revolutionaries a chance of asserting themselves under men of the Chernov and Miliukoff type.

Come what will, Russia must before long be receiving the railways and transport facilities that she so long has lacked but of which she has stood so seriously in need. She will further need and receive, thousands and even millions of pounds worth of agricultural machinery and of other goods which she cannot supply herself, and they will be poured into her distributing centres as soon as the transport routes are open, to be utilized in expanding her agricultural and other industries which have been brought to their present level of perfection, thanks to the milliards of money that France and, in a lesser degree, her Allies have lent Russia as we lent to Latin America to help develop her latent resources. In both cases Germany has reaped the bulk of the profits arising out of this increased trade. Are we going to allow this to continue to a far greater degree after the War than was the case previous to July, 1914—surely not ?

All the same as things stand at present, and unless we drive Prussia's and the Germanic domination out of Russia, all these magnificent orders will go to Russia through Germany unless the Allies including America can induce their people to boycott Germany commercially after peace is declared. But if America backs us up commercially as she is now doing from a military standpoint, if Germany owned Russia three times over, she could whistle for the supplies that the Slav peasantry will need and never be able to secure, for Germany cannot supply them alone.   America, as Count Ilya Tolstoy truly claims, is the only country in which agriculture faces the approximate conditions that exist in Russia, a country in which agriculture is conducted, not in terms of square acres, but on the basis of square miles.   America, owing to her machine-making genius has been able to develop her immense agricultural resources on a gigantic scale and, for this reason, it is from her that Russia must learn and to which she will look for machinery, to America and her Allies and not to Germany.

As Mr. Zinovy Preev, Editor of *Twentieth Century Russia*, points out in the first portion of his book on " The Russian Revolution and Who's Who in Russia," it would indeed be " difficult to exaggerate the significance of the part that the moderate element has played, and will again play for the good of Russia and the world generally in connection with the Russian Revolution—so deep is its meaning, so full is its promise, so rich are its possibilities, not only for Russia itself but for the world at large.   On the other hand, the vistas opened by the Revolution are so vast and flooded with such dazzling sunshine that one might be carried away on the wings of imagination to the most distant regions of political and social speculation."   At the time there was no doubt that the intervention of the Revolution saved Russia from an ignoble peace with Germany and prevented the whole Allied cause from being wrecked as a result of Russia's falling out of the struggle, whether wilfully or under the weight of a crushing defeat.   Since this is so, Russia deserved her letter of congratulation from the ex-President of the United States, the latest of her Allies, and Colonel Roosevelt also deserves a word of praise for the tone and wording that he chose for conveying his message.   Meanwhile let us remember that those in Russia best able to realize the value of this letter and the need of following the advice given, are still looking to the Allies for help.

This, I am not ashamed to own on this last day of March, is still my view also of Russia and her future. Russia which, months ago, would have entered Berlin in triumph, side by side with her Allies if her aristocracy had not been so permeated with traitors, with pro-Germans and actual Germans.   These men and women were around the Tsar, were at the supreme command of the Army, were in the diplomatic and other services to such an extent that the masses, over 70 per cent. of whom are illiterate, when the "heavens fell about their ears," thought that no one could any longer be trusted, once he held rank and position above their own.   To-day, therefore, it goes without saying that the mass of the Western Russians, at least, have lost faith in every one and know not where to turn for guidance and help.   Like a beautiful horse which, after having been ill used, hit on its nose and about the head by its own master, suddenly finds itself loose, the Russians at the moment are unwilling to approach anyone.   Try to treat with them and they show their heels, having found that kicking out vigorously, right and left, has so far been the only sure way of keeping themselves free from oppression and ill-treatment.

The problem now to be solved is to find out how to win back the confidence of Russia, and to teach her people to trust first their own leaders and then their Allies. Meanwhile, whilst this is being done, wily Germans, as dangerous if not as clever and successful as Rasputin was, abound everywhere, holding the thong and the halter behind their backs, and advancing with corn and sugar in their other hands.   This being so, who can blame, or be surprised at the half-starved Russians if, seeing no one else at the moment able or willing to help them, they take the sugar and nibble the corn, without noticing the danger lurking behind these gifts.

But cannot we also do as well and better than Germany ? Cannot the British public be induced to remember that Russia, like the horse, has become what she is through constant ill-usage and oppression ; that if she shows her teeth and her heels, it is only from nervousness and not through vice.   So long as this is so, and so long as we, in our turn, can maintain the belief that the heart of Russia beats true, we must and will succeed in the end in showing her who it is that has been the true cause of all her misery in the past, and who is most likely to help her help herself in the future.

Since writing the above I came across a short notice in the *Evening Standard* of March 8 of Mr. R. Wilton's book, " Russia's Agony," in which it is rightly claimed that this experienced authority, writing out of the fulness of his many years of personal and intimate knowledge of that country, still bids us to be hopeful as to its future.   Her agony is not the agony of death but of " a living, breathing organism struggling to find expression whilst wrestling against the fiend of Bolshevism "—that is, against Mob Rule.   The typical Russian, the reviewer justly claims, is not a Bolshevist, but the follower of and a believer in such great Russian leaders as Rodzianko, and he then goes on to tell us that of the disastrous influence of the pro-German element at Petrograd there is a vast accumulation of proofs.   Take one of them.   At the end of 1916 the British Ambassador (Sir George Buchanan) warned the Tsar that the food crisis (which overturned the throne three months later) was even then imperilling his future.   The whole business of supply must be entrusted to the Zemstvos or County Councils.   The Tsar thanked our Ambassador and consulted his wife.   She, in her turn, consulted Rasputin, who did not approve.   Nor did the German mentality of the Tsarina approve.   Such a delegation of powers to the Zemstvos would undermine the stability of the throne. The weak Tsar assented.   He dreaded his wife's anger. His attitude towards her, his submission to her leading strings, were summed up in one short reply made to an old general who had expostulated with him on the subject of Rasputin's influence: " I prefer five Rasputins to one hysterical woman."

Now all these mediæval clogs on the prosperity of the country have vanished.   Bolshevism will follow them; and the real Russia will reassert herself.

" From an economic point of view," Wilton tells us, " Bolshevism is an impossibility.   It offers no practicable method of feeding and clothing the people.   All who could leave the cities have fled home to their villages.   They will soon tire of village life.   And how are they to return to their lathes or looms if industries remain the sport of socialistic experiments ?   These industries will outlive Bolshevism, and attain a much greater extension than before. . . ."

Knowing this and much more, is why I pointed out in *Tropical Life* last January, that we must continue to have faith in and not despond over Russia; she is very sound at the core, and we all know that, unlike the boy's apple, it is all core.   Petrograd at the moment is only like a cankerous growth on the surface, which will be cured in time.   Mr. Preev, who is probably the best known and most reliable " moderate " writer on Russia in London, confirms this belief, for he claims that our present dis-appointment has produced a feeling of hopelessness quite unjustified by the real facts of the Russian position, and has led to a foolish and dangerous attitude over the present situation. Despite the present demoralized state of that misguided country, however, her military weakness and her internal difficulties still remain one of the most important factors of the Grand Alliance. The Russian problem concerns not only Russia herself, but her Allies as well. She is the axis round which turns the whole question : Which will win, the Allies or Germany ? It is, therefore, of the utmost importance that the Allies recog-. nize the fact that Russia as a whole is healthy, sound and loyal to our cause ; her present cankerous growth will soon be cured once a start is made, and we feel sure that a " move " will be apparent before long.

This view of the state of affairs in Russia is confirmed by a statement that I have just received from one of the leading men in Anglo-Russian financial circles in which he points out the urgent need that exists for us to have patience and to continue to cultivate the good-will of Russia and to go on helping to develop her agriculture and commerce in every way possible, and then goes on to say, as I have done, that the feeling of disappointment created in the minds of the people of the Allied countries by the kaleidoscopic changes in the political situation in Russia since the Revolution is caused almost entirely in consequence of its effect in postponing the victorious conclusion of the War. The economic aspect, which is second only in importance to the military one, has consequently remained in the background, and thus the vital importance to the Entente countries of the maintenance of the closest relations with the Russian people has been lost sight. of.

The permanent form of Government which may be evolved eventually, or the political status of any of the contending parties, are not questions which affect this issue. Our future relations with Russia are of such vital importance both to the people of Russia and to ourselves, that the time has come when the ·business and labour interests of Great Britain should take action. The moment has arrived when practical help must be given to Russia in the re-establishment and development of her industrial and economic life. The policy of silent sympathy and patronizing pity can accomplish nothing, and should be immediately replaced by an active policy of help and guidance.

For the purpose of urging this question upon our Government an influential committee of leading industrial and labour representatives of Great Britain is in course of formation, upon which it is hoped all important interests will be represented.

Russia is a country which covers about one-fifth of the habitable globe, and its natural resources in all the essential materials for the establishment, maintenance and development of every kind of trade and industry are practically unlimited. At the present moment Russia's resources are virtually untapped, although many important industries already established in the country show the extent to which Russia could contribute a large proportion of the world's requirements of food stuffs, oil, minerals and metal, flax, hides, cotton, tobacco, &c.

The importance of the means by which the resources of Russia will be eventually developed must be appreciated if the present War is not to be lost economically after it has been won militarily.

To this end it is necessary to consider from the economic point of view the relative positions of Great Britain and Germany in the world's trade. Both are essentially industrial countries, which are dependent upon considerable supplies of foodstuffs and raw materials from other countries. The British Empire through its Dominions and Colonies has at its disposal large supplies of raw material, which, as the War has proved, were being slowly dominated and controlled by Germany, through her policy of peaceful penetration; in fact, a large proportion of the entire raw material resources of the British Empire was more or less under German influence in some form or other. Now that this influence has all been, or will shortly be, eliminated, Germany will find herself forced to seek other sources of raw material supply. By turning to Russia she finds at her own doors a vast reservoir of raw materials in the hands of a nation unable of itself to develop the same, and these she aims at using for her own profit and to the detriment of Russia and the other Allies.

In addition to the natural resources above referred to, Russia possesses a population approximating 180,000,000, of whom 85 per cent. are peasants or agricultural workers. There are, therefore, in Russia, the main essentials of material and labour, for the establishment and development of great industries.

With Russia under the economic domination of Germany a position would arise in time which might seriously jeopardize the economic life and progress of the

British Empire. To prevent the German economic control of Russia is therefore a matter of vital importance, not only to the financial and industrial interests of this country, but also to the working classes. Just as industry is dependent upon raw materials for its maintenance and prosperity, so are the working classes dependent upon industry for their means of livelihood. Consequently it is equally to the interests of the working man and to those of the other classes of the community that Germany should be prevented from obtaining the control of Russia's vast supplies of men and materials.

This problem should be faced energetically and promptly, by the combined business and working interests of Great Britain. The manner in which this can be effected is only by a liberal and open extension of technical, commercial and financial assistance to the people of Russia, in the development of their country, and the establishment and expansion of their national industries, coupled with the supply of the urgently needed necessaries of life at the earliest possible moment.

Unfortunately owing to the stress and pressure brought about by the War, the financial, industrial and labour interests of this country have not found time to consider the trend of the present economic condition of Russia. It is felt, however, that the position has only to be clearly set out for its obvious importance to be recognized.

It has now become apparent that the attitude of passive sympathy maintained both by our Government and our people towards Russia has been a huge mistake. Instead of going out and helping them we have overpraised them for their successes, and unwarrantably reproached them for their failures. To make this clear it should be emphasized that 70 per cent. of the agricultural population are inarticulate and illiterate. It is therefore not only unjust but unfair to blame the entire nation for the misdeeds of a few.

While it is admitted that Russia's shortcomings have been great, we must admit that we ourselves are not altogether free from blame. Practically nothing has been done—and what little has been done has been conducted in a haphazard manner—to educate the Russian masses and bring them to see the justice of the aims of the Allies in the War. The Russian people can and must be made to see that their whole future and the future of the country they love can only be assured by loyal co-operation with the Allies.

Propaganda work on an extensive scale is essential to counteract the false conception of Great Britain which is inculcated in the minds of the Russian people in a skilful manner by our enemies, and wholehearted offers of technical and financial assistance must be made in the establishment and furtherance of their industries. The appeal must not be addressed to any one class or section, but to the whole country.

It is suggested, therefore, that a large influential and representative mission of British finance, industry and labour should proceed to Russia at the first possible opportunity with the full support of the British Government, to present the case for the Allies to the Russian people, and to offer them practical help in their business and economic development. Such a mission would be assured of the heartiest welcome in Russia, and should find—provided it is not hampered by official or diplomatic restrictions—a very fertile ground for the sowing of its seed.

While it is not possible at this stage to lay down a definite programme, the objects can be indicated broadly. The mission would devote itself to reaching the Russian people outside the centres of German influence. The need is therefore at once to form an influential committee, which committee shall, by means of deputation, press these views upon the British Government before it is too late.

In face of the above, one was glad to see in the *Sunday Pictorial*, of March 17, the following claim by Mr. Hall Caine as to the need of making England and Russia understand each other better. "War," he told us, "is a terrible intelligencer, and two years of the struggle on their western frontier told the Russian soldier a fearful if partial story. If we could have shown him (as by moving pictures) what great things he was fighting for, and that the nations of the West were shedding their blood in the same cause, it would not have been possible for him to have been led to believe (as most cruelly and criminally was done), that he was bearing the whole burden of the War. And if we, on our part, had been permitted to see the Russian peasants, in those first blind and evil days, being marched on to the battlefields without proper food, without shoes and often without arms, to be mown down like grass before the scythe, we should have sent succour in time, and so have saved the Russian people from the unscrupulous Jewish-German-Russian schemers who are now hurling them to destruction and their country to death."

IF YOU WISH TO HELP WIN THE WAR

by extending the areas (above all by increasing the yield
and improving the qualities of those areas already) planted
with Cacao, and thus add to the value of and profits
from British-grown Crops,

READ THE

Fermentation of Cacao

Based on the Experience, Investigations, and Reports of leading
authorities on this controversial but highly important subject.

Edited and with an Explanatory Introduction

By H. HAMEL SMITH.

Cr. 8vo, 318 pp. 35 Illustrations. Price 10s. net, postage 1s.

The Foreword is by Sir GEORGE WATT, C.I.E., &c., Formerly Reporter of
Economic Products to the Government of India and Author of many books
on the chief economics, tropical and sub-tropical crops. In the course of his
remarks, Sir George Watt claims that "the book will become a classic on the
subject it deals with so ably . . . the opinions of our authorities are certain to
be tested at the plantations, and out of the new experience thus gained must
evolve the future system of manufacture," not only for cacao, but for tea and
other crops.

"On this account, as the book gives comparative results of experimental
investigations into the Fermentation, Oxidation and Drying of Coffee, Tea,
Tobacco and Indigo, as well as Cacao, it is certain to attract the attention of
all those interested in the production, curing, shipping or buying of these crops.

As with our book, "Coconuts—the Consols of the East"—this work on the
Fermentation of Cacao has been much discussed in the International press and
reviews and criticisms have been published on the opinions advanced, extending
from a few paragraphs to a number of pages, issued in pamphlet form.

JOHN BALE, SONS AND DANIELSSON, Ltd.,
83-91, GREAT TITCHFIELD STREET, OXFORD ST., LONDON, W.1.

IF YOU WISH TO HELP WIN THE WAR

by increasing the output of Sugar within the Empire, especially in India and the West Indies,

READ

The High Price of Sugar,

and How to Reduce it by increasing the production within the Empire

(Second Reprint).

By H. Hamel Smith.

Price 1s. net, postage 3d.

This work, although extending to only 54 pages, has attracted much attention. The Indian Press has commented freely on the ideas advanced and welcomed their publication, whilst centres competing against our own sugar acknowledge the "strength" of the arguments advanced.

The Agricultural News of Barbados, the hub of the sugar world in the West Indies, points out that the gist of the pamphlet rests on the idea that unattached labour is becoming more and more scarce, whilst the area under cultivation grows larger and larger; above all, the demand for tropical produce is growing so enormously that it would become necessary in the near future to produce the largest possible crops per acre by intensive cultivation, and discard extensive methods as needing too many hands.

The book itself states as much on the cover, when it says:—

Even 5,000,000 tons, including India, would make a good start, and that means, on Java's basis, only 1,250,000 acres under cane for the whole of the Empire, or half of the area now planted in India alone. What an immense saving of labour, which could then be devoted to other industries, such yields would mean compared with our requirements under existing conditions. The fact that in the near future every worker will be (if he does his duty) worth two ordinary ones before the War, should alone cause the authorities to see that those who have the land and employ the labour to cultivate it, know how to appreciate and how to use both to the best advantage, and that too without the labourers being overworked to a degree that can render them useless to their family or themselves and a burden to the community at large.

JOHN BALE, SONS AND DANIELSSON, Ltd.,

83-91, GREAT TITCHFIELD STREET, OXFORD ST., LONDON, W.1.

13

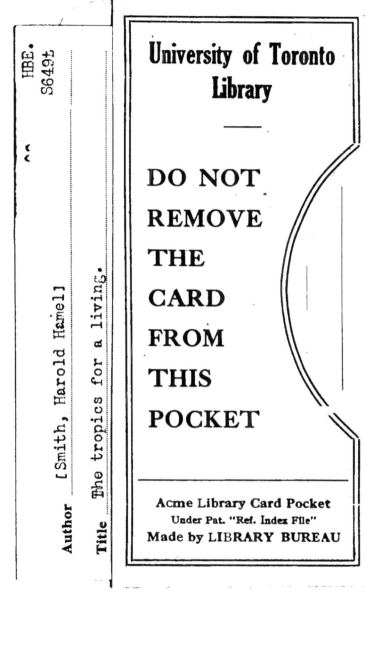

University of Toronto
Library

—

DO NOT
REMOVE
THE
CARD
FROM
THIS
POCKET

Acme Library Card Pocket
Under Pat. "Ref. Index File"
Made by LIBRARY BUREAU

CPSIA information can be obtained
at www.ICGtesting.com
Printed in the USA
BVHW040545101118
532319BV00026B/1110/P